BENEDICT CUMBERBATCH

THE BIOGRAPHY

BENEDICT CUMBERBATCH

THE BIOGRAPHY

JUSTIN LEWIS

JOHN BLAKE

Published by John Blake Publishing Ltd,
3 Bramber Court, 2 Bramber Road,
London W14 9PB, England

www.johnblakepublishing.co.uk

www.facebook.com/johnblakebooks ⬛
twitter.com/jblakebooks ⬛

First published in hardback in 2014
This edition published in 2015

ISBN: 978-1-78418-332-5

British Library Cataloguing-in-Publication Data:

A catalogue record for this book is available from the British Library.

Design by www.envydesign.co.uk

Printed in Great Britain by CPI Group (UK) Ltd

1 3 5 7 9 10 8 6 4 2

Papers used by John Blake Publishing are natural, recyclable products made
from wood grown in sustainable forests. The manufacturing processes
conform to the environmental regulations of the country of origin.

Every attempt has been made to contact the relevant copyright-holders,
but some were unobtainable. We would be grateful if the
appropriate people could contact us.

CONTENTS

INTRODUCTION

In 2010, when Benedict Cumberbatch was cast in the lead role of Christopher Tietjens in the lavish television adaptation of *Parade's End*, its American co-producers wobbled at what they felt was an audacious choice for such an major part. 'HBO said, "Who is this Benedict Cumberbatch?"' recalled the director of the series, Susanna White. 'We said everyone will have heard of him by the time *Parade's End* comes out.' Within a few months, White would be proved correct.

After BBC1 broadcast the first episode of *Sherlock* on 25 July 2010, its lead actor became very famous very suddenly. But as with all supposed overnight successes, the night had been a long one for Benedict Cumberbatch. At thirty-four years of age, he had already been a professional actor for a decade, with numerous credits in theatre, television, cinema and radio. What had marked him out early, though, was a refusal to chase populist parts for their own sake. He had always opted for the route of quality work, and had never committed to long runs of a television series. This enabled him to avoid being typecast in one role.

It looked as if landing the part of Sherlock Holmes would change all that, and he would be fixed in the persona for good in the public eye. Nearly 10 million people in Britain alone watched the first series. Yet some smart career decisions have meant that he is not exclusively associated with Sherlock Holmes.

For starters, Cumberbatch's exposure as the detective is limited: the series are just three episodes at a time, every couple of years; this is the antithesis of the ongoing, never-ending soap opera, or the 24-episodes-a-year standard of American network television. By being occasional, *Sherlock* always feels like *special* television. 'I just want to bring people in a little bit to the idea of sitting down on a Sunday three consecutive weeks,' Cumberbatch told America's National Public Radio in 2012, 'and having that water-cooler moment, that really was a sort of national sensation in the UK. It was an extraordinary cultural moment.'

The other reason why Benedict Cumberbatch can never be just Sherlock Holmes is that, career-wise, he will not keep still. He has portrayed Stephen Hawking, Horace Rumpole, Frankenstein, William Pitt the Younger, Alan Turing, Julian Assange, Vincent Van Gogh, the Duke of Wellington and Khan in *Star Trek*. He has collaborated with creative giants as diverse as Steven Spielberg and Sir Tom Stoppard. He is in one of the funniest situation comedies of recent times, BBC Radio 4's *Cabin Pressure*. He has been celebrated for a great deal of theatrical work: Shakespeare, Rattigan, Ibsen.

Perusing the Cumberbatch CV, it is clear that he craves and welcomes variety in his work. He does not have one acting mode. For a while, it looked as if he had cornered the market in upper-class buffoons, but that has broadened. 'I've often played men who are affable enough, if a bit silly,' he once said, but denied he felt typecast. 'I like to do a variety of parts so that people won't get fed up seeing me.'

Cumberbatch rarely discusses his private life, but there is a great deal of gossipy, fizzy approval towards him, daft but usually affectionate. It's the kind of good-humoured joshing that top pop stars receive. There's an Internet site devoted to pictures of Otters Who Look Like Benedict Cumberbatch. He has been compared to meerkats, and even the racehorse Shergar. Caitlin Moran, the *Times* columnist, believes he might be 'the first actor in history to play Sherlock Holmes who has a name more ridiculous than "Sherlock Holmes"'.

Even when his collaborators talk about him now, it's often a wry nod not just to his skills as a performer, but a tribute to just how famous he is. 'He's a handsome, remote genius,' offered *Sherlock* co-creator Steven Moffat. 'He's impersonating a glacier but actually he's a volcano – or actually that's what I imagine his frantic and amorous female following are thinking.'

Benedict Cumberbatch himself, while delighted with success, feels more ambivalent about being famous. He welcomes the fact his status gives him access to more ambitious roles, but is less sure about being public property as himself. 'They know you from the trail you leave with your work,' he said in early 2013. 'They assume things about you because of who you play and how you play them, and the other scraps floating about in the ether. People try to sew together a narrative out of scant fact.'

His discomfort with the excesses of the tabloids has led him to more or less dispense with discussing his own private life, and preferring to highlight his work, a preference this book mostly shares. For Cumberbatch, the work is the whole point of being a celebrity. But then, Benedict Cumberbatch is indeed that most unlikely of celebrities. He regards fame in itself as transitory. 'I don't want to complain or explain. It's part of a predictable pattern. It's a thing that will pass.'

CHAPTER 1

BEGINNINGS

Weighing nine pounds, Benedict Timothy Carlton Cumberbatch was born on Monday, 19 July 1976 at Queen Charlotte's Hospital in London. He made his public debut at just four days old when his photograph appeared in the *Daily Mirror*. It was no accident, as both his proud parents were professional actors, familiar to millions of television viewers.

His mum, Wanda Ventham, had most recently been a regular in the ITV serial *Emmerdale Farm* before Benedict's arrival, but her acting CV already stretched back 20 years with a string of credits in television and theatre. Brighton-born in 1935, Wanda began acting at the age of sixteen, and after a brief period at art school, transferred to the Central School of Speech & Drama in London.

When she finished her course, she spent one year as part of

the resident theatre company at Royal Bath. She could easily have had a stint in Shakespearean drama; director Peter Brook offered her the chance to join the Royal Shakespeare Company, but she had to decline as she was pregnant with her first child. 'I'd love her to have a "*Cranford* moment",' Benedict reflected in 2010 about his mother's possible missed opportunities in theatre, 'but for that you have to have a huge backlog of classical roles.'

With her first husband, a businessman called James Tabernacle, Wanda became a parent for the first time in 1958. The couple named their daughter Tracy, and when grown up she would become a picture frame restorer. Even when her half-brother Benedict was met by screaming fans at premieres, there were those who would make a bee-line for his mum Wanda. 'She still gets fans coming up to her on the red carpet,' Tracy would say in 2012, 'and Ben will ask her, "What are you doing?" She will say, "I was once famous as well, you know."'

Wanda juggled motherhood with West End theatrical farces such as *Watch It, Sailor!* (1960) and *Rock-a-Bye Sailor!* (1962), but her fame increased sharply from 1963 when she became a regular in the BBC television series *The Rag Trade*. Co-starring Sheila Hancock, Peter Jones and Barbara Windsor, it was one of the first hit situation comedy series where the action took place in the workplace rather than at home. It led to further guest roles in *The Saint* and *The Likely Lads*, and starring roles in one-off dramas and original plays by the likes of Fay Weldon and John Osborne. Sci-fi devotees remember her fondly from roles in three different *Doctor Who* stories (starring respectively William Hartnell, Tom Baker and Sylvester McCoy), and from the 1970s series *UFO*, set in the year '1980' and an early attempt by Gerry Anderson to move away from the puppet series he had created towards live action. In those days of three-channel television – BBC1, ITV and (from 1964) BBC2 – a single appearance could be watched by many millions of people, and Wanda became a familiar face.

Wanda's work covered dramatic theatre, comedy and action roles. She even did a few cult horror films, like *The Blood Beast Terror* with Peter Cushing in 1967, and 1974's *Captain Kronos – Vampire Hunter*. She would turn up on quiz shows such as the game about obscure words, *Call My Bluff*, and the antiques panel game, *Going for a Song*. She would play opposite the top actors of the time – Edward Woodward, Beryl Reid, Leslie Phillips and a young Julian Fellowes – as well as the titans of TV light entertainment, like Les Dawson, Morecambe & Wise and The Two Ronnies. Many series she appeared in are all but forgotten now – *The Rat Catchers*, *Rivera Police*, *Watch the Birdies* – but she was constantly in work and her list of television and theatre credits has continued into the 21st century.

The same could be said of Wanda's second husband, whom she met in 1970 on the set of an ITV drama serial called *A Family at War*. Four years her junior, Timothy Carlton Cumberbatch had quite a distinguished ancestry: he was the grandson of Henry Arnold Cumberbatch, who had been the British Consul General in Turkey, and the son of Lieutenant-Commander Henry Carlton Cumberbatch. Henry had been a decorated submarine officer during World War I, and was a key figure in British high society, before marrying Pauline Ellen Laing Congdon in 1934. Five years after that, Timothy was born, but shortly afterwards, his dad returned to the forces at the outbreak of World War Two.

After the war, the young Timothy was educated at Sherborne public school in Dorset, and (like his future wife) trained at the Central School of Speech & Drama. He graduated in 1961, became a member of the Southwold repertory company, and by the mid-1960s was a regular both on TV, and at London's Royal Court theatre, 40 years before his son Benedict would appear in plays like *Rhinoceros* and *The Arsonists*. Timothy featured in productions of Edward Bond's *Saved*, N.F. Simpson's *The Cresta Run*, and *The Knack... and How to Get It* by Ann Jellicoe. But during rehearsals for the latter in late 1965, personal tragedy struck the Cumberbatch clan when Henry died suddenly. 'My father arrived home,' related Benedict four decades on, 'and there was a hearse in the drive. He said, "Don't leave that there, that'll be the end for him", and they said, "Sorry, that is why it's here".'

Aside from theatre work, Timothy was constantly on television, performing with Ronnie Barker, Joanna Lumley, Leonard Rossiter, Eric Idle, and his future wife. Having met on *A Family at War*, Wanda and Timothy soon began a relationship, and set up home together in Kensington in West London. In April 1976, they married, and three months later, their son Benedict was born.

A full analysis of both Wanda and Timothy's stage and

screen careers would easily fill a book of its own. Their list of credits was already long and illustrious when Benedict arrived on the scene, and would continue to grow.

Wanda decided to return to work in early 1977, when Benedict was six months old. Immediately, she and Timothy landed guest roles in the ITV courtroom serial *Crown Court*, where they appeared in the dock playing warring spouses. From time to time, the couple would appear together in the same productions, but more often than not, one of them would work in theatre, the other in television, to make sure that at least one parent was at home to look after their son. Many years later, Benedict's mother described their new arrival as 'a whirlwind – he never stopped'.

Crown Court was made by Granada Television in Manchester, the city where Benedict would study at university in the late 1990s, and Wanda in particular would appear in several other series for the company. *Fallen Hero*, in which she starred as the wife of a rugby player who has to retire from the sport after injury, was a popular series, but it required her to work far away from the family's London home.

So in 1980, the last year before young Benedict started school, Wanda endeavoured to make her workload as light as possible, in order to spend more time with him. By now, the boy had started to become aware of exciting events like Christmas. 'He is a bit puzzled,' Wanda told the *Daily Express* at Christmas 1979, 'because he was taken by friends to see two separate Father Christmases, and he can't understand why there were two faces!'

Possibly the first person to predict greatness for Benedict Cumberbatch was the veteran American actress Elaine Stritch. Perhaps best known in the UK for the London Weekend TV sitcom *Two's Company*, she was so impressed by the sight of the youngster walking across a field in red dungarees despite a nearby bull, that she proclaimed, 'That child is going to be a star.'

Rarely out of work, Wanda and Timothy remained familiar faces on stage and screen into the 1980s, but they were neither household names nor from wealthy backgrounds, so the acting path was not one that brought guaranteed riches. 'They saw the pitfalls of it,' their son would say in 2013. 'You don't know where your next job is coming from, and it's unstable, into which they were having a child – me. You want stability for your children ... something better.'

Benedict remembered the Kensington of his earliest years as 'run-down; smalls hanging out in the smog, riots in Notting Hill'. Indeed, his first school, a pre-preparatory one which he attended from 1981, was actually in Notting Hill. It was here that he made his stage debut. Even Benedict Cumberbatch's starting point in acting was the school nativity play, but he did bag the part of Joseph, and received his first reaction: laughter. Admittedly, the script for the nativity play doesn't often call for the boy playing Joseph to push the girl playing Mary off the stage. But it wasn't about the audience; it was about his co-star. 'I didn't really understand it, and I wasn't intending to play to the house. I was just furious about how self-indulgent she was being.'

A restless toddler, Benedict showed little sign of controlling his energy during his first years in education. His headmistress at the Notting Hill school wrote on an end-of-term report: 'Ben is slightly more controlled but must try to be less noisy.' The naughtiness was present when outside school too. 'I used to expose myself in front of religious places,' he would remember. 'I was a very hot, bored boy and was surrounded by people who were older than me who were goading me. One day they said, "Go on, pull your pants down!" I obliged willingly.'

Then there was the occasion when Wanda took him to the theatre for the first time. Dad Timothy was in the play itself, and the excitable boy was mesmerised by the sight of the stage. When taken backstage, he couldn't stop himself from shouting from the wings: 'I want to go on!' His mother had to stop him from running on and disrupting the production. Later on in childhood, his excitement could curdle into embarrassment; as Wanda expertly goofed around in Ray Cooney stage farces, he would feel awkward: 'the audience loving her being caught in all those compromising positions and me, aged eight, absolutely mortified.'

Both Wanda and Timothy were determined that their son should have the most rounded of educations. In 1984, when Benedict was eight, he was packed off to Brambletye Prep School, near East Grinstead in West Sussex. He remained something of a tearaway there, although his disruptiveness was rarely nasty. 'It was all a bit *Just William*,' he would recall. 'I got into fights. I was pretty naughty.' More often than not, it was directionless mischief. 'I had a problem focusing. I probably had Attention Deficit Hyperactivity Disorder, or something on the border of it. I was always performing, doing silly voices.' He was wild about action-packed television and film too, especially from America: *Buck Rogers*, *Star Trek* – and films like the *Star Wars* trilogy. Television and action films were about his only real obsessions at this stage. 'I was never obsessive about anything I watched when I was a kid,' he told *SFX* magazine in 2013, 'except maybe *The A-Team* and *Airwolf*. And I loved *Knight Rider* and *Baywatch*.'

His teachers tried to re-direct his energy in a more constructive fashion. For a time, he was taught the trumpet, which he feels explains the pronounced lower lip he would develop. 'I have trumpet mouth,' he would tell the journalist Caitlin Moran. But he would show real promise on stage. At ten years of age, he was cast in a Brambletye school production of *Half a Sixpence*. As Ann Kipps, the female lead, he would belt out show-stoppers like 'I Don't Believe a Word of It', as sung by Julia Foster in the 1967 film version. He was increasingly able to temper his behavioural excesses. 'I realised there were ways to channel the energy that didn't involve being disruptive. Getting parts in school plays became my focus.'

By the late 1980s, Brambletye had its own purpose-built theatre, with a seating capacity of 300. It was opened by one Judi Dench. It was there that, in 1989, his penultimate year at the school, 12-year-old Benedict made his Shakespearean debut in a production of the comedy *A Midsummer Night's Dream*. He took the part of Nick Bottom, a bumbling weaver with acting aspirations. It was a role bursting with comic potential, and apparently according to the school magazine, he did extremely well. 'Benedict Cumberbatch's Bottom will be long remembered,' it supposedly stated. If this is true, it's not a bad first review, unfortunate wording aside.

Benedict's housemaster at Brambletye was Andrew Callender, who also taught the boy. He found it easy to recall his sporting prowess – notably at rugby and cricket – but it was his thespian abilities which were unusually prodigious. 'Benedict was a remarkable young pupil,' said Callender in 2012. 'His acting came to the fore very early on. He had boundless energy.'

As the 1990s dawned, Benedict's days at Brambletye were coming to an end. The school's headmaster had an idea for where the boy should go next. He suggested to his parents that maybe the ideal place for Benedict could be the school he had attended himself: Harrow. There he might find the structure and responsibility to help him continue his journey through the educational system.

Brambletye had not been a cheap educational option. Harrow would be pricier still. Throughout the 1980s, Benedict's parents had taken numerous stage and screen jobs to ensure that their son's school bills would be paid. By 1989, Wanda was playing Rodney's mother-in-law Pamela in *Only Fools and Horses*, and touring in stage farces by Ray Cooney.

Harrow was not an inexpensive option, and Wanda and Timothy needed a scholarship in order for Benedict to attend. 'I'm not a hereditary peer,' Cumberbatch remarked years later. 'I wasn't born into land or titles, or new money, or an oil rig.' Yet despite his relatively modest background when compared to many of his peers, Benedict Cumberbatch would feel extremely grateful for his education at Harrow.

CHAPTER 2

AN INCREDIBLY
PRIVILEGED BUBBLE

Benedict Cumberbatch's five years at Harrow School began in the autumn of 1990. He had turned fourteen in July of that year. Around two-thirds of the funding towards his education there had come from his grandmother, whose family owned a tea plantation in India.

He arrived at the 400-year-old school, populated by around 800 pupils. Fagging and corporal punishment were still commonplace. 'One night, while I was doing my homework, there was a terrible commotion. It seemed like the entire school was chasing this one boy who'd been caught "fiddling".'

Harrow had been a prestigious school for centuries. Its alumni included seven British Prime Ministers, including Robert Peel, Stanley Baldwin and Winston Churchill, the poet Lord Byron, the novelist Anthony Trollope, and the creator of Horace Rumpole, John Mortimer. But Benedict felt like an outsider to begin with. 'I was a very middle-class kid by most standards,' he said in 2005. 'I was surrounded by Lord Rothschild's son, Prince Hussein's son, dignitaries, princes and peers.' Many of his contemporaries in the 1990s were from far wealthier backgrounds. 'Everyone was always going on fantastic holidays, and I would be like, "Yeah, I'm going to see my gran in Brighton."'

He soon 'fell in with a nice bunch of teachers', a few of whom – like drama teacher Martin Tyrell – gave him the impetus to develop his acting abilities in the school productions. And it wasn't long before he found like-minded peers in the classroom. 'I was gregarious and found a coterie of brothers I'd never had before.' He had an inbuilt confidence, partly spurred on by the love and support he had always been shown by his parents. He did not feel entitled to be at Harrow, but felt he was able to investigate what was going on. He was not naturally clever, but he was good at learning.

Letters home to his parents were sincerely, blissfully happy. There was a brief period when he was targeted by a school bully, and his sense of confidence momentarily dissolved. Then he remembered himself. He pinned his enemy against the wall. No further bullying took place.

It is abundantly clear, checking through back issues of Harrow School's weekly magazine, *The Harrovian*, that Benedict Cumberbatch was one of Harrow's star drama pupils. But his first mentions came not from stage appearances, but from his contributions on the sporting field. Even in his first year, he was part of the Yearlings' rugby team, and would soon join the Junior Colts cricket squad, who would play matches against Eton, Radley and Wellington. In his third year, he would lead the Junior Colts for a while, when the resident team captain was indisposed.

According to *Harrovian* reviews, 'B.T.C. Cumberbatch' gets his first name-check for performance in 1991, after participating in a concert involving the 'Shells' (the most junior year at Harrow) on 3 March. But it was in the summer of that year that he made a breakthrough. June found him performing material from Geoffrey Willan's comic school stories about Nigel Molesworth, and reciting from Shakespeare's *The Tempest*. Most notably, that same month, he was cast in a production of the Bard's *A Midsummer Night's Dream*. Given that Harrow was an all-boys school, there were no girls to play the female roles in the play. Three years after Bottom, Cumberbatch was assigned the part of Titania. 'Cumberbatch was every inch the imperious Fairy Queen,' reported *The Harrovian* in its 15 June issue. 'His ringing tones filled Speech Room, and he displayed a mature control of gesture and movement that promises much for future productions. What most impressed here was the sense of danger this young actor breathed into the fairy kingdom.' 'Even then, I was conscious of being typecast,' Cumberbatch told *The Sunday Times* later. 'After rehearsals, I'd be backstage, whipping off my Cleo Laine-style Titania wig and changing into my rugby kit.'

Incidentally, fans of comedy at the school had an extra treat that Saturday night. Several 'Old Harrovians' (i.e. former pupils) presented their own special interpretations of *A Midsummer Night's Dream*. One was the writer and founder of Comic Relief, Richard Curtis, who had been head boy at Harrow in the mid-1970s. He presented a specially written 'Ode to Shakespeare by Edmund Blackadder'.

It was around this time that Cumberbatch met a future co-star for the first time. Much later, Rebecca Hall – the daughter of theatre director Sir Peter Hall and the operatic soprano Maria Ewing – would become good friends with Benedict. They would appear together in the film *Starter for 10* and the TV series *Parade's End*. But at the time, Rebecca was eight years old, and she was only in the audience because the best friend she had accompanied had an older brother in Benedict's class. 'You could already see what he was going to be like when he was middle-aged,' Hall would tell the *Daily Telegraph* in 2012. 'He is a one-off. It is the fate of people who are unique for others not to notice their talent straight off the bat. Benedict was never going to be the next anybody. He was always going to be just who he is.'

In the year below Cumberbatch at Harrow was Laurence Fox, later star of *Foyle's War* and *Lewis*. Fox enrolled at the school in autumn 1991, as did Patrick Kennedy, who would subsequently work with Benedict on screen: *Parade's End* (again) and *Cambridge Spies* on TV, and in the films *Atonement* and *War Horse*. At Harrow, Cumberbatch and Kennedy would appear together several times: Arthur Miller's *Death of a Salesman*, with Benedict as Willy Loman and Patrick as his son Biff, was well-received, as was the 1994 staging of Shakespeare's *The Taming of the Shrew*, where Cumberbatch's Petruchio landed him the tag of 'the supreme communicator' in the pages of *The Harrovian*.

By that stage, Cumberbatch was enough of a young man to be cast in exclusively male roles: as already mentioned, Petruchio, but also Clarence in *Richard III* (May 1993). Prior to these, though, he was often cast as women. In late 1991, he had stormed it as the maid in Georges Faydeau's 1907 farce, *A Flea in Her Ear*. 'A delightful cameo,' *The Harrovian* called his appearance. 'He had mastered the farce style to enchanting effect.' His Rosalind in Shakespeare's *As You Like It* (May 1992) would be described by Harrow's drama teacher and stage director Martin Tyrell as 'the finest since Vanessa Redgrave's.' 'I have seen pictures of that,' elaborated Cumberbatch much later, 'and I look like I am possessed by a woman.'

Also in his second year, he had landed the central role in *Pygmalion* as Eliza Doolittle. *The Harrovian* theatre reviews were mixed. Its write-up of this production (autumn 1991) praises how 'convincing and commanding' was Cumberbatch's portrayal of Eliza Doolittle, but regretfully notes that 'this performance lacked individuality and he never really made this amazing role his own. At times he veered from Shakespearian rhetoric to a highly convincing impression of Audrey Hepburn'. It's worth remembering of course that this is the school play being reviewed, not press night at the Old Vic, and Cumberbatch was still only fifteen at the time, an age when few with acting aspirations have established their own personal identity, let alone mastering the identities of others. It is forgivable that he would be channelling the star of *My Fair Lady* at that age. Soon after this, his voice broke and he began to be cast in male roles and would shine playing men of all ages.

The teenage Benedict, compelled to take on women's parts in the plays due to a complete lack of female pupils, felt frustrated by Harrow being a boys' school for another reason: it made him shy around the opposite sex. 'Having your adolescence at an all-male boarding school is just crap,' he has said. 'I was rubbish with girls for a long time.' This wasn't helped by an arrested physical development. 'I was a very late developer – very late. Fifteen, 16 – maybe even 17. But the one grace of an all-boys boarding school is that you could lie about what you'd done on your holidays.'

Acting was not the only performing he did. He also did fairly well at public speaking. On 29 October 1991, he made 'a witty and confident speech' on the subject of fame as part of a Junior Final. It was a curiously prescient choice of subject, given how high his profile would be 20 years on, and while there is no known record of what he actually said on the subject, perhaps the experiences of his parents gave him an insight into how fame works.

He clearly excelled at recitation. In March 1994, his penultimate year at Harrow, he almost won the Lady Bourchier Reading Competition, held at the school. In the final round, he read passages from Graham Swift's prize-winning novel *Waterland*, and from Tobias Smollett's *Peregrine Pickle*. 'All his readings had colour, while the prose passages had excellent narrative drive,' wrote the school magazine. Cumberbatch was placed as a joint runner-up by the special guest adjudicator, 'Stephen Fry, Esq.'. It gave an early indication that, as well as acting, Cumberbatch was a terrific reader of prose and poetry, a skill which would lead to plenty of voice work years later, especially in radio.

But there was undoubtedly a pull towards acting which Cumberbatch experienced. Were it not for an unexpected attack of nerves, his screen debut might have happened in his mid-teens. When former pupil Andrew Birkin was busily casting for his film version of Ian McEwan's *The Cement Garden*, he went back to his old school to seek out new talent. The uneasy subject matter – incest between teenage siblings – caused Cumberbatch some discomfort, especially the prospect of having to take his clothes off. 'I was terrified. I was really prudish at that age, and I didn't want anyone seeing what I looked like. So I didn't audition.' The chance to share the limelight with a young Charlotte Gainsbourg (Andrew Birkin's niece) was gone, but the very fact he'd been offered the opportunity to audition made him feel that he might have a future in this acting lark. 'I think that was the moment when I stumbled into realising that acting could be a thing for life rather than just something I did during term time.'

* * *

By his third year at Harrow, it seemed no production would be complete without Benedict Cumberbatch. Whether it was

Russian drama or farce or revue, he was one of the stars of the school's drama offerings. He had joined the Rattigan Society, named after yet another Old Harrovian: the dramatist Terence Rattigan, who had been one of the giants of British theatre in the 1940s and 50s.

Though they attended Harrow 65 years apart, Cumberbatch strongly identified with Rattigan. Both had spent much of their early lives in Kensington, they were in the same house at Harrow (The Park), and both spent plenty of time poring over books in the school's Vaughan Library.

On first seeing the numerous rows of books, Cumberbatch felt overwhelmed. 'I thought, I probably won't have a lifetime long enough to read the first shelf – let alone the first room, let alone the whole fucking library. I've always been after the idea of betterment, to understand the world around me.' His attitude to self-education would later extend into adulthood, where it would be typical for him to research a given role thoroughly.

The Rattigan Society would visit London regularly to watch plays in the West End. In early 1993, Cumberbatch was entranced by a revival of Rattigan's *The Deep Blue Sea*, starring Penelope Wilton and directed by Karel Reisz. Indeed, he was blown away by the mix of subtlety and great emotional pull of the play. 'The big moment. I realised Rattigan had a profound depth. Among all the wit, when the mask slips it's painfully raw.'

In June 1994, Cumberbatch made his own splash in a Rattigan revival. Back at Harrow School, he flourished in *The Browning Version* as the Classics master Arthur

Crocker-Harris. Written in the late 1940s, *The Browning Version* is set at 'a Public School in the South of England', which many have interpreted as being Harrow. 'Crocker-Harris' character moves between iron resilience and emotional collapse,' wrote *The Harrovian* in its 18 June issue, 'and Cumberbatch moved through each stage of his character's progression with considerable ability. He is to be congratulated on a performance to which he evidently committed himself fully.' Sixteen years later, in *After the Dance*, Cumberbatch would make an even bigger impact in a Rattigan play.

Another production which had a strong connection with his future career took place in 1994, in a Harrow staging of Tom Stoppard's *Rosencrantz and Guildenstern Are Dead*. The play brought Stoppard to prominence in the 1960s, and in 2010, when the playwright made a rare return to television with his adaptation of *Parade's End*, he specifically wanted Cumberbatch for the lead role of Christopher Tietjens. (It seems appropriate to mention here that in November 2013, Cumberbatch would appear in a special extract of *Rosencrantz and Guildenstern Are Dead* as part of an evening of celebrations marking the fiftieth anniversary of London's National Theatre.)

Sometimes, original material would be developed for Harrow School productions. Often, these took the form of revues, consisting of short comedy sketches and songs. Occasionally, something more ambitious would be tried. In November 1992, a brand new musical was premiered over four nights. *Ain't Life Good!* was loosely based around the plot of the classic Frank Capra movie, *It's A Wonderful Life*. Cumberbatch, playing a heavenly Blessed Soul, was just one of over 100 people involved in the production, which reportedly played to packed houses.

Such was the reaction to *Ain't Life Good!* that the following summer, it was put forward to compete in the South Bank Youth Music Festival competition. In the final round, held at the Queen Elizabeth Hall in London on 1 November 1993, it was judged to be Best Original Work. It marked the first time that Cumberbatch had been part of a prize-giving performance outside of his school gates.

Cumberbatch's singing abilities have rarely been called upon since his schooldays, but from the reviews of the time, it sounds as if he already possessed burgeoning vocal skills. At a Swing Band Concert just before Christmas in 1994, his guest spot on 'Minnie the 'Moocher' was such a hit with the audience that he was compelled to reprise it as an encore. Weeks earlier, he also did well in David Calhoun's *City of Angels*, which marked the opening of Harrow School's new Ryan Theatre in November 1994. 'Cumberbatch perfected the character of Stone,' wrote *The Harrovian* in its 8 December issue. 'His whisky beaten, cigarette stained voice aptly captured the personality of the philandering private eye.' It also noted his ability to make his singing voice be heard over the band, and even showed some promise as a dancer, a skill he had seemingly rarely used thus far. (Cumberbatch would later see a West End production with his parents, and at the time of writing, is preparing to film a big screen version, under the title *The Lost City of Z*.)

Whether in a starring or a supporting role, it's evident that Cumberbatch was a superlative ensemble player. He did not act in a vacuum, he was not playing the big star, and he was co-operative with his fellow actors. But then, he was not drawn to acting because it was an opportunity to 'show off'. Having both his parents in the business gave him a reality check about making acting a career choice. 'Because I saw the working practices behind what they did, it didn't carry a lot of mystique. I knew about the peripatetic nature, the uncertain income, what it can do to your social life … all of that.'

Benedict's acting ambitions were not entirely supported by his parents to begin with, even though both were stalwarts of British stage and screen. 'They were like, look at us, how out of control our lifestyle is, how money's a huge ebb and flow.' Indeed, part of the whole game plan of sending their son to Harrow in the first place was to wean him off the notion of wanting to be an actor. Ventham and Carlton were hopeful that a balanced education would push him towards an alternative, more secure career than the one they had both pursued. It seemed their 'plan' had not worked.

Cumberbatch later reflected that he lacked focus in his final year at Harrow (1994–95). He confessed that, now eighteen years old, he had preferred 'pot and girls and music' to studying. But there still seemed to be no let-up when it came to other extra-curricular activities. In sport, he had drifted from rugby and cricket to abseiling, and had become a mainstay of the school's paragliding regiment. He was still fanatical about art – 'My canvases were the walls of deserted squash courts. Where else would you be indulged like that?'

– and in February 1995, a 'huge scissors sculpture in metal and string' he had made helped The Park win a House Art Competition at the school.

But inevitably it was as a stage presence where Benedict Cumberbatch had made his greatest impact at Harrow. One of six departing pupils of 1995 to receive an Evelyn de Rothschild Leaving Scholarship, he was singled out for greatness in July of that year by the headmaster in an end-of-term speech. While Nicholas Bomford acknowledged that it was 'invidious to pick out boys for special mention when so much has been achieved as a result of collective endeavour', there was no escaping that even as a team player, Ben Cumberbatch was emerging as a star. His performances on stage, said Bomford, 'will long be remembered by those lucky enough to have seen them.' Drama tutor Martin Tyrell would later describe him as 'the best schoolboy actor I've ever worked with'.

What to do next? He had considered law as a possible profession. For his parents, jittery about the insecurity of the acting profession, this would have been a relief. 'A lot of people told me that barristers never knew where their next job was coming from, and that you had to trek all over the country, and it was very hard work. It sounded a bit like acting, so I stuck with that instead.' It also occurred to him that his reasons for chasing the law as a career lay in acting anyway. He was a big fan of John Mortimer's *Rumpole of the Bailey* on television, starring Leo McKern. Had he just wanted to study law so he could become Horace Rumpole?

He finally abandoned any aspirations to work in legal

circles when he visited the law department at Manchester University. He changed his mind; other law students reminded him of 'the living dead', and above all he realised his attempts to change career had been to 'show off to my parents that I was capable of that'. Pursuing an acting career would be precarious and unpredictable, but so could just about any other career. His five years inside 'an incredibly privileged bubble' at Harrow School had left him in no doubt about what he really wanted to do: he wanted to be an actor, just like his parents.

CHAPTER 3

BIG WIDE WORLD

With Benedict at Harrow, Wanda and Tim had increased their stage work commitments. In 1991, for the first time in 20 years, they appeared together in a touring production of the Ray Cooney farce, *Out of Order*. In its West End run, the play won the Olivier Theatre Award for Best Comedy. The couple would also be regulars in three series of the BBC sitcom, *Next of Kin*, with Penelope Keith and William Gaunt. In 1997, having played Cassandra's mum in *Only Fools and Horses*, Wanda would appear as the mum of Deborah (Leslie Ash) in another hit sitcom, *Men Behaving Badly*. But most of their work would be in the theatre now. Their son would come and watch them perform, often with increasing discomfort as his mum especially would play roles requiring her to be in some or other compromising position. 'I had to say to her, sorry

Mum, I just can't bear to see that gag one more time. I was so sensitive to it, she must have wondered if I was gay.'

After leaving Harrow in the summer of 1995, Benedict took a year out before university. He wanted to spend some time abroad, and in order to fund his trip spent around six months working in a London perfumier. The second half of his gap year found him in Darjeeling, West Bengal, India, where he taught English to Buddhist monks for an organisation appropriately called GAP. He was able to live with the monks, and witness all their daily rituals, including working and praying. 'They taught me about the duplicity of human nature, but also the humanity of it, and the ridiculous sense of humour you need to live a full spiritual life.'

The monks also taught him how to meditate, something that would prove an invaluable aid in his acting career. It gave him 'an ability to focus and have a real sort of purity of purpose and attention, and not be too distracted. And to feel very alive to your environment, to know what you are part of, to understand what is going on in your peripheral vision and behind you, as well as what is in front of you. That definitely came from that.'

There were sober moments. He would watch mourners carry corpses to the river to be burnt. 'It's not a charming ancient tradition,' he pointed out. 'You are inhaling the smoke of a burning body.' But his experiences in Tibet were not without laughter either. On one occasion, his new friends were endlessly amused by the sight of two dogs having sex in a back yard. 'The monks were on the floor laughing at these sentient beings' pain and ridiculousness, these two dogs just stuck together. "Kodak moment, sir!" Brilliant!'

Another time, his life was in danger, not for the last time. With four friends, he set off on an expedition to the mountains of Nepal. Bereft of guidance or sufficient protective clothing, the ill-equipped party soon ran into difficulties. 'We got altitude sickness and then amoebic dysentery,' Cumberbatch would recall. 'We were lost for a day and a half, trekking at night and squeezing moss to get water. We slept in an animal hut that stank of dung and had hallucinogenic dreams because of altitude sickness.' Salvation only came when they followed a trail of yak droppings and made it back to safety. 'It was a pathetic expedition,' he told journalist Caitlin Moran over 15 years later. 'We were woefully under-prepared. I had simply an extra scarf my mother had knitted me and a piece of cheese.'

Safely back in Britain, Cumberbatch began his three-year degree at Manchester University in the autumn of 1996. Despite Harrow School's location – slap-bang in the middle of the town, and not that far from Central London – he had felt a little cosseted there, and yearned for something grittier. 'I needed to be out of the danger of tying a cashmere jumper round my neck. I wanted something a bit more egalitarian. I didn't want just an extension of my public school, I wanted less exclusivity.'

He had considered Oxbridge for a time, but while both Oxford and Cambridge had drama societies and revue groups – most famously the Oxford Revue and the

Cambridge Footlights – neither university offered a degree course in drama. He opted for Manchester University, as it had a long and respected connection with drama and performance. In the late 1970s, all three writers of *The Young Ones* – Rik Mayall, Lise Mayer and Ben Elton – had studied there, as had Mayall's co-star Adrian Edmondson. The 1980s intake had included Doon Mackichan (*The Day Today*, *Smack the Pony*) and *Goodness Gracious Me!*'s Meera Syal, while from the 1990s onwards, *Peep Show* creators Jesse Armstrong and Sam Bain, *The Thick of It*'s Chris Addison, the Chemical Brothers, Professor Brian Cox and most recently, the comedian Jack Whitehall have all been Manchester graduates on various other courses. Several playwrights of excellence also attended the university, including Robert Bolt (perhaps most famous for the play *A Man for All Seasons*) and *Our Friends in the North* writer Peter Flannery.

At Manchester, Cumberbatch's contemporaries on his drama course included Olivia Poulet, who hailed from South-West London, and who was two years his junior. In their final year, 1999, they would begin a relationship which would last 12 years. Also in their year was a young Mathew Horne, future star of the BBC1 series *Gavin & Stacey*, who was training to be a stand-up and who was writing a dissertation about the performance styles of Steve Coogan.

Cumberbatch's own 30,000-word dissertation was on the output of film director Stanley Kubrick. His supervisor for the project was Michael Holt, who later remembered that the youth arrived at the university with some impeccable references from his previous school. 'I remember one of his masters from Harrow calling me to tell me what a great talent was arriving. And indeed he was.' Holt recalled someone who was extremely popular with fellow students, could be pleasant and thoughtful, but had visions of becoming a brilliant actor rather than a superstar. 'He knew it was something you had to work at. He wasn't starry-eyed. He had a professional attitude.'

The drama course presented Cumberbatch with all sorts of new challenges. 'We did a practical course in prisons and probation, which meant learning about the penal system and forms of rehabilitation, and then going in with a project for a month and a half to Strangeways, two other category C facilities and a probation centre. For a posh bloke with a silly name, to be in a world like that was extraordinary.'

We put on a ridiculous amount of plays, sometimes three at a time. You would be doing a show,' Cumberbatch told US TV talk show host Charlie Rose in 2014, 'you'd be rehearsing one, and you'd be getting ready to stage the other. Three different characters and three different worlds, and a great stretch in training for practice in the old days.'

Off-duty, as it were, Cumberbatch had made all sorts of new friends ('a thoroughly healthy – and unhealthy – mix'), and he could party hard, but was for a time floored by glandular fever. Even so, it was becoming apparent that he had been right to follow acting as a career of choice. His parents were becoming resigned to his decision, but in a positive way. The truth was, whenever they came to see a play he was in, whether it was *Glengarry Glen Ross* or

Amadeus, he clearly had such striking potential. 'My parents were sanguine about it in the end. My dad came up to me when I was in a production and said, "You're better now than I've ever been." From that moment, I thought, "OK, if I've got his blessing, I'm going to do it."'

Cumberbatch's work during the late 1990s was rarely reviewed, but just after graduating from Manchester, he was spotted by a handful of press titles. On 18 August 1999, during that year's Edinburgh Festival, he was cited as one to watch by the *Daily Mail*'s resident gossip columnist. Nigel Dempster wrote that he was 'wowing audiences' at the Greyfriars Kirk House venue in Edward Albee's two-hander, *The Zoo Story*. He had a connection with Benedict's family – he was quick to acknowledge that Tim Carlton was an 'old school friend' from their days at Sherborne School in Dorset in the early 1950s.

The Zoo Story was being performed by a theatre company called Tunnelvision. It was about two characters and a park bench in New York's Central Park. Peter is trying to read, but Jerry wants to talk about the lonely life he leads. The review of the play in *The Scotsman* – frequently the first port of call for anything to do with the Edinburgh Festival – celebrated Cumberbatch's versatility. 'Benedict Cumberbatch's performance as Jerry is imaginative and dynamic. He is the sort of actor who could sustain interest and variety in a one-man show in which he played 20 different parts.' He was just one future name who was being bookmarked as one to watch that summer at Edinburgh, where Miranda Hart was in a duo called The Orange Girls, and Cambridge graduates David Mitchell and Robert Webb were establishing themselves as a comedy double act.

Following Edinburgh, Manchester graduate Cumberbatch returned to London. While his girlfriend Olivia Poulet joined the National Youth Theatre, he embarked on one more year of education, this time at the London Academy of Music & Dramatic Art (LAMDA). He even gained his first agent, and for a time experimented with a name change. Just as his dad had done over 40 years earlier, he ditched 'Cumberbatch' in favour of 'Carlton'. His reasoning, he later explained, was for simplification; Cumberbatch was 'a bit bumbly and messy', and he assumed there was no way he could use that name as a professional actor. He soon had second thoughts, though, especially when he changed agents. 'I wasn't getting very far and my new agent suggested I revert. Benedict Cumberbatch was a mouthful of a name, but an unforgettable mouthful. They said it's a great name, it will get people talking about you.'

At the end of January 2000, he made his first notable television appearance, in an episode of the nostalgic ITV Sunday night drama series set in 1960s northern England, *Heartbeat*. His parents had both appeared in the series: Tim played three different characters over the programme's 18-year duration, while Wanda had played the same character in four episodes during the 1990s. Despite his many, much more prominent successes on television over the years, it is a curious statistic that Cumberbatch's debut in *Heartbeat* attracted the biggest national TV audience of his entire career to date. Sandwiched in between *Coronation Street* and the firefighters' drama series *London's Burning*, nearly 15 million people watched that episode of *Heartbeat*. In fact, in that week only *Coronation Street* was watched by more of an audience.

Yet it was a one-off. He would not appear on TV again for well over two years. After his one-year course finished at LAMDA, he found other work hard to come by. For six months or so, there was nothing. 'It can be dispiriting when you've put your heart and soul into something and the results aren't instantaneous.'

There were a few visits back to his alma mater. On 6 May 2000, during his final term at LAMDA, he made a comeback appearance at Harrow School in *The Taming of the Shrew*, once again as Petruchio, 'with an ingenious mania ... an amiable arrogance which was simultaneously hilarious and sympathetic'. In September, he guested as Jack Worthing in a production of Oscar Wilde's *The Importance of Being Earnest*, with Peter O'Toole's teenage son Lorcan featuring as Algernon. Cumberbatch was helpfully flagged once again in the pages of the *Daily Mail* by Nigel Dempster, but *The Harrovian* review also proudly highlighted the comeback kid. 'An actor of whom we shall surely hear more,' it remarked. 'He portrayed all the signs of a natural professional.'

A few months later, he was back at Harrow as part of CAMERA, a theatre group he had formed at university, to perform *Kvetch*, a drama by Steven Berkoff, in which he played George, a Jewish wholesaler. It was performed for staff and upper school 'due to the content of the play'. It's worth noting that Cumberbatch was by no means a name, but such was his reputation in drama at the school that his guest spot was so warmly received – and reviewed in the school magazine as 'a genuine crowd-pleaser'.

For the most part, though, actual acting jobs were scarce in the months after LAMDA. He scraped together a living as a waiter in restaurants, but there was little more than that. 'I was on beans and toast. I had an actor friend who said we were enjoying the lemon rind years, meaning we'd eat the lemon rind in our drink if we could only afford one.'

After an upward trajectory through his schooldays, and a high-octane life at university, Cumberbatch realised the real work was only just beginning. In the bubble of student drama, you're encouraged all the way. Outside that in the wider world, it was harder to establish oneself. 'You're instilled with confidence from that,' he would say many years later, 'and then you get rejection.' Fortunately, though, some proper stage work was not far away.

CHAPTER 4

PROFESSIONAL ACTOR

In the spring of 2001, Benedict Cumberbatch could finally give up waiting tables. He was selected for two stage productions at the Open Air Theatre that summer in London's Regent's Park. Staging Shakespeare there was a summertime tradition that stretched back some 70 years. He would feature in the cast of two of the Bard's comedies: *A Midsummer Night's Dream* and *Love's Labour's Lost*.

As we have established, Cumberbatch had already made his mark twice before in *A Midsummer Night's Dream*. Aged twelve, his take on the bumbling Nick Bottom the weaver had been a hit in the Brambletye Prep School production. A few years later, at Harrow, he was Titania. A decade on or so, with the comic performer Gary Wilmot playing Bottom, Cumberbatch would play Demetrius. Director Alan Strachan had revived the production the previous summer in Regent's

Park, transplanting it from the 1590s to the mid-nineteenth century.

Most of the cast of *A Midsummer Night's Dream* also spent the summer of 2001 on a second Shakespeare comedy, again directed by Strachan. In *Love's Labour's Lost*, Cumberbatch played the King of Navarre in a Wodehousian style, as if he were Bertie Wooster. His masterly portrayal of bluster and insecurity was met with some excellent national press reviews. 'Finds humour and silliness where none previously existed,' said the *Daily Mail*. 'A pleasant young blade,' remarked *The Sunday Times*, and went on, 'A bit of a wag, a bit of a lad, fancies himself, not entirely wrongly, as sophisticated.' In a quirk of fate that was to become a habit over the years, he found himself in the cast alongside someone who knew at least one of his parents – in this case Christopher Godwin. 'He'd worked with my father in [Michael Frayn's] *Noises Off*. I love the continuity of acting. It's really lovely to be acting with people from my parents' generation.'

Even though traditional theatre had been performed outside centuries before, contemporary audiences accustomed to ceilings would be taking a risk by watching plays outside. If weather conditions were idyllic, an evening of outdoor Shakespeare could hardly be bettered. In a dreary and damp British summer – and 2001 was one of far too many – it could be gruelling.

On one Saturday night, when the *Independent*'s theatre critic was present, the downpours were so persistent that near the halfway point, the actors had little choice but to run for cover. Such were the risks of performing theatre outdoors. Legend has it that two elderly audience members were once overheard discussing a production of *A Midsummer Night's Dream* they had watched in similarly wretched conditions. 'That was the best *Dream* I've ever seen,' declared one. Her companion replied: 'Yes, pity it had to be a wet one.'

All the same, Cumberbatch's King of Navarre in *Love's Labour's Lost* had made such a mark that it gained him a nomination in the 2001 Ian Charleson Awards, a prize given to the best performance in a classic play by an actor aged under thirty. Inaugurated in 1991, the Award – sponsored by the National Theatre and *The Sunday Times* – had been named in honour of the highly acclaimed Scottish actor whose life had been cruelly cut short the previous year, at the age of just forty. Among the winners and nominees over the years have been Jude Law, Tom Hollander, Helen McCrory, Marianne Jean-Baptiste, Dominic West, and Ben Whishaw.

Cumberbatch would not feature among the top three prize winners in 2001 – Claire Price, Zoe Waites, James D'Arcy – but he would be shortlisted again in 2006, just months before his thirtieth birthday would have excluded him from the running. This time round, he was placed third for his performance as Tesman in *Hedda Gabler*. He was so affecting and convincing in the role that he persuaded the judging panel that 'the play was as much his tragedy as Hedda's'. To Cumberbatch's enormous pride and satisfaction, he was congratulated at the ceremony by another actor who had excelled as Tesman when a young man – Sir Ian McKellen.

In the summer of 2002, Cumberbatch returned to Regent's

Park for a further double-header of open-air Shakespeare (as well as a revival of Joan Littlewood's *Oh! What a Lovely War*). If *Romeo and Juliet* was coolly received by the critics, his performance as Benvolio stood out for several of them, with one – the *Guardian* – arguing that he 'seems to carry the whole weight of the tragedy on his frail shoulders'. *The Stage* praised 'a commanding performance, making much from the comparatively small role to appear the stronger of the Montague rebels'.

The more modernist setting of *As You Like It*, relocated to the Edwardian 1920s, was generally deemed more successful. Back at Harrow in the early 1990s, he had triumphed as Rosalind, but now he was playing opposite that character as the intense and impetuous Orlando. For some he was a little too intense in the part. 'Cumberbatch once or twice falls to ranting,' wrote the *Sunday Telegraph*, but went on, 'he more than makes up for it with his ardour and openness.' It was a convincing portrayal of a love affair in the view of several press pundits, who were most disappointed that the press night performance had to be stopped early, due to more heavy rain. The weather scarcely improved over the next few days, but the cast battled on, while the audience cowered under brollies. The *Glasgow Herald* commented that Cumberbatch and Rebecca Johnson 'echo Andie MacDowell and Hugh Grant's sodden *Four Weddings* climactic embrace, but this time entirely authentically.' 'Both these actors display exceptional promise,' enthused *The Stage*.

'In true British spirit, it has to get really wet and dangerous before the show is stopped,' said Cumberbatch. Yet at least in torrential rain, a cast and an audience suffer together. At one *As You Like It* performance, he faced an early exit alone when he lost his voice. The awful moment occurred just after Orlando had whispered the line, 'I cannot speak to her!' A lone member of the 1,000-strong audience chuckled aloud at the unfortunate predicament facing the actor. As his understudy took over his lines, a despondent, voiceless Cumberbatch cycled home.

He encountered another embarrassing situation in the spring of 2003. It took place offstage, but it was mortifying nonetheless for the rising star. Casting was taking place for *The Lady from the Sea* at London's (thankfully indoor) Almeida Theatre. At the audition, partly down to a self-confessed inability to remember names easily, he accidentally and repeatedly called the Almeida's artistic director Sir Trevor Nunn 'Adrian Noble', at the time the artistic director of the Royal Shakespeare Company.

Fortunately, Nunn cast Cumberbatch anyway. *The Lady from the Sea*, which marked the theatre's relaunch, was an unsparing emotional drama from the 1880s by Henrik Ibsen. The production starred Natasha Richardson, whose mother Vanessa Redgrave had delivered a stunning performance in the central role of Ellida 25 years earlier. It told the story of a married woman living in the mountains who still yearns to be free, both for the sea and for a sailor she once loved. Now married to a country doctor, and with two young daughters, she loses another baby at just five months of age.

Cumberbatch was in a supporting role, as an ailing but

self-important sculptor by the name of Lyngstrand. It was a part that required him to master the emotive and the darkly comic. 'What made him funny,' he later recalled, 'is that he had no idea how ridiculous he was. When people were laughing at me in the audience, I tried to put a bit of white noise out there to block it out.' The pomposity of Lyngstrand was the sort of role he was being offered more and more, which he was already a little concerned about. 'Gaucheness is a default mechanism with me, so it's immediately something people see I fit into a box of. But when you go home and look at yourself in the mirror, the one thing you don't want to be is that person all the time.'

Cumberbatch was a more familiar name to the public by March 2005, when he was back at the Almeida in another Ibsen revival – this time 1890's *Hedda Gabler*. Director Richard Eyre, fresh from presiding over a West End version of *Mary Poppins*, had claimed to have had the idea to revive the play after reading a copy of *Hello!* magazine in a dentist's waiting room, in which there was an interview 'with a rich, posh young woman who was celebrated for being celebrated' and who confessed to having 'a great talent for boredom'. 'Mmmm, Hedda Gabler lives,' thought Eyre, and on seeing Eve Best appearing in a National Theatre production of O'Neill's *Mourning Becomes Electra*, he knew he had his Hedda.

Opposite Hedda's icy contempt, Cumberbatch was Tesman, her husband and a struggling academic. He was widely praised for underplaying the foppishness of the character, instead emphasising his scholarly and thoughtful qualities. 'It's more interesting for me to play him differently,' he said. 'And it's better for the ensemble too. I've always felt it belittles both her tragedy and his to present this idea that, right from the start, they've missed the boat because she's married an idiot.' The play sold out its run at the Almeida, and from late May of 2005, transferred with the same cast for a 10-week run at the Duke of York's Theatre.

A year later, a lead role came Cumberbatch's way: George in *Period of Adjustment*, a tragi-comedy from the pen of American playwright Tennessee Williams, and not often performed. Set on Christmas Eve, George is a Korean War veteran, who has just married Isabel (Lisa Dillon) but finds it impossible to consummate the union. He is reassured by Ralph (Jared Harris), his friend from army days, that such problems are not unusual for newlyweds, but it transpires Ralph himself is experiencing a disintegration of his own marriage to Dorothea (Sandy McDade). Williams was not generally known for comedy, and *Period of Adjustment* was by no means classed as one of his greats, unlike *A Streetcar Named Desire* or *Cat on a Hot Tin Roof*, and it had not been performed in London since 1962, but the performances drew some positive comment. *Time Out*'s theatre critic wrote that Cumberbatch 'brings a virile warmth that makes us hope for the marriage'. Once again, he would be making both audience and critics alike root for a flawed character.

* * *

In addition to Cumberbatch's stage work throughout this period was a surge in television roles. If the 18 months following his brief *Heartbeat* showing in 2000 had been fallow, the autumn of 2001 found him filming *Fields of Gold*, a two-part thriller for the BBC about genetically modified crops and the way that governments collude with big business. It was written by two journalists, one of whom – Alan Rusbridger – was (indeed at the time of writing still is) the editor of the *Guardian* newspaper. It had, though, also been partially inspired by the John Wyndham sci-fi story *The Day of the Triffids*, and was focused on how scientific advances were spiralling out of control. It was broadcast in the summer of 2002.

Even in the minor roles of the cast list – about halfway to two-thirds down – Cumberbatch was eager to prepare for the part he had been assigned, and worked hard on background research, a decision that was not always popular. When working on *Dunkirk* in 2003, a documentary-drama about World War Two's unforgettable May 1940 maritime evacuation, he found himself barred from contacting the surviving relatives of his character's real-life incarnation. 'The BBC were saying, "You might upset them." I'm about to play him on screen! If that's going to upset the relatives, I might as well get it over with now.'

Another role of 2002 saw him in the opening episode of that autumn's most-talked about drama: *Tipping the Velvet*, boldly adapted by Andrew Davies from the equally bold Sarah Waters novel, and starring Rachael Stirling and Keeley Hawes. He would be subject to a great deal of good-natured ribbing from friends after accepting the part of Freddy. 'I was the boy that turned a girlfriend into the most celebrated lesbian on television. I got so much stick for that.'

At the time of writing, Cumberbatch has still only ever appeared in a few full television series, and July and August of 2003 saw the transmission of the first of these. *Fortysomething*, written by Nigel Williams and based on his own 1999 novel, was a comedy-drama about the midlife crisis, and marked the return of Hugh Laurie to television comedy nearly a decade after his last series with Stephen Fry. Laurie played Paul Slippery, a general practitioner alarmed by the impending and unstoppable onset of middle age. Slippery's crisis, in which he worries about his moribund sex life, is compounded by the amount of sex his three grown-up offspring are enjoying, not to mention his wife's bid for liberation, now that their children have come of age.

In an illustrious cast – Anna Chancellor, Sheila Hancock and Peter Capaldi among many others – Cumberbatch was Slippery's idealistic daydreamer of an eldest son, Rory. There were some concerns that the novel's setting was a bit insular, with Paul Slippery being an actor in a BBC radio drama (the media as a subject for drama rarely attracts big audiences), so his occupation and workplace were changed to healthcare, as a satire on the NHS, as well as an exploration of how a middle-aged man could rediscover his love for his wife.

Maybe on BBC2 where high ratings were not quite as vital, *Fortysomething* may have had a chance to build an audience over its six-week run. But it was broadcast on ITV – which was aggressively chasing viewers – and not even a guest cameo by Stephen Fry in the second episode could stop the ratings from tumbling. ITV panicked and shifted the series from a prime slot on Sundays to a graveyard one after 11 o'clock on a Saturday night. Repeats of the reliable *Midsomer Murders* filled the gap on Sundays. A handful of broadsheet critics continued to carry a torch for the series, but regrettably, it has never been repeated, and remains relatively obscure. Hugh Laurie, who had also directed some of the series, licked his wounds and auditioned for the part of another disillusioned medic. It would mean Laurie being resident in Los Angeles for several years making one of the most watched television series on the planet. An arrogant pedant of a man, who plays a musical instrument and lives at 221b, the character of Gregory House MD makes frequent nods towards the detective Sherlock Holmes in the way he could coldly analyse rare and otherwise undiagnosable medical conditions. It was the kind of character that fascinates a viewing audience, the kind that Benedict Cumberbatch would later get to play.

For now, though, in these early years as a professional, and as uncertain as his career could be, he was satisfied with his lot: stage and screen work gathering pace. 'You can't predict how it's going to turn out,' he said of this uncertain time. 'What happens is you do your bit, you settle, and see where you are in the grand picture of where everyone else is. You go, "Ooh, I'd like a bit of what that person's doing, and I think I can get up to that standard, and I think I could be taken seriously enough to do that.' Just as *Fortysomething* was demoted into virtual obscurity by ITV, Benedict Cumberbatch was about to play a part which would make him – if not a star – a name.

CHAPTER 5

THE SCIENTIST

In September 2003, filming began in Cambridge and London on a new film for television about Professor Stephen Hawking. Its director, Philip Martin, had excelled as a documentary filmmaker for TV, with credits including a full six-part series for the BBC in 1997 called *Stephen Hawking's Universe*, in which the scientist's theories on the evolution of the cosmos, black holes and time travel were explored.

Stephen Hawking became famous outside scientific circles with the publication of *A Brief History of Time* in 1988, which detailed his studies and explorations into the Big Bang Theory – the theory stating that the creation of the universe occurred 15 billion years ago via a gargantuan explosion. The book became a best-seller, but Hawking had long been confined to a wheelchair for many years after the onset of motor neurone disease.

The new BBC film, simply titled *Hawking*, concentrated on the period between 1963 and 1965, when he was studying for his doctorate at Cambridge University, but against the growing shadow of his illness. 'It's about the nature of time on both a deeply personal and a universal scale,' commented the film's producer, Jessica Pope. 'At the moment when his intellect was striving to grow to its full potential, his physical self was cruelly closing down.'

At the outset of *Hawking*, Stephen is celebrating his twenty-first birthday in his hometown of St Albans, Hertfordshire. Lying on the grass beside his future wife, Jane Wilde, and stargazing, he finds he is unable to get up and soon discovers that he has only two years to live, due to the onset of his illness.

The film's screenwriter, Peter Moffat, had written *Cambridge Spies* for broadcast in 2003, a four-part drama about Anthony Blunt, Kim Philby, Guy Burgess and Donald Maclean, in which Cumberbatch and fellow ex-Harrovian Patrick Kennedy briefly featured. The lead roles were taken by a new generation of promising young actors: Samuel West, Toby Stephens, Rupert Penry-Jones and Tom Hollander.

A year later, *Hawking* marked Cumberbatch's debut as a lead on television. He confessed that while the prospect of playing Stephen was a thrill, it was daunting too. 'That initial elation of getting the job passed over very quickly, because I thought, "I've got a lot of work to do".' Even so, he would discover that those pressures would lead to some rewarding moments during the making of the film, and would call it 'the most satisfying job I've done' in his career up to this point.

The task of portraying on screen someone who is still alive can be fraught with difficulties. Hawking himself had co-operated with the filmmakers, but had questioned an early draft of the script where, in one scene, his character was seen to have discussed his illness. He wondered if this was too 'soap opera'. 'I think what Stephen thinks is a soap opera is rather different from what the rest of us think,' commented director Philip Martin just before the film received its TV premiere. The affair was written up in the press as if there had been big arguments, but Cumberbatch denied it. 'The fact that he didn't like the first draft of the script is par for the course,' he said. 'We made changes to accommodate his views, and he remained continually in conference with the production team. He's been integral to the film.'

Stephen Hawking met Cumberbatch twice during the making of the film – first at a script meeting, and at a subsequent day of shooting at Caius College in Cambridge, the city in which the Professor (by now in his sixties) was still living. 'We got a call that Stephen might pop in and see it being filmed,' said Philip Martin. 'So Stephen as he is now met Stephen as he was then, in his old college quad. It must have been strange for him to see himself portrayed. He said it was really great to be played by someone much better-looking than himself.'

The young actor was nervous about meeting the scientist, especially on set. 'There he was – this incredibly intelligent, forceful presence – and there was I, a dopey actor feeling anything but intelligent.' But any anxieties soon fell away. 'There was lots of joking. He watched a bit and then said, "Very good, very realistic – but you're much too handsome."' He was a lively presence during the shoot, even if communication could be an arduous process. 'He is very keen to beat you to making the first joke,' said Philip Martin. 'The business of communicating is so difficult, he gets down to what he wants very quickly, so you have very productive meetings and he tells you exactly what he thinks.'

Someone else who visited the set was the real-life Hawking's son, Tim. 'Tim looked quite shell-shocked,' Cumberbatch told the *Radio Times*. 'He told me that he had only ever spoken to his dad through his voice synthesiser, and had only ever seen him in a wheelchair, so it was very spooky seeing me as his father, walking and talking.'

Because of Hawking's condition, casual conversation could be an involved process, and Cumberbatch longed to have more time with him to ask questions. 'You want to sit down and have a pint and ask, "Are you left-handed or right-handed? What do you look for in a girlfriend?" I couldn't because having a conversation with him is such tortuous hard work.' But he came to understand the slight awkwardness between them. 'Every now and again our eyes would catch and I'd look away and then I held his gaze for a little bit and he looked back up again and I smiled at him and he smiled back and it was fine. I suddenly realised he must be uncomfortable with this whole thing.' In 2007, he elaborated further: 'It was a bit frustrating because you're not allowed to ask him any questions. Perhaps he feels that everything you might want to know is already available in his work.'

The real-life Jane Wilde, Hawking's first wife, visited another university location shoot, this time at Trinity Hall, and was moved to tears watching Lisa Dillon and Cumberbatch playing her and Stephen as they had been 40 years earlier. 'It reminded me of how idealistic we felt then. That is one of the most difficult things to cope with, to see how it's all gone so horribly wrong,' she told the *Daily Mail* in 2004. 'But people will see how things were, and make a comparison with the present, and in that sense the timing is fortuitous.'

Confining the story mostly to just a two-year period in the distant past did mean that the team working on the film had greater freedom than they would have done had they tackled a biopic of Hawking's entire life. 'With this period of his life,' said Cumberbatch, 'we almost had carte blanche because not many people know that much about it.' This was long before *A Brief History of Time*, and long before Hawking became famous. 'Unusually in playing a real person, I had pretty much a blank canvas. There isn't even any film from those days.' There was, however, some footage of Stephen's mother, and further inspiration came from friends of Hawking's, and from Jane Wilde.

The aim was to give a performance somewhere between an impersonation and his own interpretation of the man. But Cumberbatch was determined to make the character a realistic one. 'It's very important to portray Stephen as a human being rather than as a kind of superhero icon, which of course he is. We wanted the audience to engage with this person beyond what he was struggling through with his body, so that his character and the great joy of scientific discovery and finding true love were at the forefront.'

As part of his preparation, Cumberbatch enlisted the help of a movement teacher and consulted with two men who actually had motor neurone disease. To act the role, it was essential to examine how the disease affects the body's gravity. His findings made him feel grateful for his physical condition, and every night after filming, rigorous exercise was a must. 'Every night after filming, I'd do stretching exercises to expand my limbs in a way that I couldn't during the day, while playing someone who's losing the use of his muscles.'

Emulating Hawking's declining speech patterns was also hard work, although Cumberbatch was said to have come close even during his audition. 'It was quite clearly written in the script,' he told *The Times*. 'It's slightly like the atonal palate of a deaf person because the soft palate goes, the tonal variation goes, the tongue loses its elasticity, so it's very vowelly, the consonants go. It's like me when I'm very, very hungover, really.'

The real-life Hawking had eventually lost the power of speech, although not until the mid-1980s when he contracted pneumonia during a scientific conference, and had to undergo an emergency tracheostomy. With the help of an American voice synthesiser, Hawking could now communicate – albeit slowly – by selecting highlighted words from a computer screen, which he then arranged into sentences. But he never switched the setting of the voicebox from an American accent to an English one. Cumberbatch discovered the reason why during the shooting of the film. Hawking had told him: 'I find that American and Scandinavian accents work better with women.'

Great care had to be taken so that the behaviours of someone with severe illness were not overplayed. How to display increasing severity of symptoms without acting in dubious taste? 'I thought I'd give it five stages,' explained Cumberbatch, 'so that the viewer would know where we were through the walk and talk. We specifically chose certain symptoms to emphasise, which does actually happen; one day the speech would be a lot worse than the fine motor skills.'

Cumberbatch felt strong responsibility for the portrayal, as he knew that for many, he was representing motor neurone disease on screen. 'There will be thousands of people with motor neurone disease who will have that interest in the film.' It was essential to get his portrayal right.

It wasn't just Hawking's worsening physical condition which was a challenge to dramatise. How can a narrative bring to life the subject of theoretical physics, which does not lend itself easily to visual representation in a drama? The scientist had hoped that the film might find room for his work on black holes in the 1970s and 80s, but Philip Martin – whose own background was in making science documentaries – worried it would have alienated the public. 'By the time you get to Stephen's work on black holes, the cosmology gets so complicated it's very difficult to explain.' Yet the final cut would satisfy the scientist, by then 62 years of age and a twice-married father of three. He would say of the film, simply: 'It captured the spirit of the time.'

Hawking was broadcast by BBC2 on Tuesday, 13 April 2004, opposite several middling reality TV series on rival channels: *A Life of Grime, The Games, Neighbours from Hell*. It was a much more interesting proposition. A few press critics were guarded about how effective the mix of science, romance and illness actually was, and pointed out that some of the material was factually different to the content of a documentary screened immediately afterwards on BBC4. For instance, it was stated in the latter that Hawking's first collapse had not occurred at his twenty-first, as suggested in the drama, but several months earlier while ice-skating with his parents.

But is the function of the biopic to document a life story as accurately as possible, or to encapsulate the heart and soul of its subject? Anyone's life story poured into a 90-minute drama would be reductive. What seemed to be most important here was to access the essence of Stephen Hawking in the 1960s, and the critics were unanimous that Benedict Cumberbatch had achieved just that. The *Guardian*'s Nancy Banks-Smith marvelled, 'There was a gawkiness, arrogance and charm about Cumberbatch, which reminded you of a child taking a watch apart. And putting it together better.' Over at *The Times*, Joe Joseph was also impressed at how Cumberbatch balanced the failings of Hawking's body – 'conveying Hawking's humour, his passion, his lack of self-pity, and giving the gist of Hawking's features, his melting posture, those inquisitive eyes, that sloping gash of a smile, without overstepping the mark into parody.'

In the summer of 2005, *Hawking* would win Cumberbatch his first major award: the Best Performance by an Actor at the Monte-Carlo Television Festival. He lost out at the BAFTA Television Awards when Rhys Ifans triumphed for his portrayal of Peter Cook in the single drama *Not Only But Always*, but he was delighted to be in the running for Best Actor in the first place. He insisted that he was simply delighted to be able to attend the ceremony with his mother and father, and to be able to show off the Jil Sander suit he had bought specially. He later revealed that he had often been up against fellow nominee Michael Sheen in auditions, for parts Sheen gained and he hadn't.

Benedict Cumberbatch and Stephen Hawking rarely connected again after the making of *Hawking*, but their worlds would occasionally collide. In 2010, the pair would share narration duties on a three-part documentary series for the Discovery Channel called *Stephen Hawking's Universe* (unrelated to the Philip Martin series of the 1990s), for which Hawking wrote the scripts, on subjects including time travel, alien life forms and the life and death of the universe itself. In late 2012, both attended an informal 'summit' about the nature of existence in a Central London bar with other science enthusiasts including the author Will Self and the comedian Dara O Briain.

Cumberbatch's connections with scientists were to continue. In early 2013 he played the quantum physicist Werner Heisenberg in a radio dramatisation of Michael

Frayn's *Copenhagen*. Set in World War Two Denmark, when the country was under Nazi occupation, it explored how scientific research between Heisenberg and fellow scientist Bohr (Simon Russell Beale) was under threat, due to their political disagreements. 'These are such extraordinary people,' said Cumberbatch, 'with so much on their shoulders. So much of what they did affected so many people. It's a ripe topic for drama.'

Not necessarily accessible topics, but such was the brilliance and sensitivity and intelligence of Frayn's writing that he managed to make potentially difficult material into compelling drama. 'You can't betray the intelligence of the characters for the sake of simplifying the story,' declared Cumberbatch. 'At the same time, you can't leave the audience in the dust. I've struggled with science in things I've played before, but it's important to understand what's in front of you, given the speed at which Bohr and Heisenberg deliver it, because they are that smart.'

By then, he had also portrayed a botanist (in the 2009 film *Creation*) and both Victor Frankenstein and the monster he created – of which, much more later – and was preparing to play the mathematician Alan Turing in *The Imitation Game*. He retained a personal passion for the power and importance of science. To this end, in March 2013, he was appointed guest director of the Cambridge Science Festival. 'My link to a science festival may seem a little tenuous, yet as an actor who has researched playing Stephen Hawking, Joseph Hooker, Werner Heisenberg, and both Frankenstein and his creation, I've long had a passion for all fields of science. Our engagement with it has reached a crucial crossroads.'

Ten years before this appointment at the Cambridge Science Festival, Benedict Cumberbatch had been in the city filming *Hawking*. Not only had he learnt about performance from Stephen Hawking, he had also concluded something about the value of life itself: 'Life's very precious. You've got to give it 120 per cent. Just celebrate the fact that we're alive and enjoy it.' And for him the best review came from its subject: Hawking himself. Even though the Professor was in poor health at the time, suffering from pneumonia, he was said to have enjoyed the result, and the portrayal of him. 'He's said he likes the film,' Cumberbatch reported back. 'For a man of few words those are potent ones.'

CHAPTER 6

AFRICAN ADVENTURE

The success of *Hawking* meant that Benedict Cumberbatch was in demand for television work. Small roles came and went, from a second instalment of *Heartbeat*, to Chris Morris and Charlie Brooker's satire on London hipsters, *Nathan Barley*. But for his biggest project of 2004, he was off to South Africa to film a mini-series for BBC2, which, at a cost of £5 million, was one of the channel's most expensive productions yet.

To the Ends of the Earth conflated into three parts a trilogy of novels written by William Golding: 1980's prize-winning *Rites of Passage*, and its two successors, *Close Quarters* and *Fire Down Below*. It was set in 1812 and was about the passengers and crew sailing from England to Australia squeezed on to a vessel which had once been a robust warship, but was now in sorrier, ropier condition.

The story was told almost entirely from the perspective of Edmund Talbot, a young aristocrat travelling to Sydney to take up a government post arranged for him by his godfather in his native England. Edmund documented the voyage in a journal, which would be sent back to his godfather.

William Golding had died in 1993, but his daughter, Judy Carver, agreed to share some of his private journals with the BBC, as a way of showing the estate's support and trust in their making the series. She revealed that her father had intended making the first novel a stand-alone affair, but could not resist extending the story. 'I think he said at one point, "I've left all these people sitting around in the middle of the ocean, and I keep thinking of things that Edmund would say." I think he did walk around imagining himself in the world he had created. His imagination was very strong, to the extent that he could actually feel things. He could feel the texture of the wood on the boat.'

The unpredictable climate in Britain would have made for a difficult filming schedule, and other locations like Australia and Malta were considered too costly. So it was decided to shoot the entire production in South Africa, making it the biggest television project ever made in that country. Cumberbatch (as Edmund) and a supporting cast including Sam Neill, Jared Harris (son of Richard), Victoria Hamilton and Daniel Evans made it to Richard's Bay Harbour, a few hours away from Durban, just as the BBC crew were completing months of work on constructing sections of the boat. 'We had this really brilliant mixed crew,' commented Cumberbatch, 'though it was possibly a bit colonial, because we had these Zulu boys who were literally employed to rock the boat.' Even there, the weather was often influencing the shoot. Heavy rain could come without warning, and the tides wouldn't necessarily swell at the right moments of filming.

There were other uncomfortable aspects to the shoot. Heat was one. 'The set was housed in what was basically a massive corrugated iron shed: a giant oven,' Cumberbatch told the *Radio Times*. 'The temperature was incredible. The sweat was just running off you, especially in those old, thick velvet costumes. It made it virtually impossible to do any make-up because nothing would stick to your face. No matter how much water you drank, no matter how much rest you had, some days we just had to give up and stop filming.'

One of the producers, Lynn Horsford, compared *To the Ends of the Earth* to Golding's most famous work, *Lord of the Flies*. 'It has similar themes of what happens in a closed society. There's a very strong sense of class structure – it's like Britain in miniature. It has looked incredibly intimate, like *Big Brother* on a boat.'

In fact, the gestation of *To the Ends of the Earth* had already taken five years, pre-dating *Big Brother*. The adaptation's genesis dated as far back as 1999, but the project had collapsed after the death of its original screenwriter, Leigh Jackson. Finally, Tony Basgallop was hired to complete the script when the Russell Crowe sea-based film *Master and Commander* (directed by Peter Weir) had been commercially successful, making *To the Ends of the Earth* financially viable.

As Edmund Talbot, the central character, narrator and

guide for the entire voyage, Cumberbatch represented the story's voice and conscience, the figure the viewers were asked to relate to. Over the course of the three 90-minute episodes, he was hardly off the screen. He described it as 'a nineteenth-century rock'n'roll gap year': 'It has all the same ingredients – drug-taking, casual sex and a journey of self-discovery.' Hopefully, unlike his experiences in Tibet in 1996, this would be a gap year where he would be in no danger.

Edmund was a poor sailor, but at least Cumberbatch only needed to *act* being seasick. 'He was born with a silver spoon in his mouth,' he said, 'and this is a pioneering trip, but he thinks it's going to be all plain sailing.' Among those joining Talbot aboard the craft were the anti-royalist Mr Prettiman (Sam Neill), the no-nonsense and irascible Captain Anderson (Jared Harris), a strict governess by the name of Miss Granham (Victoria Hamilton), and a well-oiled artist called Brocklebank (Richard McCabe).

The ambitious, priggish and often arrogant Edmund Talbot was not an easy narrator to empathise with, but Cumberbatch brought plenty of humanity to the part, recognising that under the bumptiousness, there was vulnerability and curiosity. 'He's always open to learning. He's a product of his time.' If Talbot's voyage began with what was described to him as 'the objectivity of ignorance', he was assured that he would be completing it, 'with the subjectivity of knowledge, pain and the hope of indulgence.' To try and empathise with Talbot's limitless self-confidence, Cumberbatch drew on his experiences back at Harrow in the early 1990s, and recalled how some of his wealthy contemporaries had already assumed a sense of authority and position, having been born into a privileged existence.

To the Ends of the Earth marked Cumberbatch's first-ever screen sex scene, with Paula Jennings in the role of Zenobia. 'We were both terribly terrified,' he said of the experience. 'You're doing it all in front of a bunch of strangers. There was a large group in a small cabin.' The character would have been sexually very confident, and in any case, because of his point of view, he would have been keen to paint himself as a sexually experienced figure. 'In the book, Edmund knows what he's doing. But I imagine that, rather like others of his ilk, his father had probably given him a chambermaid or prostitute to initiate him.'

Although a great deal of the budget (which would eventually double to £10 million) was spent on constructing the ship sets to look as authentic as possible, many of the most memorable scenes came with the more intimate moments: the tensions between characters in tiny rooms. 'We had to build all that,' said David Attwood, the director, 'just for one character to look another in the eye. But that's what it's about, I think.'

Attwood had been especially keen for the adaptation to look gritty and uncomfortable, rather than a glamorous travelogue. 'David wanted [it] to be an accurate representation of what it was like to pull off a trip on the sea in those days,' said Jared Harris, playing Captain Anderson. 'He was eager to deglamorise the idea of the beautiful high seas. He wanted to make *To the Ends of the*

Earth as frightening as it must have been. Back then, it was lethal. Everyone was taking a huge risk just by setting foot on a boat.' Sea travel was no fun, it could be rough, tedious and dangerous.

As he was on screen for just about the whole of the series, Cumberbatch was busy as could be, but said, 'Each day was a new challenge. I loved hurling around that boat on ropes, with bits of rigging falling around me in flames.' With any spare time when the cameras weren't rolling, he – like many of his co-stars – couldn't wait for the chance to let his hair down. The surroundings of South Africa offered safaris on horseback, and he spent time skydiving and learning to scuba dive.

But there were also dramas off set. Future *Gavin & Stacey* star Joanna Page (Marion Chumley, another of Edmund's potential love interests) had a narrow escape. One day, she hailed a taxi and had an alarming experience. 'The driver refused to take me back to my hotel. He drove me around for ages and said that he would only take me back if I let him take nude photos of me. I politely refused.' Page managed to get back to base unharmed but after she had returned to the UK, something even more worrying happened on the South African highways to three of her fellow cast members.

One evening, Benedict Cumberbatch, Denise Black and Theo Landey were in a car on the highway to Santa Lucia, near the South African border with Mozambique. The soundtrack to their journey was a Radiohead song, 'How To Disappear Completely', and Cumberbatch had felt about as relaxed as could be. 'It was one of the best times in my life.

Then bang! Every time I'm feeling really good, a bit of me is waiting for that bang.'

The bang began with a tyre blowing. They had no choice but to stop. Stranded in the dark, they now found themselves surrounded by six armed men, who had crept out from a eucalyptus plantation. 'They frisked each of us for weapons and valuables,' said Cumberbatch, 'then bundled us back into the car and drove us into the bush.'

Once there, the men stopped the car, the three actors were hauled out, and they were told to put their hands on their heads. The men swiftly tied the victims' hands behind their backs, ordered them to kneel down, and were put in 'the execution position' with a duvet over their heads in order to silence the shots. When Cumberbatch tried to stand up, the robbers told him to get in the boot of the car. 'I heard Denise saying, "Please don't kill him."'

It was in the car boot that Cumberbatch quickly hatched a plan: he pretended to be severely claustrophobic and claimed that in the panic he might die. 'There's a problem with my heart and my brain,' he told their captors. 'If you leave me in here, I will die, possibly have a fit, and it will be a problem for you. I will be a dead Englishman in your car.' After a few minutes, the men agreed to let him out. They took him up the hill on his own, and tied his hands behind his back once again. Then the men disappeared. After a time, the three actors made a run for it, and contacted the police. They had no money, transport or debit cards but at least they were alive, and pretty much unharmed (although Cumberbatch still has a scar from being tied up).

'I thank God I had the presence of mind to give them the idea that it would be better to keep me alive,' he would later say. Their ordeal had lasted around three hours, and for much of that time they had not known if they would survive it. 'I knew my mother was going to get a call, either from me or someone else,' Cumberbatch would recall, 'and the difference would change her life.'

Maybe what saved their lives was to remain polite and helpful at all times. That was the advice offered in an email that, by happy coincidence, Theo Landey had received only days before filming started, about to how to react in the event of a car-jacking or maybe it was because they were accustomed to being directed, even if it was usually by someone infinitely friendlier. 'It was only because we were actors,' believed Denise Black, speaking in 2011, 'and so used to taking instruction and being able to keep yapping, that we were able to talk our way out of it.' Indeed their performances were so persuasive that they had been spared.

* * *

To the Ends of the Earth was broadcast in July 2005. Like *Sherlock*'s first series five years later, it surprised some people by premiering in high summer. Surely, given all the money spent on it, it would have been better to launch in the autumn when TV viewing figures are traditionally much higher? But rather than pack the peak-time schedules with repeats, the BBC had crammed summertime with new series. While some critics reduced *To the Ends of the Earth* to the status of a period drama *Big Brother* at sea, Nancy Banks-Smith at the *Guardian* compared it with a maritime BBC favourite of the past, which in 1974 had guest starred one Tim Carlton. 'To those with warm memories of *The Onedin Line*,' she wrote, 'it will all come as something of a cold shower. This is the Navy of rum, bum and the lash. We are spared the lash.' This was no luxury liner, but a decrepit shell of a ship.

The making of *To the Ends of the Earth* was an adventure both onscreen and off. As a 'nineteenth-century gap year' for Benedict Cumberbatch, it had been a little too eventful, but by giving the performance of his life, he had probably helped to save the lives of both himself and two of his co-stars. In the aftermath of the car-jacking, he embarked on what he later described as an 'adrenaline junkie drive' – a lot of skydiving and hot air ballooning and 'looking over the precipice'. If he learnt anything from the experience, it was a determination to live life to the full. 'There is a sense of impatience and a yearning for a life less ordinary,' he told the *Guardian* in 2010, 'which is destructive, as it leads you away from harnessing the true value of things. But it also gives you fantastic knowledge. I know I am going to die on my own, which is something you don't realise until you are faced with that. A sobering but profound thought to realise early in life.'

In co-operating with his co-stars, he knew he had to be self-sufficient in life. It was a lesson learnt in his younger days in Harrow (to be both co-operative and independent), but this particular experience had shaken him out of any complacency. 'When you've been forced to look into the idea that you die on your own,' he told *The Times* newspaper, 'you go, "Oh, OK, well if I've got my own company at the beginning and the end of this life, I might as well do a few crazy things with it under my own steam".'

CHAPTER 7

CAPTAIN SPEAKING

As a counterpoint to his rising profile on television, Benedict Cumberbatch was highly sought-after in the world of radio drama and voiceover work. From the autumn of 2003, he became an increasingly familiar voice on BBC Radio 3 and 4, a working relationship that continues to this day. Over the next decade, he would participate in numerous serials, one-off plays (both adaptations and original work), plus book readings, narrations and one of the best-loved comedy series on the air.

Radio does not pay well, especially when compared to film and television, but nevertheless actors and writers express a strong commitment to working in the medium. Even in 2013, when Cumberbatch's time was dominated by Hollywood work, he would contribute to plays and series for Radio 3 and 4.

Those who rarely listen to speech radio might assume that BBC Radio 4 is only the news and the everyday story of country folk, *The Archers*, which has been running daily for over 60 years. Yet there is a lot more to it than that: documentaries, discussions and features, book and poetry readings, and specialist programmes about books, films, the arts, science, food, finance and many others. In entertainment and comedy, the network has originated and nurtured numerous cult hits, which later transferred to television: *The Hitch-Hikers' Guide to the Galaxy*, *Whose Line Is It Anyway?*, *Have I Got News for You* (which also continues to this day on Radio 4 under the name *The News Quiz*), *Knowing Me Knowing You with Alan Partridge*, *Little Britain* and *The League of Gentlemen*. Plus, quite apart from *The Archers*, it broadcasts several hours of drama every week: a classic serial on Sundays, drama serials in the mornings as part of *Woman's Hour*, and afternoon plays every day from Monday to Saturday.

For the most part, Cumberbatch's radio work has consisted of single plays, serials and book readings. He first appeared on Radio 4 in September 2003 when he featured as Edmund in an adaptation of Jane Austen's *Mansfield Park*, broadcast as a daily serial over two weeks as part of *Woman's Hour*. Within a year, he was a regular voice on the network, as a performer in single dramas and serials, as a narrator of feature material, and as a reader of book adaptations both of fiction and non-fiction. His first lead role in a radio drama came in June 2004, shortly after the broadcast of *Hawking* on television. He was Captain Rob

Collins in *The Biggest Secret*, a play specially written by Mike Walker to commemorate the 60th anniversary of the Normandy Landings, otherwise known as D-Day and broadcast on 5 June, the eve of the event. Collins is recovering in a hospital after being injured in a parachute drop, and is pleasantly surprised to be recalled for action.

From here on, Cumberbatch was all over the Radio 4 airwaves: reading books by Christopher Isherwood, Honoré de Balzac and Patrick O'Brian, reworkings of Homer's *The Odyssey*, Paul Scott's *The Raj Quartet* and Frederic Raphael's adaptation of his own novel, *The Glittering Prizes*. He would play Dudley Moore in an original play about the *Beyond the Fringe* cast of Moore, Peter Cook, Alan Bennett and Jonathan Miller. He would assume the guise of the prodigious but self-destructive Romantic poet Thomas Chatterton, whose untimely death occurred in 1770 when he was still in his teens. Furthermore, he would give a first-class performance of the American T.S. Eliot in *Tom and Viv*, about the breakdown of his first marriage to Vivienne Haigh-Wood (Lia Williams).

Elsewhere in the radio schedules, he read from Franz Kafka's nightmarish *Metamorphosis* (about a man who finds he has been transformed into a 'monstrous vermin'), and from a newly written biography about Giacomo Casanova. But in his large body of work for radio, two projects have risen above everything else. One is a legal drama in which he stars as a character he has loved since childhood. The other is an original situation comedy.

The legal drama gave him the chance to be involved in the

world of Horace Rumpole, the barrister created by John Mortimer (another ex-Harrovian, incidentally). Rumpole, let's remember, was the character who almost made Cumberbatch abandon acting for a career in law, until he realised he was obsessed by the man. In 2009, he teamed up with Timothy West to portray two ages of Rumpole. West would play a senior version, reflecting on his early days in the profession in the 1950s and 60s, while Cumberbatch would appear in the flashbacks as 'Young Rumpole'. As of early 2015, eight of Mortimer's Rumpole cases have been adapted most effectively by Richard Stoneman.

Despite showing a great deal of potential in his youth as a comedy performer, Cumberbatch has rarely tackled knockabout humour in his professional career, but *Cabin Pressure*, a Radio 4 sitcom first broadcast in 2008, has been a glorious, hilarious exception to the rule. Written by John Finnemore, previously a writer for *Dead Ringers* and David Mitchell and Robert Webb's sketch shows, *Cabin Pressure* followed the misadventures of the staff of the most cash-strapped charter airline, which had only four staff and one aeroplane.

Cumberbatch starred as Captain Martin Crieff, a pilot who had taken seven attempts to gain his licence, and who had accepted responsibility on the condition that he came very cheap. The other three regular cast members were Stephanie Cole as the bossy founder of MJN Air, Carolyn Knapp-Shappey, Finnemore as Arthur (her air steward son, so dim that he was surprised the plane could fly without flapping its wings), and Roger Allam as First Officer

Douglas Richardson, a world-weary man perpetually seething with sarcasm.

Overseeing production of the show was David Tyler, a radio producer since 1985 but who, despite many years working on TV with the likes of Victoria Wood, Paul Merton, Steve Coogan and Eddie Izzard, has never abandoned radio comedy, and has produced numerous shows over the years for Jeremy Hardy, Armando Iannucci, Milton Jones and Marcus Brigstocke. *Cabin Pressure*, like most of Tyler's output, was made through Pozzitive, an independent production company he had set up with another comedy producer, Geoff Posner.

John Finnemore had not written a sitcom series before, but he had conducted a great deal of research into the world of aviation, and realised that an aeroplane was the perfect setting for a comedy. The hierarchy of the staff led to plenty of rivalry. It was set in a confined space, and just flying a plane in the first place is a risky operation. The four primary characters – Carolyn, Martin, Douglas, Arthur – were all British archetypes: draconian, uptight, grumpy and downright idiotic. Other recurring or occasional passengers included the unreasonably demanding Mr Birling (Geoffrey Whitehead), plus a paranoid bassoonist, a snooty film actress (Helen Baxendale) and Carolyn's sister Ruth (Alison Steadman), whose cameo went some way to explaining why the siblings had not spoken in 15 years.

Like so much radio comedy, *Cabin Pressure* gradually gained popularity over the years, yet even after four series some Cumberbatch fans were unaware of its existence, not just because it was a radio series, but because for some time, it was broadcast at 11.30 in the morning when the majority of people were at work. Fortunately, it reached a wider audience in the summer of 2010 when, just as *Sherlock* was premiering on television, it was repeated in the early evening comedy slot on Radio 4 at 6.30, bridging the gap between the six o'clock news and *The Archers*. Six-thirty is a good slot for a programme on Radio 4: people are heading home from work or making a meal and winding down. A good laugh always helps after a tough day.

Could *Cabin Pressure* have transferred to television? It would certainly have been nice for such a funny and fast-paced show to become better-known, although part of the joy of the series as a radio-only enterprise was that it was perfectly possible to go anywhere in the story without the need for building lavish sets or visiting far-flung locations. The episode titles reflected the wide geographical canvas for the series: each week's episode was either given a title of a grand international destination (Abu Dhabi, Boston, Cremona etc.), or a more modest British one (Ipswich, Ottery St Mary, Wokingham).

As of early 2015, Benedict Cumberbatch had made more *Cabin Pressure* than anything else on radio or television: 25 of its 26 half-hour episodes. By its third series in 2011, he was a big star, and not quite always available for recordings any-more, but he only missed one recording (when Tom Goodman-Hill deputised as Martin). Even for series four, he managed to squeeze it into his busy international filming schedule, and the six episodes had to be taped in London in two marathon Sunday sessions. As the show was recorded in front of a live studio audience, there was a mad rush for tickets by this stage in the run, and wild cheering as well as respectful applause over the signature tune: the riotous overture to the opera *Ruslan and Ludmilla*, by the Russian composer Mikhail Glinka.

In November 2013, it was announced by BBC Radio that *Cabin Pressure* was to end. A two-part finale would be taped in early 2014, and broadcast in time for Christmas. It would end the series on a high, with its trademark mix of rich, vivid characters, surreal ideas and inspired jokes. All that, plus some delightful cast interplay. *Cabin Pressure* is already sorely missed, but at least it came to an end before the comedy grew stale.

He had shown his comedy credentials in *Cabin Pressure*, but Cumberbatch had become a star because of *Sherlock*. The combination of comedy and stardom meant it was only a matter of time before he got the call to do a panel show. In October 2010, he became the latest guest host for *Have I Got News for You* on BBC1. Although Angus Deayton had done a sterling job as chairman and scriptwriter on the show since its inception in 1990, from 2002, a different guest host chaired each show, from Bruce Forsyth and Charlotte Church, to Alexander Armstrong, Jo Brand and Kirsty Young, and countless others.

An apprehensive Cumberbatch had been a fan of *Have I Got News for You* since his teens. 'My family and I used to make it a routine TV date to relish,' he said, just before the recording. 'Like a moth to the flame, I am terrified but cannot resist.' He was the first host of the 40th series, with regulars Paul Merton and Ian Hislop, and guests Victoria Coren and Jon Richardson. 'From people I know who have done it before, it is really good fun, however heavy the laundry day may have to be the next morning.'

Suddenly, then, Cumberbatch was being asked to be himself (rather than play someone else) on television. It was a pleasant surprise. 'With fame, you do get the most extraordinary perks and experiences, whether it's chairing programmes or having a voice in the political field, because you happened to have a large audience who listened to you for three nights a year ago. It's both beneficial and odd, the usual yin-yang thing. But by and large, good.'

* * *

By 2006, Cumberbatch's voice work was spreading beyond radio to audiobooks and advertising voiceovers. He had the sort of voice you might recognise, even if you couldn't yet quite put a name to it. In time, his voice would help to sell pet food, ice cream, insurance and cars. The live touring version of David Attenborough's BBC series *The Blue Planet* would employ him as narrator, in which his commentary over action of dolphins, whales, tropical fish, penguins and polar bears would in turn be accompanied by a remarkable music score from the composer George Fenton. On television documentaries, he would read from William Golding's diaries for an *Arena* special, commentate on footage of the southern Pacific Ocean, and narrate more of Stephen Hawking's findings into the universe.

One of his most affecting contributions in voiceover work came in 2005 with a Channel 4 film about Rick Rescorla, the Cornish-born security boss at Morgan Stanley merchant bank in New York. In 2001, Rescorla had died in the 9/11 attacks on the Twin Towers, while helping to save over 2,000 lives. But he had been predicting for over a decade that the Towers could be vulnerable to a terrorist attack and had taken every effort to tighten security at the World Trade Center, as well as advising on improving evacuation routes.

In 2012, Cumberbatch was involved in two epic events as a reader. At the end of July, he read a short piece of prose in praise of London as 'the beating heart of the nation', as part of Danny Boyle's opening ceremony for the 2012 Olympic Games. Two months later, he participated in a reading project about a gargantuan mammal. Launched as part of the Plymouth International Book Festival, *The Moby Dick Big Read* was an online reading marathon in which each of the 135 chapters of Herman Melville's *Moby Dick* was read by a different person. As well as Cumberbatch, those taking part included Stephen Fry, Sir David Attenborough, Will Self, Neil Tennant, Rick Stein, Cerys Matthews and Simon Callow. The opening section was voiced by the actor Tilda Swinton.

Cumberbatch's voice was also called upon for a new iPhone video game in 2011. *The Night Jar* had the ingenious twist of having no visual content. It placed the player on a spaceship in complete darkness, with the object of the game to reach safety by navigating via sound cues alone. Then in 2012, he became a recording artist of sorts: he performed a six-minute long spoken word piece for a compilation album assembled by the band Friendly Fires. Part of the *Late Night Tales* series, it was a stew of styles which had influenced the group, from indie heroes like Stereolab and the Cocteau Twins to the more surprising inclusion of Olivia Newton-John. His track was a reading of 'Flat of Angels' by Simon Cleary. Cumberbatch was a fan of Friendly Fires, and the feeling was mutual. 'He really got into subtleties in the text I didn't realise were there,' said Cleary. The piece was about the comedown of a house party, delivered in alternating voices. In 2013, he would contribute a second section of the tale to another *Late Night Tales* mix album, this time by the Norwegian electronic music duo Röyksopp.

* * *

But through all of this, Benedict Cumberbatch always stayed loyal to radio, whether drama on BBC Radio 3 and the World Service channel (the latter heard worldwide), or material for Radio 4 and its sister speech station, BBC Radio 7 (later, BBC Radio 4 Extra). In January 2013, just as the fourth series of *Cabin Pressure* was being broadcast, it was announced that he would feature in a new adaptation (by radio producer Dirk Maggs) of Neil Gaiman's *Neverwhere*, a cult fantasy set in an alternative subterranean version of London. It was a London where fictional characters would live alongside real historical figures and peculiarly apt that Cumberbatch was cast for this. Here is a man who has spent roughly half his professional career portraying real people, and half playing created characters – even though some of those fictional figures are so vivid and enduring, it's tempting to imagine them as real. This time he met yet another of his idols on the project, Sir Christopher Lee.

'It was extraordinary to talk to that man. I'm very new to all this so I'm still tongue-tied when I meet my heroes.'

Cumberbatch, then, loves working in the medium of sound only. Even though it generally pays less than film, television and stage, the advantages – as with all voice work – are that it is relatively quick to do, and there are no long and expensive location shoots. With a talented director and an able cast, a radio drama can be recorded in a day in a studio with artful effects and sound design. 'It's nice to intensely concentrate on and listen to the word,' he told the *Radio Times*. 'Radio's just a joy.'

CHAPTER 8

FROM SUPPORT TO LEAD

It was 2006, and Benedict Cumberbatch was approaching his thirtieth birthday. Over the next few years, he would tackle more and more ambitious roles, some minor, some major. He was becoming one of the most versatile actors in British drama, able to switch between the different demands of stage, film and TV with a seeming effortlessness. Over the next three or four years, his diary would be crammed with commitments. His film work would include some of the most acclaimed British features of the period, as well as some diverting work on lower-budget productions. On the London stage, he would excel in some interesting revivals. And on television, he would flourish in both drama and comedy.

In 2005, Benedict Cumberbatch had been one of nearly 150 actors hired for *Broken News*, a new sketch show for BBC2, which parodied television news and current affairs output. In the 1990s, Armando Iannucci and Chris Morris's *The Day Today* had been a groundbreaking and pitch-perfect distortion of slick, aggressive magazine shows and bulletins like *Newsnight*. But *Broken News*'s creators, John Morton and Tony Roche, wanted to reflect the 24-hour news channels of the twenty-first century, which had to stretch material in order to fill space, and so made great play of switching between channels in the middle of items, as if the show were being controlled by a bored, jaded viewer. 'It reflects how we've become news addicts in this multi-media age,' said Morton, previously creator of the documentary pastiche *People Like Us* and later writer of *Twenty Twelve*. 'In *Broken News*, the frenetic world of news isn't about news anymore. It's about predictions, speculations, recap, taking a look at tomorrow's or yesterday's papers – possibly even last Thursday's papers.'

Cumberbatch played a roving reporter on *Broken News*, the hapless Will Parker, whose official job title was worldly affairs correspondent for a fictional network called PVS. 'Unlucky Will is on the spot in prime locations,' he explained, 'but there are usually empty podiums behind him because the people he's waiting for don't turn up. So he fills airtime with ridiculous conversations about the person he is expecting to see.' For instance: 'Well, the speculation here in Washington has been at least as much to do with what Mr Rumsfeld isn't going to say as it has been about what he might or might not say, when he arrives any minute now behind me.'

'Will is always first on the scene,' said Cumberbatch, 'waiting for a story to break, but he's so early that he doesn't really know anything. Basically, he has to fill lots of empty space saying the same idiotic thing in lots of different ways. If you watch any big story unfolding on TV, you'll realise it's painfully close to reality.'

On another assignment, Parker found himself in Greece waiting outside a hospital for an exclusive on the potentially worrying outbreak of tomato flu. As John Morton acknowledged, 'News has started to borrow the grammar of theatre. It has become a dramatisation, which is strange because drama has been heading in the opposite direction by borrowing the grammar of documentary.'

Had *Broken News* been made any more recently, Cumberbatch would have been arguably too well-known to have been convincing in the part of Will. Part of the joke with a television satire of form is to be persuaded that the cast are real people, and several other future famous names lurked in the *Broken News* ranks, among them Sharon Horgan (creator and star of the sitcom *Pulling*) and Miranda Hart's sidekick on *Miranda*, Sarah Hadland. 'We wanted faces that could sort of slip under your radar,' explained the producer of the series, Paul Schlesinger, 'which is why we spent over three months in casting. When you look at the screen, we need you to believe that you really are watching a news network.'

* * *

After a shaky start, Cumberbatch's film work was finally starting to gather pace. By his late twenties, he had featured in a short film, 2002's *Hills Like White Elephants* (based on an Ernest Hemingway short story), and as 'Royalist' in *To Kill a King*, a drama about Oliver Cromwell and Thomas Fairfax, but little else. But in the wake of his success as *Hawking* on TV, the cinematic offers finally began to roll in.

Though he only had a small role in it, *Starter for 10* was a success. It was a coming-of-age comedy set in 1985 and adapted from a best-selling novel by David Nicholls, who cut his teeth writing for ITV's *Cold Feet*, and would later pen the even more successful *One Day*. James McAvoy played a Bristol University undergraduate and quiz addict called Brian Jackson, who had a hunger to appear on the inter-college quiz *University Challenge* (a TV fixture since the early 1960s), but whose general knowledge about social and sexual situations was less certain. 'It's about a teenager trying to fit into the world,' said McAvoy. 'That's a story that will be told forever.'

Cumberbatch's appearance in *Starter for 10* was one of the film's highlights. He played Patrick, the fiercely ambitious and pedantic captain of Bristol University's *University Challenge* team. 'He's old before his time, and very bad-tempered, all of which are attributes which I'm very much aware of myself, so that was easy to play.' But he had also drawn inspiration for the part from several contemporaries from his younger days. 'He is an amalgamation of a lot of people I was at school with and people I felt a little bit sorry for at university. They are always there at the freshers' fair, wearing a tie, bless them.' As ever, when Cumberbatch played someone irritating or arrogant, he avoided any temptation to make them one-dimensional caricatures of 'poshness', and always took care to render them more complex and human.

Nowadays, Jeremy Paxman urges dithering contestants on *University Challenge* to 'come on!', but for 25 years, its quizmaster was Bamber Gascoigne, who preferred the gentler, almost apologetic murmur of 'Must hurry you'. Gascoigne was played in *Starter for 10* – with quite unerring accuracy – by Mark Gatiss, a founder member of *The League of Gentlemen*, and a man who would a few years later be instrumental in Cumberbatch's career.

While the American funding for *Starter for 10* enabled the film to be made in the first place (Tom Hanks was one of the producers), Cumberbatch felt a little uneasy with the editorial interference that could come from the backing. 'American investment comes with editorial control. That side of your industry worries me. In a comedy drama about *University Challenge*, who cares that they might not under-stand what Heinz ketchup means?'

Cumberbatch and McAvoy quickly became good friends, and the pair had various adventures and misadventures when the cameras stopped rolling. At one point in 2006, they had defied the elements and walked up the highest peaks of the Brecon Beacons in mid-Wales, but had started their journey far too late in the day after an extended lunch during which Cumberbatch had consumed a large steak-and-kidney pie in Hay-on-Wye. 'It was fucking hilarious,' McAvoy told the *Observer* newspaper. 'We finally started walking up Pen-Y-Fan at half past three. And of course the cloud came down.' A somewhat bloated Cumberbatch, with a bellyful of pie, protested. 'But I thought: Ben, I am not stopping because of your bloody pie. We kept walking and ended up with 5ft visibility.'

McAvoy and Cumberbatch would again play lead and supporting role respectively in *Atonement*, Joe Wright's big-screen treatment of Ian McEwan's novel. Cumberbatch played a creepy confectionery businessman called Paul Marshall, one of the least likeable characters he would ever portray. *Atonement* opened in British cinemas in September 2007, and was soon followed in 2008 by *The Other Boleyn Girl*. Based on the historical novel by Philippa Gregory, this was a drama about Anne Boleyn's sister Mary, about whom relatively little was known. Here, Cumberbatch was cast as a merchant's son William Carey, who marries Mary (Scarlett Johansson). The role required him to take part in a wedding night bedroom scene with Johansson. He helpfully summarised the shoot for the *Daily Telegraph*. It sounded underwhelming and bathetic. 'I get on top of her and go "Ooh!" Knuckles whiten and I roll over, say "Thank you" and start snoring.' A sex scene lasting seconds. 'I guess it's what any man would suffer,' he later shrugged, 'when faced with beauty that intense.'

Larger roles had also come his way. In 2005, he had landed the part of William Pitt the Younger, who in 1783 had become – at the age of just 24 – the youngest man ever to be British Prime Minister. It was all part of a feature film called *Amazing Grace*, which told how William Wilberforce campaigned to abolish slavery in Britain. During the seventeenth and eighteenth centuries, an estimated 11 million men, women and children had been sold into the barbaric and undignified world of slavery, but it took over two decades for Wilberforce's campaign to succeed. The film's title came from the famous hymn of the same name, one of many penned by John Newton, formerly captain of a slave ship who on becoming a clergyman saw the light and was also instrumental in the campaign to abolish slavery.

In actual fact, Cumberbatch had a connection with the real life of the slave trade. There was a brief period when he tried to hide his unwieldy name (apparently of German origin), of which he would later say, 'LA agents think I'm a Dickens character'. Mum Wanda had tried to convince him to drop the 'Cumberbatch'. '"They'll be after you for money," she used to say,' 'they' being the descendants of Britain's slave trade. 'There are lots of Cumberbatches in our former Caribbean colonies,' Benedict elaborated. 'When their ancestors lost their African names, they called themselves after their masters. Reparation cases are ongoing in the American courts. I've got friends involved in researching this scar on human history and I've spoken to them about it. The issue of how far you should be willing to atone is interesting. I mean, it's not as if I'm making a profit from the suffering – it's not like it's Nazi money.' Even so, he concluded those Cumberbatches were likely to be 'pretty dodgy'. Was his involvement in *Amazing Grace* a pure coincidence, the *Scotland on Sunday* newspaper wondered? 'Maybe I was trying to right a wrong there,' he admitted.

Playing Wilberforce was Ioan Gruffudd, familiar to

Hollywood and the international film industry, and his commercial viability allowed director Michael Apted to surround his lead with other great British actors of every generation. These were names like Albert Finney, Ciaran Hinds, Rufus Sewell, Michael Gambon ... and Benedict Cumberbatch. 'Doing a scene with Michael Gambon,' Cumberbatch later said. 'What could be better?'

The insistence on casting well-known and talented figures rather than Hollywood stars was a conscious effort on Apted's part. Here was an opportunity to make, as he put it, 'a British-based film about a British subject, with a British cast.' This was important to him, as he did not want a 'celebrity cast'. 'I wanted to get believable performances out of people who are well known, rather than inter-national stars.'

Cumberbatch and Gruffudd got on well, on and off screen. 'He's a tremendous actor, he's breathtaking actually, and quite fun to be around,' said Gruffudd, who revealed that the two would often go ten-pin bowling during the making of the film. 'Because, more often than not,' he explained, 'we were living in Holiday Inns on some back-of-beyond industrial site, where there was only a Cineplex and bowling alley.'

Michael Apted's career had taken him from TV work in the 1960s at Granada in Manchester – the seminal *7 Up* documentary series and a new popular serial called *Coronation Street* – to feature films: *Gorillas in the Mist*, *Gorky Park* and the James Bond film of 1999, *The World is Not Enough*. 'I wasn't interested in making a dull biopic,' said Apted of *Amazing Grace*. 'I wanted to make a film that showed how heroic and relevant politics can be. I wanted to portray it as a generational battle – the young men taking on the older generation – like the Kennedys and their Camelot court were to America in the 60s.' Steven Knight, who wrote the screenplay, also had a background in television; he was one of the three creators of *Who Wants to Be a Millionaire?*, one of the best-selling TV formats in the world. Additional help was sought from Wilberforce's biographer, the politician William Hague.

Amazing Grace had premiered to tie in with the bicentenary (in 2007) of the abolition of the slave trade in Britain. Two years later, 2009 marked two anniversaries relating to the scientist Charles Darwin: 200 years since his birth, and 150 years since the publication of his masterwork, 1859's *On the Origin of Species*. Darwin's vision about how the world was created had clashed with his wife's strongly-held religious beliefs, a disagreement which would deepen following the death of the couple's daughter.

Creation, starring Paul Bettany and Jennifer Connelly as Darwin and his wife Emma, was described as a combination of ghost story, psychological thriller and love story. Co-funded by BBC Films, its source material largely came from a book called *Annie's Box*, written by Darwin's great-great-grandson, Randal Keynes. The director was Jon Amiel, now busy in Hollywood, but once a television director in the UK on such masterpieces as Dennis Potter's *The Singing Detective*. Cumberbatch co-starred as the botanist Joseph Hooker, an ally of Darwin's who had tried to persuade him to complete *On the Origin of Species*, against the backdrop of family crises.

Parts like these had secured Cumberbatch a Hollywood agent by his early thirties. 'He thinks I've walked straight out of Dickens,' he quipped. Even so Stateside blockbusters were still some way off, and he liked it that way. One particularly effective low-budget home-grown feature was *Third Star*, shot in only a month in the autumn of 2009 for less than half a million pounds. It was a moving comedy-drama and the directorial debut of Hattie Dalton. He played James, a young man on the brink of his thirties who has a terminal illness, but who opts for one last hurrah, and invites three close friends on a trip to a favourite beach in West Wales to celebrate their friendship while they still have time. 'I think it explores sides of friendship that are often neglected,' said Cumberbatch. 'The streaks of competitiveness, support, love, irritation and trust are all here. But I also liked the idea that being robbed of your life too early doesn't give you the right to tell others how to live ... What I think is beautiful is that he's the one who learns the most in the end.'

The film showed the irreverence that the closest of friends can show towards each other, even when tragedy is close by. When James – his illness by now in its advanced stages – tries to offer advice to the others about how they should live their future lives, and does not hold back with his reservations about them, they groan that, 'It's like going for a walk with a sick, white Oprah'. 'It's very understated, not touchy-feely,' Cumberbatch told *The Times*, 'not that modern disease of wearing your heart on your sleeve.' It seemed a fair assessment. The relationship between the closest friends will always withstand plenty of joshing.

To look the part – slim, if not downright gaunt – other filming commitments made shaving his head impossible, but he could be strict about diet: 'I ate healthily, but there was no snacking, no drinking, no bread, no sugar, no smoking.' Even after he lost weight to look the part, he was still hard to lift off the ground, as J.J. Feild (playing his friend Miles) discovered when he needed to carry him. 'I tried to look like I was being all strong and butch,' commented Feild, 'but humans are really heavy.' When the month-long shoot ended, Cumberbatch drew a line under it by indulging in a pork belly roast.

The screenwriter Vaughan Sivell described James as 'a man losing his place in the Universe, and wanting to right everything before he goes.' Sivell was inspired to write the screenplay of *Third Star* out of the belief that a generation of affluent young people were not being rushed into maturity, as they were no longer obliged to go to war. 'The time spent bumming around lasts and lasts. Their worst problem is that their laptop won't sync with their phone. So I wanted to put pressure on these men, the time pressure that comes with someone dying, and watch what they did.' The result was a picture that packed a big emotional punch, but it was somehow life-affirming. 'It's really about friendship. There were some real tears on that set,' assured co-star J.J. Feild. 'It's a beautifully uplifting human film.'

Third Star's premiere took place in June 2010, as the closing attraction of the Edinburgh International Film

Festival. A month earlier, Chris Morris's debut feature *Four Lions* (with Cumberbatch as a negotiator), about a bungling quartet of terrorist jihadis from Sheffield who are intent on causing destruction in London, had opened in the UK.

Cumberbatch was delighted that he had been able to be versatile and flexible in the roles he was offered, across stage and screen. 'I've been complimented on my ability to shape-shift in the past, and I guess this little lot will really put that to the ultimate test. I love working in what I call the Philip Seymour Hoffman area, where you get a crack at the meaty character parts as well as the quirkier leading roles, while still retaining enough anonymity to keep things in balance.'

* * *

As the cinema career was growing, so Cumberbatch's stage work remained as adventurous as ever. The autumn of 2007 brought revivals of two long-lost twentieth-century European plays at the Royal Court in London, and he starred in both of them.

That season there was some new blood at the Royal Court Theatre, where Dominic Cooke had taken over as artistic director. As Cumberbatch explained, 'I liked the way that Dominic set out his stall by saying that he was going to question the values of the core Royal Court audience.' His other reason for going back to stage work was that he dreaded getting rusty as a live performer. 'Filming is a very fractured process,' he told *The Stage*. 'You never really know what you've got until you see the completed film.' The other advantage with live performance was that he would rarely get the chance to watch his efforts played back. By his own admission, he was not a good audience of his own screen work: 'I find it painful enough watching myself on film at cast and crew screenings.'

The first of the two plays was *Rhinoceros*, an absurdist work from 1959 by Eugène Ionesco, unperformed in London since the mid-1960s when Orson Welles directed Laurence Olivier as Bérenger, who refuses to conform with society and discovers he is isolated when everyone else follows some rampaging rhinos and ends up being morphed with the creatures. The rhinos were represented by thunderous rumbling offstage, although at times due to the location of the theatre, audiences would confuse it with the nearby rumblings of trains on the Underground's Circle Line.

'The play is able to change with the times,' said Cumberbatch, who played Bérenger in the revival. 'It was written as a dark satire on Nazism, but it's as relevant to any kind of fascism from East or West, which makes it much more than old wine in a new bottle.' It still had considerable resonance in the modern age, regarding moral panics and thinking for oneself.

Dominic Cooke had wanted to move the Royal Court's productions away from social-realist drama, a decision not popular with everyone, but his choice of Cumberbatch in the agitated lead role of Bérenger was applauded by several newspapers. 'Cooke is a great actors' director,' wrote the *Independent* after press night, 'and he releases something in Cumberbatch we have not seen before. Here, he surpasses himself.'

Many of those in *Rhinoceros*, Cumberbatch included, would form the cast of *The Arsonists*, another relatively unknown play from the late 1950s, which is about appeasement. 'It's wonderful being in an ensemble,' Cumberbatch said. 'There's a fluid approach to work. You play to each other's strengths. I think Dominic hopes the plays will feed off each other.'

Succeeding *Rhinoceros* at the Royal Court in November 2007 was *The Arsonists*, written by the Swiss dramatist Max Frisch in 1958. It had last been performed in London in 1961 as *The Fire Raisers*. Then, its director was Lindsay Anderson, later to direct *If...* and *O Lucky Man* for the cinema. Radio 3 had revived the production in early 2005 as a radio drama, with Phil Daniels as Eisenring. In the 2007 revamp, Cumberbatch played Eisenring, an icy and imposing member of a group of terrorists which moves into the house of Biedermann (Will Keen), a respected pillar of the community. Biedermann refuses to acknowledge or accept what is going on in his own home, even when 'petrol drums pile up in the corner'.

The Arsonists had been given a contemporary sheen, although to Cumberbatch's relief, not in a clumsy way. 'We are not walking around with mobiles and laptops like they always fucking do with Shakespeare,' he sighed to *The Times*. The change in British society was archly addressed at the very outset of the play. One character prepared to light a cigarette, something that would have been commonplace in theatre once upon a time, but the smoking ban in public places (then just introduced) had put paid to that, and so a group of firefighters pointed hoses at the cigarette.

* * *

With two plays at the Royal Court and the release of two feature films, all within the space of a few months, Benedict Cumberbatch's name was suddenly everywhere. The man himself knew it and called 2007's closing months 'the autumn of Cumberbatch', before immediately retracting on the grounds that it sounded a bit ominous. He was right though, and those four projects weren't the sum total of his autumn.

There was also a one-off film for television. It was a dramatisation of Alexander Masters' unconventional biography *Stuart – A Life Backwards*. Masters was an academic in physics at Cambridge University, and had met Stuart Shorter in the city in 1998 when he found him in the doorway of a shop. Stuart was a very different man to Masters – he was homeless and variously described as a 'thief, hostage taker, psycho and sociopathic street raconteur' – but the two bonded and became the unlikeliest of friends. After Shorter fatally collided with a high-speed train in 2002, Masters agonised over whether to write about their friendship, wondering if Shorter's eventful but often harrowing and violent story might only reach a select readership. 'I suppose I realised that Stuart was not classic biography material,' he told the *Sunday Telegraph* in 2007. 'As one critic put it, his was hardly the Life of Great

Achievement.' Yet in print the result sold well over 100,000 copies, and inspired Sam Mendes (one of *Starter for 10*'s executive producers) and his production company to arrange a screen adaptation.

'It's a bizarre buddy relationship,' commented Cumberbatch, who was cast to play Masters. 'They're an odd couple thrown together by circumstance.' Certainly, the distance between the pair resulted in some grim but compelling humour, although the American cable network which co-funded the film persuaded Cumberbatch not to use too much of Masters' Cornish burr. 'HBO in their wisdom said, "We don't know if it'll play in Salt Lake City."'

Tom Hardy played Stuart Shorter to Cumberbatch's Masters, a casting choice that amused the real-life author. The two looked nothing like each other. How the actor dressed was a different matter, though. 'His wardrobe is very real – whenever I see him on set, I think he must have stolen my clothes.'

Stuart – A Life Backwards was not easy viewing, nor was it without levity. 'Humour was almost the key thing,' said director David Attwood. 'There have been many films about the homeless and they're generally worthy, and – that horrible word – "gritty". The best way to tell this story is not by lecturing them, it's by entertaining them.'

* * *

The Last Enemy was Benedict Cumberbatch's last television series prior to *Sherlock*. A political thriller in five parts, it predicted the effects of surveillance technology on society and relationships in Britain in the near future. After a terrorist attack at Victoria Station in London, which kills over 200 people, the British government places restrictions on civil liberties, and armed police take over the streets.

Surveillance technology had become a controversial subject in the UK, where the average citizen could be captured on CCTV camera as often as 300 times every day, and where the nation had more surveillance cameras per head than anywhere else on the planet.

Filming began in mid-February of 2007, and lasted six gruelling months. 'I reached that point of exhaustion,' said Cumberbatch, who starred as Stephen Ezard, 'when you're too tired even to sleep. It was supposed to be set in the winter in North London, whereas we were filming in a studio in Budapest at the height of summer. We were all melting in the heat of 500 lamps.'

It also brought back some of the horror of 7 July 2005 in London. 'Everyone on my bus was in a state of panic,' Cumberbatch told the *Mail on Sunday*'s *Event* magazine in 2013. 'They had heard about the bomb on the other bus across London in Tavistock Square and started running over each other. There were kids, there were women – it was a real fight to get them down the stairs. I staggered out into the street. I was on my way to help a friend with a workshop at the Young Vic theatre and I couldn't get through to him. The phones were jammed. Everyone around me was also talking about massive explosions on the Underground.'

Ironically, writer Peter Berry had had to swiftly change

tack in the early drafts of *The Last Enemy* because of the 7/7 attacks. He had begun the series in 2005, and had managed to anticipate aspects of the calamity. 'I wrote the first episode in which bombs went off on the London Underground about a month before 7 July 2005,' Berry told the *Radio Times*. 'So I had to take those out.' It was an early example of how dystopian fantasy could be overtaken by horrific real-life events.

Despite bringing back unpleasant memories of 7/7 from time to time, Cumberbatch was excited by the concept and the execution of *The Last Enemy*. Months before the series aired, he exuberantly told one reporter about how 'I got to run around with guns and dodge explosions, which I loved, because I've always wanted to do some of that kick-ass stuff.' He was comparing it to the 1980s series *Edge of Darkness*, 'a kind of personal liberty versus state security thriller ... It's about ID cards, iris-scanning and the extremes that surveillance can be taken to, which are terrifying.'

Peter Berry, formerly a writer on *Prime Suspect*, felt similarly strongly about the notion of ID cards being introduced into British society. 'The idea of having to account for yourself to someone who has power over you is so appalling. You may not have to carry it, but if you don't, you will have to report to a police station within 24 to 48 hours. I don't want to live like that.'

Cumberbatch's character Stephen Ezard is a mathematician just back from China, who becomes embroiled in a global conspiracy after he tries to establish what has happened to his brother Michael (played by Max Beesley), who was killed by a landmine while working for a charitable organisation in Afghanistan. 'He is complicit with the government,' Cumberbatch said of Stephen, 'becoming a puppet for it and not realising what he is getting involved in.' Ezard has obsessive-compulsive disorder which he could relate to, even if he wasn't technically a sufferer. 'I have been known to check my temperature and worry too much about symptoms. And I do have threshold anxiety. I have this thing where I have to check the gas is off two or three times.'

Ezard's obsessive sense of detail, in some ways a dry run for the character of Sherlock Holmes a few years later, was exploited with some extremely long and complicated speeches for Cumberbatch to learn. 'It's a bit of a stretch. The other day, I had a vast tract of dialogue and Peter had written quite complex lists into it.' Line-learning did not come naturally to him in the first place. 'I struggle to learn by rote. When I was younger I had to spend double the amount of time learning French vocabulary.'

Another very different challenge came when Ezard embarked on an affair with Michael's wife Yasim (played by Anamaria Marinca) and Cumberbatch faced another sex scene. 'Sex scenes are never easy and shouldn't be easy,' he shrugged. 'Even if you were single and fancied the pants off them, it would be hard because it's such an unnatural thing to do in front of a film crew.'

The role of Stephen Ezard proved a rich one for Cumberbatch, a mix of the dynamic and the intellectual.

'Stephen is an awkward, accidental hero, but there's a vitality to him. He is running around handling guns, coming across bodies, escaping bullets and policemen, living underground, being tortured, being driven around in the boot of a car ...' It was quite a role.

The Last Enemy reached the screen in early 2008, as part of a BBC1 drama schedule that also included *The No. 1 Ladies' Detective Agency*, the *Life on Mars* spin-off *Ashes to Ashes* and *Lark Rise to Candleford*. In the next couple of years, Benedict Cumberbatch appeared in a variety of guises in TV drama. His first work for ITV in nearly five years was as ex-policeman Luke Fitzwilliam in *Agatha Christie's Marple*, starring Julia McKenzie, in which he shared the screen with Jemma Redgrave, Sylvia Syms, Shirley Henderson, David Haig, Hugo Speer, Tim Brooke-Taylor and others. Fitzwilliam would team up with Miss Marple to solve the mystery of a spate of deaths shortly after a glamorous young American woman arrives in the village of Wychwood-under-Ashe.

* * *

Having played a politician (William Pitt the Younger), a botanist (Joseph Hooker) and a biographer (Alexander Masters), the next of Cumberbatch's real-life roles was as a legendary painter. In 2010, he was the tortured nineteenth-century Dutch artist Vincent Van Gogh, in a TV drama-documentary to coincide with an exhibition at London's Royal Academy celebrating his life and works. Presented and co-written by Alan Yentob, the host of the arts series *Imagine*, *Vincent Van Gogh: Painted with Words* was based around excerpts from a series of letters exchanged between Vincent and his younger brother Theo (Jamie Parker). The correspondence documented every stage of Van Gogh's adult life, right up to his early demise in 1890, aged only thirty-seven. But the film was careful to also include many of his canvasses, featuring works less commonly seen than 'Starry Night' or 'Sunflowers'. As would be expected by now, Cumberbatch brought a dimension of humanity and sensitivity to Vincent, rather than the popular image of a man out of control.

Painted with Words came a few months after a two-part television film called *Small Island*, in which he was cast as a 'little Englander'. Bernard is a dull banker-turned-landlord in the London of the 1940s, who is suddenly called up for World War II. After his departure, his wife Queenie (Ruth Wilson) takes in lodgers who have sailed on the SS *Empire Windrush* from Jamaica to Britain. Gilbert (David Oyelowo) and Michael (Ashley Walters) have faced an uneasy and hostile reception in London, while struggling with low-paid jobs and casual bigotry. When Bernard returns home several years later, having been missing presumed dead, he discovers the strong feelings Queenie has for Michael. For his contribution as Bernard, Cumberbatch received a nomination in the Best Supporting Actor category at the 2010 British Academy Television Awards, while Oyelowo's starring role was shortlisted for Best Actor.

The BBC drama department had announced earlier in 2009 that it intended to try to make more period productions based in the more recent past, and not simply keep remaking

Dickens or Austen favourites. *Small Island* was a compelling example of the success of this strategy, moving and well-acted from all sides, and ultimately led to other post-war period drama productions such as *Call the Midwife* and *The Hour*. For Benedict Cumberbatch, though, sudden fame would arrive in 2010 via an evergreen favourite brought bang up to date.

CHAPTER 9

OUT OF
THE FOG

On 19 December 2008, the BBC announced that it would be producing a new contemporary take on the Sherlock Holmes character and stories, originally created by Sir Arthur Conan Doyle in the late nineteenth century, but remade in countless stage plays, films and television series over the decades.

The two men responsible for the reinterpretation had been creative giants in British television for some time. The Scottish writer Steven Moffat, formerly an English teacher, had taken over from Russell T. Davies as the showrunner of *Doctor Who* in 2009, but his writing career went all the way back to the imaginative and amusing children's series *Press Gang* at the end of the 1980s, which made stars of Julia Sawalha and Dexter Fletcher. The sitcoms *Joking Apart*, *Chalk* and *Coupling* had established him with grown-ups, before he had modernised Robert Louis Stevenson's *Dr Jekyll and Mr Hyde* for James Nesbitt in 2007's *Jekyll*. He was first exposed to the work of Sir Arthur Conan Doyle at the age of ten, when his parents considered a film version of *The Hound of the Baskervilles* on TV to be 'too frightening', and sent him to bed. Soon after, though, they gave him a copy of *A Study in Scarlet*, the first Holmes story. He was immediately hooked.

'It's not too much of a stretch to say that Arthur Conan Doyle invented the TV series,' Moffat would reflect. 'He looked to all the fiction magazines and they were all serialised novels or short stories. He thought to himself, the short stories are great but they don't bring you back next week or next month. What about a continual series of short stories featuring the same character? You'll always have a reason to come back next month. Now, *that* is the TV series.'

Moffat's co-creator on *Sherlock*, Mark Gatiss, also had a background in comedy. He was one-quarter of the League of Gentlemen, whose macabre humour had gravitated from fringe productions, to radio and then television, but he also had a serious interest in film history, particularly horror cinema. He was a devotee of Conan Doyle's work. 'I retreated into Sherlock Holmes,' Gatiss said of his boyhood in County Durham. 'I wanted to live like an 1895 detective, not in a grim post-industrial town.' He immersed himself in the purple-covered Penguin editions of the stories, and marvelled at them. 'The Holmes stories are all dialogue and you can read them in 20 minutes. Whenever I meet someone who hasn't read them, I always think they have got so much fun to come.'

The two men knew exactly who they wanted for Sherlock Holmes. There was only one man for the job – and Mark Gatiss had worked with him three years earlier, on the film *Starter for 10*. 'It was vital to nail the casting,' said Gatiss. 'Benedict was the only person we saw for Sherlock. It's very difficult to get someone with that amount of command, which he really has.'

Their Sherlock of choice had thoroughly enjoyed several past interpretations of Conan Doyle's enduring icon, most notably Jeremy Brett's reading for ITV's *The Adventures of Sherlock Holmes* in the 1980s and early 90s. But as someone who liked to be surprised by his career and do all sorts of acting jobs, Cumberbatch was not one to speculate about long-term ambitions or dream roles, and the prospect of *Sherlock* was no different. 'I didn't really have a dream to play this character,' he said. 'That's the one question that I never have an answer for: what jobs do you really want to play? I came to this role very flattered that they were very seriously considering me for it.'

Finding the right person to play Holmes's companion took longer. An early possibility was a young actor called Matt Smith, who came to audition for Dr John Watson. 'Matt gave a very good audition,' Steven Moffat later revealed, 'but he was clearly more of a Sherlock Holmes than a Dr Watson. There was also something a bit barmy about him – and you don't actually want that for Dr Watson.' Only a few days later, Smith auditioned for the part of *Doctor Who*, a show

Moffat had recently taken over. Enormous acclaim would follow, and as the set of *Sherlock* was next door to that of *Doctor Who* in Cardiff, it wasn't long before Matt and Benedict were constantly bumping into each other. 'We have lovely mornings,' said Smith, just appointed the new Doctor, 'where we go, "Hi Sherlock!" "Hi Doctor!" I think they should do an episode [with Sherlock Holmes]; these two great minds going, "Ding-ding-ding! Whatcha got?"'

Soon after seeing Matt Smith, the *Sherlock* producers tested Martin Freeman, who had featured in Richard Curtis's 2003 romantic comedy *Love Actually* and revived Arthur Dent for the movie of Douglas Adams' *Hitch-Hiker's Guide to the Galaxy* (2005), but was perhaps still most famous for his role as the lovelorn Tim Canterbury in the original BBC2 TV series of *The Office*. At his audition, it was obvious that he was the perfect Watson to Cumberbatch's Holmes. 'When Martin left the room after reading with Benedict,' recalled Gatiss, 'Steve said, "Well, there's the series before our eyes!"'

'Once Benedict was there,' said Steven Moffat's wife, the producer Sue Vertue, 'it was really just making sure we got the chemistry for John – and I think you get it as soon as they come into the room. You can see that they work together.'

Vertue had met Moffat a decade earlier when they worked together on his sitcom *Coupling*. Her mother was Beryl Vertue, a pioneering independent force in entertainment for nearly five decades. In the 1960s, as agent to comedy giants like Spike Milligan, Tony Hancock, Ray Galton and Alan Simpson, Vertue recognised the potential in international television sales. She sold the formats of hit British sitcoms like *Steptoe and Son* and *Till Death Us Do Part* to American TV networks. After a spell as a film producer, she returned to television in the early 1990s and started up the production company Hartswood Films, which enjoyed a string of hit shows: *Men Behaving Badly*, *Is It Legal?*, and the afore-mentioned *Coupling* and *Jekyll*.

Beryl Vertue and her producer daughter Sue were both eager to embrace Cardiff as the primary location for *Sherlock*. 'There is a lot of enthusiasm there,' said Beryl, 'and some very interesting locations. A production leaves a lot of money in a town. Apart from the crew you have cars, hotels, food, restaurants, couriers... All those things are a big financial advantage.' The location of Cardiff as a production base for the revival of *Doctor Who* from 2005, plus spin-off series such as *Torchwood* and *The Sarah Jane Adventures*, meant it soon became a nerve centre for other established BBC dramas like *Casualty* and new shows like *Merlin* and *Being Human*. The city had become a major tourist attraction – visitor numbers had increased by more than 40 per cent. It was much less expensive to film in and around Cardiff than in London.

It was while working on *Doctor Who* as staff writers that Moffat and Gatiss had hatched their plan to revive the idea of Sherlock Holmes. On their many train journeys back and forth between London and Cardiff, they discovered they were both huge fans of Holmes and Watson. They had enjoyed the idea of Basil Rathbone and Nigel Bruce in the 1940s playing the two characters as contemporary figures, rather than as hangovers from Conan Doyle's Victorian era.

'Modern-dress Holmes,' they thought. 'Someone should do that again!' After discussing this at length, they decided that they should be the ones to do it – before someone else got the chance.

Finally, the two of them, plus Sue Vertue, met up to strike a deal. Appropriately, the venue chosen was a restaurant in London's Piccadilly called the Criterion – the very first place Holmes and Watson had dined in Conan Doyle's original books. Work would begin on a pilot in January 2009.

From the outset, the plan was to be faithful to the characters of Holmes and Watson, but transplant them to the world of twenty-first century London. The look of *Sherlock* would be bang up to date; fustiness would be out. It was the antithesis of a period piece. 'Conan Doyle's original stories were never about frock coats and gaslight,' said Moffat. 'They are about brilliant detection, dreadful villains and blood-curdling crimes. Frankly, to hell with the crinoline!' Gatiss agreed. 'What appealed to us about doing Sherlock in the present day is that the characters have become almost literally lost in the fog. While I am second to no one in my enjoyment of that sort of Victoriana, we wanted to get back to the characters, and to why they became the most wonderful partnership in literature.' In addition, the two leads were relatively youthful – Cumberbatch was 32 at the time of the pilot, Freeman a slightly more senior 37 – which meant that the show would challenge the convention of Holmes and Watson being middle-aged. Add to that a sartorial elegance for Holmes. 'A modern take on Sherlock requires a modern look,' declared Gatiss. 'Benedict brings that to the role. He's in this sharp suit and a stylish overcoat, which gives him a great silhouette.'

Benedict Cumberbatch's Sherlock Holmes would remain the eternally super-confident detective, with a determination to outwit both criminals and the police. Some were concerned that the modern setting might make solving the cases too easy. The nineteenth-century Holmes, they argued, had not had the luxury of Google or a mobile phone to help him escape a trap. But Cumberbatch insisted this was missing the point: 'He uses technology as a resource. This man contains things that technology, no matter how efficient it is, cannot know. He's one step beyond because he's human.' In other words, the human mind has a flexibility and spontaneity that no computer (no matter how sophisticated) could possess, and Sherlock was attracted by science, technology and the Internet. 'He's brilliant at collating information,' said Cumberbatch. 'And he's as equally engaging on an intellectual level as he is on the understanding of human nature.'

'I am sure [Holmes] would have loved to have had the technology we have now,' said Paul McGuigan, who would direct most of the first two series. 'In the books he would use any device possible and he was always in the lab doing experiments. It's just a modern-day version of it. He will use the tools that are available to him today in order to find things out.'

With no deerstalker, and nicotine patches replacing the crutch of his pipe, the new Sherlock would have access to mobiles, laptops and MP3 players. Watson would have a blog. Holmes would fire off text messages (innovatively, these would appear onscreen, as would characters' inner thoughts) and run a website called The Science of Deduction. But their base would remain the famous central London address of 221b Baker Street (above a greasy spoon cafe), Holmes's devious nemesis Moriarty would still be an enemy, and other supporting characters would be present, like Mrs Hudson the housekeeper and Inspector Lestrade (played by Una Stubbs and Rupert Graves respectively).

Holmes would also still play the violin. Cumberbatch was a novice to the instrument, but needed to at least look like he could play it – even if it was just holding the bow correctly. Help on this matter came from Eos Chater, a member of the string quartet Bond. 'I would never insult the musical profession by saying that I had learnt the violin,' said Cumberbatch. 'I am desperately trying to convince people that what I am playing looks realistic. I have had some lessons.'

There was some discussion about whether Sherlock would take drugs in the new series. After all, in Conan Doyle's works, Holmes had been addicted to morphine. Might the super-sleuth be reliant on street drugs nowadays? Steven Moffat brushed aside the idea. 'In Victorian times everybody was taking some kind of drug, largely because there was no such thing as a painkiller. It is a very different thing to say that Sherlock Holmes would be a coke addict now.'

It seemed only natural to make the new Holmes and Watson series as up-to-date as possible. 'When you read the stories, you realise Holmes is an extraordinary modern man in a modern metropolitan London,' insisted Mark Gatiss. 'They weren't period stories to the people that were reading them, so we worked off exactly the same principle. We are not only keeping the essential character of Holmes, we are restoring it.'

Dr John Watson's background for *Sherlock* bore strong similarities to how the character was introduced in Arthur Conan Doyle's very first Holmes story. In *A Study in Scarlet*, written by Conan Doyle in 1886 and published a year later, Watson was a wounded army medic returning from the frontline in the Second Anglo-Afghan War of 1878–80. Gatiss realised that this resonated with present-day Afghanistan. 'It is the same war now, I thought. The same unwinnable war.'

Once back in London, and with post-traumatic stress disorder, the military doctor would have no home or circle of friends. 'He's come back home to nothing,' said Martin Freeman. 'The one thing we know about ex-service people is they can find civilian life really hard to adjust to.' Before long, Watson would be introduced to Sherlock Holmes by a mutual friend who knew Watson at Barts Hospital, and the pair would start flat-sharing in – where else? – Baker Street.

* * *

Stepping into the shoes of Sherlock Holmes was a daunting prospect. How many Holmes had there been in 125 years? Some studies suggested at least 200. Benedict Cumberbatch may have been guessing when he said, 'I am probably the

71st Sherlock.' The first incarnation on screen occurred as early as 1900, though all trace of that has long gone. Still in the silent film era, there was a short in 1910 called *Arsène Lupin contra Sherlock Holmes*, and almost fifty 20-minuters in the early 1920s with the Englishman Eille Norwood in the starring role. But it was in 1939 that the first truly famous Sherlock Holmes made his debut. Starting with *The Hound of the Baskervilles*, and sporting the trademark cape and deerstalker, Basil Rathbone (with Nigel Bruce as Watson) would star in 14 films in seven years.

Since Rathbone, the roll call of Sherlock Holmes actors has included Peter Cushing, Roger Moore, Stewart Granger, Ian Richardson, Tom Baker, Christopher Lee and Nicol Williamson. Peter Cook teamed up with Dudley Moore as Watson for a desultory *The Hound of the Baskervilles* remake in the late 1970s. Even John Cleese had been Sherlock – in the 1973 television one-off, *Elementary My Dear Watson*, written by the absurdist playwright N.F. Simpson. Most recently, there had been two TV Sherlocks: the Australian Richard Roxburgh (in the BBC's 2002 remake of *The Hound of the Baskervilles*) and in 2004, Rupert Everett in *Sherlock Holmes and the Case of the Silk Stocking*.

Perhaps the boldest break with the traditional Holmes image came in 1988. The film *Without a Clue* assigned Dr Watson (played by Ben Kingsley) to solving the crimes, for which he dreamt up a literary creation: an inebriated unemployed actor called Holmes, played by Michael Caine. It wasn't an incarnation the young Benedict Cumberbatch had enjoyed. 'There have been some pretty awful adaptations, some really, really painful ones. Michael Caine – let's not go there.'

Cumberbatch's personal favourite was Jeremy Brett, the star of ITV's *Adventures of Sherlock Holmes*, whose decade-long stint in the lead role might have lasted still longer, had it not been for his untimely death in 1995. Even so, Brett – and for that matter, Rathbone – had inhabited period pieces. 'Jeremy Brett was wonderful,' said Cumberbatch, who had watched him avidly as a youngster, 'but that doesn't put me off at all. We're moving away from a Victorian period so it's a great scope for freedom and interpretation.' Indeed, it wasn't as if the intention of *Sherlock* was to eliminate all previous incarnations, but to add to them. 'We're setting out to do something new,' said Cumberbatch. 'Why should we serve up what people have already had so sublimely?'

Martin Freeman agreed that it was like starting afresh. 'I think you can get into trouble if you try to hang your hat too much on what other people have done,' he said. 'Those people haven't done this script. We're not playing the novels, we're not playing the films. We're doing this script.' Besides, it wasn't as if reboots didn't happen elsewhere in popular culture. 'Steven [Moffat]'s rationale was that we update Ian Fleming with Bond all the time,' said Freeman. 'We're not seeing Daniel Craig in the Fifties. Arthur Conan Doyle's stories are certainly rich enough to do that with.'

Ultimately, Moffat promised that despite the setting, *Sherlock* would reflect the core values of the two central characters. 'Everything that matters about Holmes and

Watson is the same. Other detectives have cases, Sherlock Holmes has adventures – that's what matters.'

Because Holmes was not a policeman but a private detective, he was not bound by police procedures and doing everything by the book. He could be much more unconventional and shadowy in his working methods. The police had come to nickname him 'The Freak'. He was also a man not just of thought but of action. 'Holmes was a good shot and a martial arts expert,' said Cumberbatch, 'and although he's very much of the thinking school rather than an action school, he is also supposed to be an athlete – which I enjoyed quite a bit.'

Cumberbatch regarded *Sherlock* as a mystery series set apart from most of the many detective and cop series on television. He put it down to the central character having a mind like a computer: '...this almost supernatural but achievable ability to tie in the amazing amount of detail from a crime into some kind of narrative and then he uses his sensory qualities with his database of knowledge in his hard drive to make sense of it. He can scan a situation through touch, taste, sight, smell and an incredible amount of acquired knowledge.'

The character of Sherlock Holmes is so enduring and vivid that some have assumed him to have been a real person. The fictional chat show host Alan Partridge (aka Steve Coogan) once insisted that he had lived, but he wasn't alone in his delusion. In fact, some believe Holmes to be not just real but still alive, evidenced by the volume of correspondence which still reaches The Sherlock Holmes Museum in London's Baker Street.

How much of Sherlock was in Cumberbatch? And how much of Cumberbatch was in Sherlock? Frequently entertaining and animated in conversation, he was careful to emphasise that *Sherlock* was a scripted series, and he was still just acting when on screen. 'Because I talk a lot – probably because I'm nervous and can't quite edit the thoughts into something a bit more pithy – I get pinned into the same mania bracket, or having the same level of energy.' Far from it, he insisted. 'I'm very lazy in comparison to Holmes and I operate at a far lower speed.'

Benedict Cumberbatch's Sherlock Holmes is a talkative, pedantic sort. 'He is one step ahead of the audience, and of anyone around him with normal intellect,' he said. 'There's a great charge you get from playing him, because of the volume of words in your head and the speed of thought – you really have to make your connections incredibly fast.' But this did not make him a superhero, more a highly observant human being capable of deducing something from the tiniest fragment of evidence.

Steven Moffat had always been fascinated by the character of Sherlock, precisely because his was a skill, not a superpower from the gods. There would always be an explanation. 'Sherlock Holmes *explained*,' said the *Doctor Who* writer. 'Superman never told you how he flew, he just did. The Doctor never says a word about how the Tardis can be bigger on the inside, it just was. But Sherlock can't wait to tell you how the trick is done – and I couldn't turn the pages fast enough to find out.'

What he sometimes lacks is a sense of empathy, and he has

a tendency to speak without thinking, like Gregory House or Basil Fawlty. Death and murder can be an emotive subject for many, but it can excite Sherlock Holmes.

The lack of empathy and unflinching eye for detail means that Sherlock can have a macabre attitude when finding a corpse. Watson has more of a conscience. 'Sherlock likes the game of it,' commented Martin Freeman, 'whereas John is, at first, horrified by how Sherlock treats a dead body as a game.' 'Holmes needs grounding,' said Cumberbatch. 'He is too maverick for what he is trying to achieve. Watson is a reality check but, like a moth to the flame, needs the adventure. London is the battlefield.'

Freeman was in no doubt, even as the pilot was being made, that Cumberbatch was a dream of a co-star. 'I'm fast learning Benedict is perfectly cast. He has a really strong and assured way with language, and he's quick and able to play quick thinkers as a result, people who are mercurial.' And to play Holmes, to be able to think quickly, is a must.

* * *

Even before *Sherlock* was given a chance to take flight, yet another Holmes would appear. This time, it was Robert Downey Jr. in Guy Ritchie's film, with Jude Law as Watson. Having a big feature film reach the screen while a TV series based on the same characters was being made could have knocked everyone's confidence on *Sherlock*. 'I did feel threatened,' Cumberbatch later admitted. 'Robert Downey Jr. is amazing. They've crammed it into a Warner Brothers type action role, which is terrific in its way, but I must admit I was horribly, schoolboyishly relieved when the press gave it a bit of a kicking.' Still, Holmes is a tough character to gain full control over. 'I don't think we're in competition with it. He's the most-played fictional character, so who am I to be precious about it?'

The premiere of the *Sherlock Holmes* movie on Boxing Day 2009 might have meant that the Sherlock hour-long pilot would have been delayed until the following year, but in the event, that pilot would never be broadcast. Instead it would be remade and transmitted as the first of three feature-length stories.

When newspapers revealed that the Sherlock pilot (an embryonic version of 'A Study in Pink') had been 'shelved', in May 2010, some titles protested that £800,000 had been wasted on something the viewers would never see. The *Sun* even assumed that the pilot must have been sub-standard. However, the purpose of making a television pilot is to try something out. 'As with the rest of the industry,' explained a BBC statement, 'we occasionally use pilots to experiment with the best ways of telling stories. As a result of this pilot we commissioned a series of three 90-minute episodes.' So the series would go ahead, and for those who wanted to see the 'lost' pilot, it would be on the DVD release as a bonus. Making that pilot had not only convinced the BBC to go ahead with a series, but also persuaded international broadcasters to buy it. So much for it being a waste of money.

Knowing the story wouldn't go away, Mark Gatiss went on to elaborate on what had really happened.

'We were originally going to make six 60-minute episodes. Then the BBC said, "We want to make this more like event television, so we want three 90-minute episodes."' So the team set about remaking and expanding the pilot but having been happy with the efforts of director Coky Giedroyc, they decided to make the first version public. 'We thought, "Well fuck it, we're just going to show people the pilot." It's different, but we would have been very proud to put it out.'

Besides, the temporary burial of the pilot was necessary. The first version of 'A Study in Pink' had a similar plot, and mostly the same cast. But for the 90-minute version, it had been rewritten and extended substantially. It looked and sounded very different. The more devoted fans would welcome its presence as a bonus feature on the DVD, as an interesting comparison with the subsequent series, but for casual viewers, the major changes in style and content for the series were too dramatic and risked looking confusing. It was important when establishing a new series to be as clear and distinctive as possible.

As director for the series, Paul McGuigan was shown the scripts, and the unbroadcast pilot episode. He had a specific vision for how the series should look. 'One of the first things he said,' Steven Moffat told American radio station NPR, 'was you want to think Sherlock Holmes is behind the camera too. You want to see the world as Sherlock Holmes sees it. And that informs an awful lot of his work on the show... to give you the Sherlock's eye-view of the world all the time.'

The shooting of *Sherlock*'s first series was complete by the late spring of 2010. Filming mostly went well, although after weeks of outdoor filming during a bitterly cold winter, Benedict Cumberbatch suffered a bout of pneumonia at one point. Missing a day of the shoot, he was prescribed some antibiotics from the doctor, but then on the next day had to film a key fight scene. 'I think my opponent could have almost literally knocked me down with a feather,' Cumberbatch told the *Daily Mirror*. 'I certainly wasn't landing any meaningful punches. I was feeling so spaced-out and flaked out.'

Cumberbatch had a reputation for working hard, and despite his determination to keep himself in trim (plenty of swimming, yoga and honey), sometimes this led to lapses in his health. Not only had glandular fever floored him back at university, but during the Royal Court double-header of *Rhinoceros* and *The Arsonists* of 2007, he had developed a stomach ulcer. The pneumonia on *Sherlock* came from overwork, as he admitted several months later. 'I was in utter denial,' he told *The Sunday Times*. 'I was throwing myself into it with no rest, having fun because I love the character so much. Basil Rathbone and Jeremy Brett may be the ideal Victorian heroes, but I want to be the modern one.'

A Study in Scarlet had been Conan Doyle's first Sherlock Holmes story, way back in 1887. Over 120 years later, it had been retitled 'A Study in Pink', and would be the first of three feature-length episodes of *Sherlock*. Holmes and Watson would investigate a series of suspicious deaths triggered by a serial killer, whose murders had been contrived to look like the victims had taken their own lives.

Originally the series had been intended for BBC1's autumn season of 2010, but the Corporation had a rethink and instead brought it forward to three Sunday nights over July and August. The series creators panicked; they did not feel ready. 'We were sitting around with our heads in our hands,' recalled Steven Moffat. '"There isn't enough time to do this. It will broadcast to no one."'

Summer is generally a poor time for a high-profile new series to launch. The media industry and the general public are either on holiday, or at least winding down. Major television series traditionally launch in autumn, winter and spring. Summer, with the extra hours of daylight, is the time for sporting events, repeats, *Big Brother* and experiments. The omens did not look good for *Sherlock*.

To spread the word, the production team took to the social networking site Twitter to try and drum up support for the new show. But they were not expecting mass appeal. They hoped for 4 million to tune in, if that, and maybe some decent reviews.

On the evening of Sunday, 25 July, Benedict Cumberbatch was racing on his motorbike to the home of Steven Moffat and Sue Vertue in South-West London to watch the episode premiere on BBC1 with them. Unfortunately, he was held up. As Moffat wrote on Twitter: 'B. Cumberbatch coming to my house to watch Sherlock but he's stuck in traffic. On Baker Street.'

Baker Street? Too much of a coincidence, surely? 'I think he may have made that up, to be honest,' said Mark Gatiss, much later. 'But it's a really good lie.'

CHAPTER 10

SHERLOCK FEVER

When Benedict Cumberbatch finally made it to Steven Moffat's house that Sunday night, the party could begin in earnest. They would have to watch 'A Study in Pink' on delay. It wasn't long before everyone present realised that the show and its stars were big news. A casual glance on Twitter found that just about everything about it was trending. 'People were talking about it with this passion,' said Moffat. 'As if they were lifelong fans – when of course, they'd not seen it 90 minutes ago. Everything had changed in 90 minutes.'

Launching a new television series is stressful enough, especially when you're reinventing well-loved fictional characters. And in an age when users of social media websites and online forums can make their opinions known immediately, it is even more unnerving. 'I had a certain amount of trepidation,' said Mark Gatiss, 'but we were always very confident [that] as soon as you saw a couple of minutes you'd get it. However the extent to which people got it took us all by surprise.'

Gatiss's expectations towards the reception of *Sherlock* had already been boosted when members of The Sherlock Holmes Society had reacted approvingly to a preview showing. 'They all loved it. You can imagine that there wouldn't be any more ossified or reactionary group of fans. One of them thought it was the best on-screen depiction he'd ever seen.'

Cumberbatch too was amazed by all the praise, even if there was a grudging air to some of it. 'If I had a penny for every time a fan of the originals had come up to me and said, "I didn't want to like this, but I did", I'd be rich.' He admitted that some had wanted the show to crash and burn: 'We silenced a lot of the doubters. Knives were sharpened. I think a lot of people thought, "That'll never work."'

Almost nothing new is a guaranteed hit in television. Before a frame of footage had been shot for *Sherlock*, the BBC had conducted some audience research into what sort of following the programme might get. Focus groups tend to be conservative in nature, and nervous about anything too different. The findings regarding *Sherlock* seemed to bear this out. 'We were told it would not work,' said Ben Stephenson, head of the BBC's drama department, 'that it would get an old audience, it would get a small audience.'

In fact, the first episode of *Sherlock* was watched by more people than anything else on TV that night. Rival channels were dominated either by showings of oft-repeated films like Jim Carrey's *The Mask* or by series into their umpteenth runs: *Coast*, *Taggart*, *Big Brother*. Next to these, *Sherlock* at least represented something brand new, and over 7.5 million viewers tuned in, almost double what the makers had been hoping for. Within days, it was being heralded specifically as a reason to preserve the BBC. Culture Secretary Jeremy Hunt made a statement that the programme was 'a very good example of the BBC at its best, investing in new programming', but maintained a cut to the BBC licence fee was still likely. Moffat hit back. Reducing or even freezing the licence fee would affect the quality of shows like *Sherlock*. 'These shows are expensive and difficult,' he said, 'and require huge amounts of backing and huge amounts of nerve, particularly on the part of the commissioners.'

The first reviews had surpassed just about everyone's expectations; the critics were smitten by *Sherlock*. 'A triumph,' announced the *Independent*'s Tom Sutcliffe, 'witty and knowing without ever undercutting the flair and dazzle of the original. It understands that Holmes isn't really about plot but about charisma.' Elsewhere in the same paper, David Lister branded it as 'the ultimate buddy movie' and paid tribute to the decision to cast Cumberbatch and Freeman: '...whoever is responsible deserves a BAFTA.' The *Daily Telegraph* paid special attention to the portrayal of Holmes: 'Cumberbatch's sleuth is just the right balance of psycho-nerd and winning eccentric, the sort of person you'd love to have as your flatmate, if you could stand the mess.'

Cumberbatch's take on Sherlock Holmes was undoubtedly

compelling as a leading character, if an unlikely hero. Was he cool or simply cold? Flawed and spiky, he was often hard to like, but he had added a humane sheen to an obsessive, analytical being. He accepted that he could be driven when it came to work, 'but I'm not asexual and I'm not veering towards wanting to achieve everything at the expense of everyone around me. It's all healthy stuff to play and get out of your system but it's not stuff I want to take with me into my own life.' He still found it marvellously liberating to be rude in the skin of the character, 'because you can't be in real life. I think people love the idea of someone who's that hard-nosed and purposeful.'

Rather than making the character an all-knowing one (which risked making him smug), it was important to make Holmes's knowledge selective. He could be ignorant about things for which he had no passion or interest. The gaps in his knowledge helped make him believable. 'If you don't have those bits, he looks like a demi-god,' argued Mark Gatiss. 'It is so exciting to have a person that doesn't know that the earth goes round the sun or the name of the Prime Minister, because why does it bother him?'

One of the most impressive feats of Cumberbatch's performance on *Sherlock* was having to remember and deliver some fearsome and complicated monologues, uttered in a torrent at high speed. He was used to having to get the lines right, having worked in theatre so much, where the first take is your only take. But even so, Moffat and Gatiss's speeches would test him to the limit. 'I practise at home,' he said of the line-learning marathons. 'There is a lot of midnight oil burned. Sometimes it feels like, rather than acting, you're being a machine. I don't mean that in a negative way. Holmes is just very ... still. Still, but fast.'

He has revealed that he could not learn these speeches 'parrot fashion'. Instead, he explained: 'In rehearsals, repetition, "actioning" the script, a Stanislavski-based method of understanding the why, what and how of the part by applying transitive verbs to each line, association with that action, the cue line and any blocking all act as triggers to remember the line.' Although he acknowledged that 'a patient assistant director or girlfriend' was helpful too.

A maverick and an outsider, then, Sherlock was no super-hero. His skills were not otherworldly, or magical, but achievable through effort and wit. It was this drive, rather than inspiration or god-given talent, which was hard to match – and Cumberbatch admitted that his fascination for Holmes made him all the more curious in his spare time about human behaviour and motivation. He would silently analyse those around him in public; he might gaze at train passengers, at their clothing and baggage, and try and gain an insight into what their lives might be like. 'You can't help but go there in your mind,' he said of this casual but compulsive quest into the human condition.

Benedict Cumberbatch's Holmes was an unorthodox romantic lead, but a romantic lead all the same, certainly in the eyes of many viewers. Certain co-stars agreed. 'There's nothing more unattractive,' said Una Stubbs (aka landlady Mrs Hudson) in the *Radio Times*, 'than a man who thinks he is attractive. I think the fact that Benedict doesn't think he's attractive is so attractive to women. Discerning women.' Some press commentators agreed. 'He is notable as a heartthrob,' wrote Zoe Williams in the *Guardian*, 'for his very un-bestiality, his refinement, his piano player's hands, his indoor complexion, his humming brain.'

Cumberbatch's reaction was one of bemusement. 'I look in a mirror and I see all the faults I've lived with for years. Yet people go nuts for certain things about me. It's not me being humble. I just think it's weird.' Still, in terms of career progression, it had its good points. 'It builds a momentum. I've got the most fantastic opportunities, and that attention has been a huge help. As long as it helps me find good roles, my response is, "Bring it on!"'

Nor was Sherlock a romantic icon. 'He's not some alpha male who always gets the girl,' said Cumberbatch. 'He's a misfit who hacks people off.' And he could be obstructive if anyone else might be lucky in love. For example, he gets in the way of John Watson's dates with a fellow doctor in the second story, 'The Blind Banker'. 'Sherlock isn't socialised, and John likes that about him,' commented Martin Freeman. 'But it also infuriates him!'

The enigmatic but profound friendship between Holmes and Watson in *Sherlock* was hard to explain or quantify. Mark Gatiss made an attempt at explaining it regardless. 'They form a unit,' he told *The Sunday Times*. 'John Watson is gradually making Sherlock Holmes more human, and Sherlock Holmes has given John Watson his mojo back.'

There were viewers and Internet commenters who interpreted the relationship as going beyond friendship. The

Sherlock scriptwriters would often nod teasingly towards these theories, but there was nothing substantial beyond that. 'Much as Sherlock adores John, and he's fond of him, there's nothing sexual – all the jokes aside,' said Cumberbatch, but said of the quips, 'the problem is, they fuel the fantasy of the few into flames for the many. People presume that's what it is, but it's not.' Some on the Internet have let their imaginations run riot, wildly and explicitly, on the matter. 'There are a lot of people hoping that our characters and ourselves are rampantly at it most of the time,' said Martin Freeman. He brushed aside the fantasies as 'tongue-in-cheek', but maintained that, ultimately, their strength as a twosome was the way they complemented each other, as in so many friendships and relationships: 'They give something to the other that is lacking in their life.'

Besides, Cumberbatch denied there was much sex appeal in the character of Sherlock to begin with, or at least not consciously. He explained that Holmes had abstained from sexual activity because he is busy in other areas of life. 'Not every man has a sex drive that needs to be attended to,' he argued. 'Like a lot of things in his life where he's purposely dehumanised himself, it's to do with not wanting the stuff that is time-wasting, that's messy. To the Victorian eye he's an eccentric, but I think he has purposely repressed those things.'

The affection and respect between Holmes and Watson, while it could be awkwardly expressed, was certainly there. 'It is about the things that wind each other up and the things that they genuinely love about one another as well,' said

Freeman. 'We all certainly saw it as a love story. These two people do love and kind of need each other in a slightly dysfunctional way, but it is a relationship that works. They get results.'

* * *

Sales of Conan Doyle's original novels trebled after the first *Sherlock* episode aired, but the series viewing figures dipped by around a million for the second story. In 'The Blind Banker', a terrible fate awaited anyone who saw mysterious ciphers on walls around the City of London. The drop in viewing figures was not in itself too much to worry about – most new shows lose a quarter or a third of the audience in the second week – but reviews were lukewarm towards aspects of the plot, especially the portrayal of a band of Chinese smugglers known as the Black Lotus. A warmer reception greeted 'The Great Game', the final episode, written by Mark Gatiss, and which found Holmes up against a devious bomber. Not before time, it unveiled Sherlock's shadowy enemy, James Moriarty, played by Andrew Scott, who introduced an Irish accent to the character for the first time. In Steven Moffat's view, Scott brought a terrifying coldness to the part: 'He has this amazing ability to conjure up this sort of blank-eyed desolation of a man too clever. Too clever to exist, almost.'

Scott's identity in the role of Moriarty was not revealed before broadcast. Gatiss delighted in keeping such secrets from the viewers, which was quite an achievement in an age where news travels faster than ever, especially via social media. Indeed Gatiss had managed to keep his own role (as Holmes's brother Mycroft) under wraps, and some had been misled into believing *he* would be Moriarty. Neither Scott nor Gatiss appeared in the publicity material cast lists, nor in the *Radio Times* billings. When so much television kept telling you what was going to happen next, Gatiss was a great believer in holding certain things back: 'If every now and then you pull a fast one so that the moment of transmission still means something, it can be just wonderful.'

Many were surprised and disappointed that *Sherlock*'s first series was comprised of only three episodes, in an age where most American television series make 13 or even 24 episodes every year, and even high-profile high-concept British series like *Doctor Who* manage up to a dozen. But the prospect of making more *Sherlock* had the problem that Steven Moffat – as the showrunner and head writer on *Doctor Who* too – would have to accommodate those commitments. The BBC, delighted with the first series ratings for *Sherlock*, acknowledged that it wasn't a question of 'if' more would be made, more 'when' and 'how'.

There were two possible options for the second run of *Sherlock*. Either there would be another trio of 90-minute films, or a slightly longer series of hour-long episodes. BBC drama head Ben Stephenson believed that the 90-minute option would feel like 'less of a detective show and more of an adventure show'.

Over the first three *Sherlock* episodes, viewing figures had peaked at 9 million in the UK. It would be a huge international sales success for the BBC, which licensed the episodes to 180 territories worldwide. Viewers in the United States were treated to them from October 2010 on the non-commercial US network PBS. From August, teasers from the show had been included in a promotional campaign onscreen, which partially borrowed a slogan from Holmes himself: 'The Game Is On This Fall'. Indeed it was. It would be pitted against another critical favourite: HBO's gangster series *Boardwalk Empire*. But for American audiences, and to the great regret of the production team back in the UK, each 90-minute episode of *Sherlock* would be cut by eight minutes to accommodate sponsorship announcements. 'We try to cut the bits which aren't essential to the story,' admitted Sue Vertue at Hartswood, 'but they are often the lovely character scenes.'

Populist but smart and critically feted, *Sherlock* would be an obvious contender for prizes in awards ceremonies. Its first plaudits came in October 2010, when it picked up two gongs at the Crime Thriller Awards sponsored by the opticians chain Specsavers. The show itself won the coveted TV Dagger prize, seeing off the competition of *Wallander*, *Luther* and *Ashes to Ashes*. But Cumberbatch himself was recognised individually, accepting the award for the Best Actor category from the star of *Silent Witness*, Emilia Fox. The following January, he battled it out with Matt Smith and *Ashes to Ashes*' Philip Glenister for the National Television Awards' Best Drama Performance, but all three were trumped by the more senior David Jason, retiring from his role as Jack Frost in ITV's *A Touch of Frost*.

Victory would be Cumberbatch's again, however, at the

Broadcasting Press Guild Awards that March, when he beat Hugh Bonneville of *Downton Abbey* to the Best Actor award. In September, he was Best Actor of the year at the *GQ* magazine awards – where recipients in other categories included Matt Smith, Hugh Laurie, Bill Nighy, Professor Brian Cox and George Osborne.

Then in May, there were the BAFTA Television Awards Best Actor, for which Cumberbatch was up against Jim Broadbent (*Any Human Heart*), Daniel Rigby (Eric Morecambe in *Eric and Ernie*) and *Doctor Who*, aka Matt Smith. *Sherlock* itself was shortlisted for Best Drama, while Martin Freeman was in the running for Best Supporting Actor. Though again, Cumberbatch missed out on the top prize (Rigby won), both the show itself and Freeman collected gongs on the night itself, which coincidentally took place on Conan Doyle's birthday: 22 May.

* * *

The fanbase for *Sherlock* and Cumberbatch now extended to Russia and the Far East. He had to become used to the attention of the public, which had suddenly grown extremely devoted. After giving his all each evening in theatrical productions like *After the Dance* and *Frankenstein*, an exhausted Cumberbatch would face excitable Sherlock fans outside the stage door. 'I had done a long day and I said, "I don't wish to be rude...", and they said, "We've come all the way from South Korea". People came from Russia, Japan... everywhere.'

It was on a visit to Japan where he found himself the centre of attention to a bewildering degree. 'I was mobbed at the airport. There were a few people who were interested to talk to me about everything to do with my life at the moment, and to let me know that I'm very big on the Internet, which I have sort of got wind of.'

The level of devotion, then, bordered on surreal. 'It's strange to have that sort of intimacy from strangers when it's all through your work. A lot of "I know you don't know me but I'd like to spend the rest of my life with you" stuff, which is odd.' But there was a humorous side to this idolatry. Take, for instance, a page of lookey-likey pictures he was sent by a fan: 'Sid from *Ice Age*, a horse, a llama, a hammerhead shark and a meerkat'.

Between the broadcast of series one of *Sherlock*, and the making of the second batch in 2011, Benedict Cumberbatch had been busy with plenty of other work, including the filming of *War Horse* and *Tinker Tailor Soldier Spy*, so it felt peculiar returning to do it again. He was unused to making television series – all his previous ones had been single series, and it was only on radio in *Cabin Pressure* where he had become accustomed to several series of something. Even if the public were only just getting used to it, would he already feel like it would be more of the same?

'When I went back it felt like a pale impression,' he admitted. 'It felt like I was impersonating something I'd seen on the telly last year. It now had this life that was completely outside what we had done before in front of a camera. We had been part of the audience, and the audience reaction to it, for a lot longer than we had actually been playing the roles.' Or was it just that he didn't like revisiting the Holmes hair? 'I was short and blond in *Tinker Tailor Soldier Spy*. I really didn't like coming back to this hair. I can't think of a wittier or even accurate comparison, but I just think it makes me look a bit like... a woman.'

One development in series two would be the way that Holmes' icy analysis would start to thaw and gain a little humanity. 'His methods are devilish,' said Cumberbatch, 'but he's got good at the core.' But Holmes' ultra-observant working methods would remain. 'You see extraordinary depth in the smallest detail. It's joining the dots. That's the fun thing, building a narrative. You do try to piece together personal stories from bits of information.'

The three episodes in Sherlock's second series would be 'A Scandal in Belgravia', 'The Hounds of Baskerville' and 'The Reichenbach Fall'. 'A Scandal in Belgravia' was a reworking of the very first Conan Doyle short story about Holmes: *A Scandal in Bohemia*. It picks up from where 'The Great Game' left off, with Holmes and Watson escaping the clutches of Moriarty, and finds the monarchy's reputation threatened by incriminating photographs. Soon the occupants of 221b are up against terrorists and a government conspiracy.

The source material for the second story, 'The Hounds of Baskerville', is – of course – from *The Hound of the Baskervilles*, the third of the Holmes novels, and probably the best-known of them all. Sherlock Holmes is asked to investigate the presence of a supernatural hound on the moors of Devon which has been terrorising nearby residents, especially one aristocratic family. When Charles Baskerville dies, there are fresh fears that the hound is still at large. Instead of centring the story round a country house (as in the original), it was set around a sinister research base specialising in animal experimentation.

The third story, 'The Reichenbach Fall', was a rebooting of the 1893 story, *The Final Problem*. The original tale included the notorious battle on a ledge at the Reichenbach Falls in the Swiss Alps, which sent Holmes falling to his apparent death, and was indeed intended by Conan Doyle to bid farewell to Sherlock. The author had wanted to go back to writing fiction of a more 'serious' nature. But although he had intended to kill off Sherlock Holmes in *The Final Problem*, overwhelming public demand over several years made him rethink this decision, and he was finally persuaded to resurrect him in *The Adventure of the Empty House* in 1903.

In fact, Conan Doyle could be quite scornful about the popularity of Sherlock Holmes. In 1923, he bemoaned: 'If I had never touched Holmes, who has tended to obscure my higher work, my position in literature would at the present moment be a more commanding one.' Sometimes Conan Doyle could neglect the plots of Sherlock stories and not even finish them properly. 'The readers would often be waiting and waiting,' said Mark Gatiss, who with Steven Moffat had little choice but to create proper endings to some of Conan Doyle's originals, 'and suddenly we were destined never to find out why the murderer did it, because the ship they were on sank in a storm. Basically, someone comes round and says to Conan Doyle, "Do you want to come out?" And he says, "Hang on, I'll just finish this and I'll be with you in five minutes."'

For the remake of *The Final Problem*, 'The Reichenbach Fall' would find Professor Moriarty making a return to break into the Tower of London, Pentonville Prison and the Bank of England, puzzling everyone as to how he was able to do it. But the climactic confrontation between him and Holmes would take place not in Switzerland but on the roof of St Bartholomew's Hospital in London. The rooftop scenes were some of the earliest to be shot for the new series, and it wasn't long before snaps of Cumberbatch made it into the press – pictures of Sherlock apparently being taken to hospital after falling off the roof. But did he jump, or was he pushed by James Moriarty?

Moffat and Gatiss had decided to give Moriarty the psyche of a suicide bomber, reasoning that he had no particular ambition to survive his dastardly deeds unharmed. 'The villains that chill us are the ones who aren't compromised by the need to survive,' said Moffat. 'People whose eyes you look at and there's no sign of anything human.'

Although all three stories in series two were loosely based on Conan Doyle originals, various motifs and themes were dropped in from some of his other works. 'Almost all of the stories are not long enough,' said Moffat, by way of explanation. 'We did "The Great Game" and that's adapted from about 28 Sherlock Holmes stories.' But then, Sherlock was less about the intricate and cunning plotting (as intricate and cunning as it could be) than about the characters in those stories. 'The engine of the plot has to be the adventures,' said Mark Gatiss, 'but what people really love is the banter and the rows, and the proper feeling between them, which really leaps off the screen.'

As in the first series, Steven Moffat, Mark Gatiss and Stephen Thompson would write one story adaptation each. Thompson's previous series as a writer included the BBC legal drama *Silk* and *Doctor Who*. Between them, the three would tackle a trio of 'big stories' from the Conan Doyle canon. They could have delayed these until later in the run, but chose not to. 'Knowing we were a huge hit, instead of making people wait years and years,' said Moffat, 'we thought, "To hell with deferred pleasure, let's just do it now – more, sooner, faster. That also means we see three different sides to Sherlock.' Meaning 'Sherlock and love', 'Sherlock and fear' and 'Sherlock and death'.

The filming schedule ran smoothly until early August 2011, when unforeseen events forced the production to close ranks. As riots broke out in streets in and around London and other cities, gangs of looters began trying to vandalise the set, attempted to steal scaffolding poles, and at one point picked up some rigging to attack an old pump engine. Production was shut down temporarily, and Mark Gatiss sent the following message on Twitter: 'Scene incomplete owing to approaching looters. Unbelievable times.'

Cumberbatch was upset by the attacks in general, and watched the news coverage on TV with growing alarm and anger. He was left in no doubt as to the motives of many of

Above left: A young Cumberbatch poses for the *Hawking* photocall in July 2004.

Above right: Parents Wanda Ventham and Timothy Carlton and actor Mark Gatiss attend the IMAX 3D Premiere of *Star Trek Into Darkness* in May 2013.

Below left: David Furnish, Evgeny Lebedev and Cumberbatch attend the Grey Goose Winter Ball to benefit the Elton John AIDS Foundation in October 2011.

Below right: Cumberbatch and Martin Freeman pose with their BAFTA for Best Drama Series for *Sherlock* in May 2011.

Above: Tom Hardy, Colin Firth, Gary Oldman, Cumberbatch and John Hurt arrive at the UK premiere of *Tinker Tailor* in September 2011.

Below left: Jonny Lee Miller and Cumberbatch accept their joint Best Actor Award for *Frankenstein* at the 57th Evening Standard Theatre Awards in November 2011.

Below right: At the after party with Best Actress winner Sheridan Smith.

Above: Resuming the eponymous role on the set of *Sherlock* in London in April 2013.

Below left: Filming a scene for *The Imitation Game* in London in November 2013.

Below right: Brad Pitt and Cumberbatch attend the *12 Years a Slave* premiere during the 2013 Toronto International Film Festival.

Above: Cumberbatch, Allen Leech, Alex Lawther and Matthew Beard accept the Ensemble Performance Award onstage during the 26th Annual Palm Springs International Film Festival Awards Gala in January 2015.

Below left: Sheltering co-star Keira Knightley from the rain at the opening night gala screening of *The Imitation Game* in London.

Below right: On the red carpet with fiancée Sophie Hunter for the 72nd Annual Golden Globe Awards in January 2015. All pictures © *Getty Images* those involved. 'I'm a Prince of Wales Trust ambassador, so I'm all about giving youth an education, a voice and a chance not to take the wrong road. But those eejits saying they're doing it for socio-political reasons? Fuck off, no you're not, you're on a jolly and you're getting away with it!'

He knew all too well that an outburst such as this was likely to be met with some ridicule. 'I come from an incredibly privileged bubble, so the minute I open my mouth I can sense the comeback of "What the fuck do you know?" But my sympathy is with the people who do know what they're talking about, who have been brought up on estates and live morally decent, contributing lives and who have seen opportunists destroying all their work.'

* * *

One of the most talked-about cast additions for Sherlock's second series was Lara Pulver, previously Section Chief Erin Watts in *Spooks*. She played Holmes' love interest, Irene Adler. 'Irene and Sherlock just get each other to the core,' said Laura Pulver. 'They are so similar and so different on so many different levels. What was great was just pushing each other's buttons and seeing what exploded.'

Irene is a dominatrix with the very same capability as Holmes of making ingenious analytical leaps and participating in mind games. 'She doesn't suffer fools gladly,' Cumberbatch told the *Guardian*. 'He [Holmes] has a blind spot which is female emotional intuition. He's very good at guessing the kind of everyday circumstances in the sexes, the normal nuances of courtship. What she has is much more complicated than that.'

So this would be no conventional love story, but two complex people who have a similar worldview. Or as Martin Freeman pithily put it, 'Holmes happens to be falling in love with someone who is as insane as he is!'

One scene between Sherlock and Irene in 'A Scandal in Belgravia' would be much-discussed: he underwent a whipping from her. 'It was really painful, Lara went for it,' Cumberbatch told the *Sun*. 'I don't know how people get pleasure out of that kind of thing, I genuinely don't.' For her part, Pulver quipped that she was only doing what he asked her to do. 'Benedict said, "It's all right, Lara, you can hit me harder. I was like, "Oh *can* I now, Benedict Cumberbatch?"'

The whipping scenes were not the most controversial in the episode, however. For her opening scene as Irene, barely two minutes long, Pulver was naked. 'When I read that script, I didn't even flinch,' she said later. 'It was just a moment in the storytelling. For it to have become such a focus of that episode kind of shocks me. It is naive to think it wouldn't be mentioned, and yet it still shocks me.'

'A Scandal in Belgravia', which opened the second series of *Sherlock*, was broadcast at 8.10pm on New Year's Day 2011. British television operated a policy that nine o'clock marked a watershed in terms of content. Anything before then purported to be 'family viewing'; anything after that time was skewed towards a more adult audience. Around 100 viewers (out of nearly 10 million) contacted the BBC to complain about the first Pulver scene. 'That was ludicrous,' she commented. 'You saw more of Benedict when his sheet fell down than you did of me.' 'It's not supposed to be a source of stimulation for the audience,' argued Cumberbatch, who pointed out the counter-support for the scene.

Ultimately, it was all great publicity for the series, and as the BBC observed, pre-watershed should not mean anodyne. 'We had lots of conversations about it,' said drama head Ben Stephenson, 'and I think we were right in thinking it's a bit of a cheeky show.' In fact, 'A Scandal in Belgravia' proved to be the most popular single programme in the history of the BBC's online catch-up service, the iPlayer. Over 2.5 million people watched it when it was made available, beating a *Doctor Who* episode from 2010.

But would Steven Moffat really kill off Sherlock Holmes after just six instalments of the programme? No one seemed to be giving anything away. '[He] is not afraid of controversy,' conceded the BBC. 'Nobody would put it past him to kill off Sherlock as it would be a dramatic twist.' The ultimate in dramatic twists, in fact. Moffat shrugged off the idea of it being beyond the pale: 'Robin Hood died. Sherlock Holmes had a famous death. This is our version of the story and we can do what we like.'

The second series had won round doubters of the previous one. One *Radio Times* senior writer had dismissed the first series as 'beautifully crafted but hollow'. Barely 18 months later, the same journalist branded it 'a grown-up drama for people like us. And you can't say that very often. The script is literate, witty and clever, full of lines that sing out with intelligence.' It was quite clear that *Sherlock* was a unanimous TV smash hit, and Benedict Cumberbatch was a star.

CHAPTER 11

PUBLIC CUMBERBATCH

After 2004, when he had starred as the young Stephen Hawking, Benedict Cumberbatch steadily became increasingly well-known, but remained able to carry on his day-to-day life as normal. Rarely was he snapped by the paparazzi or approached by members of the public. 'I don't get spotted,' he said in 2007, 'Maybe a girl will stop me in the street and ask: "Did I snog you at my cousin's wedding?", but that's it.'

The first series of *Sherlock*, in July and August 2010, changed all that. At thirty-four, he was suddenly a visible public figure. He later described the trajectory as 'a horrific fairground ride'. Yet even before this, he was perceptive about how fame can distort one's perception of the world. Having become accustomed to preparing for acting roles by observing society around him, it was going to be tough to continue with this when he himself was going to be the centre of attention. And he was also now almost too busy to ponder and reflect. 'One of the fears of having too much work is not having time to observe. And once you get recognised, there is nowhere for you to look any more. You can't sit on a night bus and watch it all happen,' he explained. 'There are ways of not being recognised, of course, but planning is essential. Existing in the public space with any kind of private dimension is a fun game to play. That involves hats and glasses and just trying to keep a low profile in an Inspector Clouseau disguise.'

Success had brought financial stability, although some anxiety lingered about those of his contemporaries who had not secured the breaks in the way he had. 'When you start getting jobs, and see your mates from drama school, you have this innate sense of guilt that it's not fair that others aren't doing exactly what you're doing. It's soul-destroying. There is a kind of weird guilt about doing well.'

Had he become a household name at the right moment? He couldn't be certain. 'If I'd had fame early on,' he told the *Guardian*, 'I'd have been able to abuse it in the way that a young man should. I've been working to this, but a lot of the fruits of it I can't really enjoy.' Faced with an intense level of adoration, it was still scrutiny. How would he cope in the circumstances? A big worry came with the group of people who would refer to him by the name of his most famous role. 'You get known as "Sherlock". That's not just from people who can't be bothered to remember "Benedict Cumberbatch", and who can blame them, because it's such a strong signature.' But then again, to his relief, it wasn't as if George Clooney was called by his *ER* character name 'Doug Ross' anymore.

Cumberbatch was starting to get used to TV appearances under the character name 'Himself': chat shows, breakfast TV, entertainment juggernauts like *Alan Carr: Chatty Man*, *The Jonathan Ross Show* and *The Graham Norton Show*, perched on a sofa next to the likes of Kerry Katona, the Red Hot Chili Peppers and even Harrison Ford. 2010, though, was when the tabloid newspapers became interested in Benedict Cumberbatch. To them, he was not merely a successful and highly acclaimed actor, he was a celebrity. He was there not just to talk about his various films and TV shows, but to be photographed, and maybe to discuss his personal life.

He had always had a wry way in interviews, and was prone to being playful. Television and radio interviews would usually demonstrate an irony in the voice if he made a joke, but the face-value style of the tabloids could never quite do justice to this patter on the page. One of his first experiences of having a joke decontextualised came at the *Sherlock* press launch. 'I'm always cast as sort of slightly wan, ethereal, troubled intellectuals or physically ambivalent bad lovers. I'm here to tell you I'm quite the opposite in real life. I'm a fucking fantastic lover!' The remark would follow him around, much to his chagrin. 'That got everywhere,' he groaned only weeks later. 'Everyone was coming up to me, going, "So, how good are you, exactly?" Jesus Christ...' Mostly, he would politely distance himself from the idea that he was a sex symbol. 'People see a value in you that you don't see yourself. So when I'm told of my sex-symbol status and all that nonsense I find it laughable, silly. I've been looking at this same old mush all my life.'

He was flattered by his devoted female fanbase, but was also careful. A Twitter account called @Cumberbitches had started up, sharing information and gossip about the object of its desire. As of September 2013, 60,000 fans had signed up. He felt uncomfortable with the account name, and opted instead for 'Cumberbabes', and eventually 'Cumberwomen' and 'Cumbergirls'. 'It's not even politeness. I won't allow you to be my bitches. I think it sets feminism back so many notches. You are... Cumberpeople.'

When *Sherlock* initially made him a star on television, Cumberbatch was still in a long-term relationship with Olivia Poulet, whom he had met on their drama degree course in Manchester. By the mid-noughties, Poulet's star had also started to rise, with minor roles on television in *The Inspector Lynley Mysteries* and *The Rotters' Club* leading to her first co-starring credit: as the young Camilla Parker Bowles in *Whatever Love Means*, an ITV drama about the romance between Camilla and Charles, Prince of Wales. Later she would perhaps be best known on television for playing Emma Messinger, the cynical Tory spin-doctor on Armando Iannucci's *The Thick of It*. Cumberbatch and Poulet made a reluctant showbiz couple, rarely giving journalists more than the most basic of information. 'We are good friends,' Poulet had tantalised the *Sunday Telegraph* in 2005. 'We've been good friends for a long time. But then we were not such good friends for a bit. And now we're good friends again.'

In the autumn of 2007, they moved from West to North London, from Shepherd's Bush to Hampstead. Here, they bought a flat with a roof terrace described by Benedict as 'my sanctuary'. The prospect of marriage was rarely raised publicly by either of the pair, but by his mid-thirties, he had godchildren, while she had nephews, and he regularly announced he was broody, even hoping he might reduce his workload in order to embrace parenthood. 'I know you pick up an amazing amount of stamina the minute you become a dad, but I would like to be a young dad. I would love to have the ability to juggle a career and have a young child.' His was not a secure profession. Acting, like many jobs in the creative arts, is feast or famine, but despite this, he was insistent he could make it work, given the chance. 'Children are expensive,' he was quoted as saying in the pages of the *Daily Telegraph* newspaper, 'but as an actor, if you freak out about economic maturity you'll never step out the front door. Everyone I know who has done it says you will never regret it. Your life doesn't stop when you have children.'

He told *The Sunday Times* in the summer of 2010: 'We both want children, but not necessarily right now, and not necessarily with each other. We're great as we are for now.' They had even appeared together in *Sherlock*'s second story, 'The Blind Banker'. But in March 2011, with both parties' careers in the ascendant, they chose to part amicably after 12 years together. Single again, but still with a great fondness for his ex, Benedict confessed that his broodiness was still present, but recognised, 'the reality of children is you have to be in the right place with the right person.' The split with Poulet would bring some unwelcome attention from the press for Cumberbatch, and he was doorstepped by reporters and photographers. 'It was unnerving to think they knew where I lived,' he told the *Radio Times*.

After their break-up, Poulet continued in *The Thick of It* on BBC2, played Carol Thatcher (daughter of Margaret) in a Channel 4 biopic, and shone in a revival of Caryl Churchill's *Top Girls* in the West End. She also wrote comedy sketches with the writer-performer Sarah Solemani, a drama script about women in their thirties for the BBC, and a screenplay about four young women who had rowed the Atlantic Ocean.

The newly-single Cumberbatch suddenly became one of showbusiness's most eligible bachelors, regularly linked to other women in the gossip columns. Later in 2011 the designer Anna Jones accompanied him to the Venice Film Festival where *Tinker Tailor Soldier Spy* was opening, but if this was a relationship, it seemed relatively short-lived. Photographs circulated, too, of him with the supermodel Lydia Hearst, and he was seen out and about both with the Russian model Katia Elizarova, and with the actress Liv Tyler in Los Angeles. The gossipmongers could get carried away, though. There was the night he was snapped by a swarm of paparazzi in the company of a mystery woman, who turned out to be his personal assistant. 'We got papped to the point that I couldn't actually see, and I had to put my head down. Immediately, they presume,

"Ah, beautiful blonde..."' The personal assistant was also his niece.

Even after the end of his long-term relationship with Poulet, he remained keen to start a family but knew that he wanted to find the right person. 'There are always moments and meetings and chance encounters,' he said in the summer of 2012. 'But to make meaningful relationships is very hard at the moment. Also, I was in a very long, long relationship all through my twenties and early thirties, so I know about looking for the right one, I guess.' 'One of his regrets,' his half-sister Tracy Peacock was quoted as saying, 'is that he hasn't found someone to settle down with. I think they would have to be someone not in the acting profession, someone who was happy to hold the fort while he went off and pursued his career.'

It's one thing to have your stage and screen performances becoming the centre of attention, quite another to find that you yourself are scrutinised and spotted. At least to begin with, Cumberbatch didn't mind being recognised, and found that meeting the public was mostly painless. 'You do get a few spiky people who want to have a go, but I can just about deal with them. I've got the energy for it. It might be different if I was older.' But it was at the deli counter in Tesco's when he realised he had crossed the line into superstardom. 'The staff all stared at me. A younger guy split off from the group and said, "Mate, I'm not being funny but you know that series *Sherlock*? You look quite a lot like him." I said, "I am Sherlock".'

He admitted that he was unprepared for being in the

constant glare of the media. 'I hadn't really made myself a target,' he said, citing his roles of Hawking, Pitt the Younger, Van Gogh and Frankenstein – four roles sufficiently different to prevent any kind of consistent personality from breaking through. Now not merely a famous actor, it was presumed that he was a Personality. And with the arrival of celebrity can come a sense of loss. 'Just because I'm in my thirties,' he told the *Radio Times* in August 2012, 'it doesn't make the weirdness of no longer being private any less. I don't think it matters whether it happens when you're 25 or 55. Something is suddenly taken away.'

Personality and celebrity can be a trap, and Cumberbatch has to date dealt well with becoming a star, with a few wobbles. Genial and charming in company, he was mostly happy to sign autographs for fans, but would quip that afterwards he would have to 'have ice cubes put to my wrists'. Occasionally, he would lose patience a little and wonder aloud about the value of signing autographs. 'What is this need for proof we all have? Why do people need me to ruin the front page of a book with my terrible signature so that they can prove that they've met me? Will no one believe them otherwise?'

An over-sensitive reaction? Perhaps, but if you haven't sought the limelight for its own sake, adjusting to the constant attention is not easy. You are recognised by people you don't know. They know all about you, or at least the version of you that they've read about. There's an argument that once someone is in the public eye, part of the job is to be professional and polite with the public. But it is still a job, and the problem with fame is that it is impossible for other people to relate to you directly, especially if you're an actor. Do the autograph hunters expect Sherlock, or Cumberbatch, or the Cumberbatch with the celebrity sheen? Being famous is still an act.

To Benedict Cumberbatch, fame with permission was fair enough. For the more obsessive fans, he expressed concern, although often more for their own welfare. But without any permission or warning, the attention could feel intrusive and unpleasant. He did not appreciate opportunists trying to take his picture without asking. 'I feel it's cowardly and a bit pathetic,' he said. 'Just ask me if you really want me to have a photograph with you.'

In March 2013, he was at home one night when he discovered that someone was watching him from another property nearby and live-tweeting his every move. 'It was the strangest fan experience that I've ever had. It was such a strange and a direct thing to see these tweets. I found it really worrying and very hard to deal with.' The tweeter quickly deleted the messages and baked a cake by way of an apology. Cumberbatch would say little more about the matter, and did not contact the police, but it did underline the fact that you couldn't escape attention if you were a celebrity, especially with 24-hour media coverage and social media (Cumberbatch does not tweet). 'The sad thing is I don't really have anonymity any more in the UK, as it has got just like it is in America.' He didn't mind being spotted sometimes, or stopped – but it was a strange life for it to happen all the time.

Cumberbatch knew that the rate he was going, he was unlikely to become much more famous: 'It won't last on quite the same level, but what you have to do is just treat each bit as a job and get the best out of those experiences. If you constantly walk around in a bubble of excitement you wouldn't be able to do any work.' The answer was to try and remain grounded with his nearest and dearest, who even if he had wanted to get too grand, wouldn't have let him. When he was sent an outsize black whip with a red heart on the end by an anonymous admirer, he couldn't resist mentioning it on a TV chat show... only to discover that the fans who sent it were some of his friends.

* * *

Cumberbatch had wanted success, not necessarily fame. If he had sought recognition it was for the work, not for him as himself. This was a bit of a shock, and the almost unanimously positive reaction on Twitter shook him slightly. He half-expected 'people abseiling down into our garden just to get a sneak peek at us.'

After three and a half decades of being Benedict Cumberbatch, he was now being called Sherlock in the street. But he had devised a wry response: 'When people come up to me and ask, "Are you Sherlock Holmes?", I say, "I just look a bit like him. I'm not actually Sherlock."'

CHAPTER 12

IN DEMAND

Despite his rise to fame in cinema and on television, Benedict Cumberbatch had not abandoned stage work. The Royal Court hired his services again in spring 2008, this time with Katie Mitchell on directorial duties, for a domestic drama by Martin Crimp. In *The City*, Chris's marriage to Clair (Hattie Morahan) is falling apart when the company he works for is restructured, and he loses his job.

As usual, Cumberbatch conducted considerable research for the role of Chris, in which he contacted and visited support groups for the redundant. For one scene, he was obliged to visit a meat counter in a supermarket, because his character had to take on a new job as a butcher.

The City marked the first time the childless actor had to portray a dad on stage. He was especially nervous about one specific scene, a confrontational one with a child actor, but ultimately felt reassured. 'I was worried, but there are studies showing that young actors are very strongly aware of the difference between fiction and real life.' Great care was taken in rehearsals with these junior performers, whose parents were always made aware of what was going on.

If anything, it was the audiences who could be more troublesome. During the press night performance, a mobile phone ringtone sounded persistently for several minutes. 'There was a moment when Hattie broke off,' said Cumberbatch, 'and I thought about stopping and saying, "OK everyone, we're only 20 minutes in, so we're going to ask that the phone be turned off and we're going to start again." I had this speech all ready, but I was repressing it and repressing it.'

Worse was to come on a subsequent night. At the end of the final act, one audience member called out, 'That was absolutely awful!' 'What annoyed me,' Cumberbatch said, 'was that the audience had been sitting in silence at the end of this very puzzling play, and then someone decided to hijack their entire thought process.' Such is the peril of live theatre – it can elicit an instant reaction, and not always a welcome one. For him, compelling the audience to concentrate was a modern problem in the theatre. 'Texting and talking have become a real problem, but you have to understand that you can't demand their attention, you have to command it. You have to make them behave by your acting, not by shouting: "Behave!"'

Riskier still is live television drama, where there is no safety net for retakes. In 2009, Cumberbatch took part in a project organised by the Sky Arts channel called *Theatre Live!*: a season of plays which were being transmitted on TV as they were being performed. Of course, in the early days of television – before videotape became commonplace – all programmes were live, drama included, and if a play was to be 'repeated', the cast and technicians had to reassemble and perform it again. All sorts of things could go wrong; worst of all, in 1958 a key actor in the ITV play *Underground* suffered a fatal heart attack (offscreen) during the live broadcast, and the other actors had no choice but to improvise the story so as not to draw attention to the missing performer.

Cumberbatch's parents, Wanda Ventham and Tim Carlton, were active in those early days of television drama. They were just starting out as professionals, and so were already well prepared for pitfalls, having an abundance of stage experience behind them. Such a background means one can cope more easily with various disasters, and Cumberbatch was no different, but *Theatre Live!* was to prove a nerve-wracking collision of live television and live theatre. There was no second chance if anything went wrong.

The play was called *The Turning Point*, written by Michael Dobbs, perhaps best known for his political drama, *House of Cards*. 'So much of modern broadcasting is safe and desperately over-controlled,' said Dobbs, 'but live drama, with all its risks, promises something that will keep everyone on the edge of their seats – audience and actors alike.' Cumberbatch would play the spy Guy Burgess in a play about a meeting in 1938 between himself and Winston Churchill. At the time, Churchill was in between stints as

Prime Minister and felt to be in the political wilderness, while Burgess was one of the Cambridge Five spy ring, passing secret information to the Soviets.

Despite the growing number of screen roles coming his way, Cumberbatch remained passionate about theatrical work. 'It's the best place to be,' he said. 'I know it sounds wanky, but as an actor the more I do it, the more I need to do it. I know I ought to say my ambition is to take over the world and be the lead in everything, but I'm really happy with the way it is going.' It was all experience, and in 2010, he would proudly tackle a part and production by a playwright close to his heart.

* * *

In 2010, as the centenary of Terence Rattigan's birth approached, it was time for his work to be reassessed. During the 1940s and 50s, Rattigan was one of the most celebrated of British playwrights. He wrote about a small sliver of society, but with such insight into the human condition that even if you weren't upper middle-class, it was quite possible to relate to the emotional make-up of his characters. He wrote about the class he knew, but he still understood humanity. It was about the stiff upper lip of British society, but it was about that moment when that stiff upper lip would tremble. His many plays were about human vulnerability. Rattigan's private life had to remain private, though; homosexuality would not be decriminalised in Britain until the late 1960s.

Like Benedict Cumberbatch, Terence Rattigan grew up in Kensington, West London, and was educated at Harrow School. He gained a scholarship to the school after his father, a top diplomat, was forced to take early retirement. The two were even in the same house at the school, The Park, and both excelled at cricket. He arrived there in the late 1920s, over 60 years before Cumberbatch. At Harrow, one of Benedict's most acclaimed performances had been in Rattigan's 1948 play, *The Browning Version*, in which he played a classics master called Andrew Crocker-Harris, a man forced into early retirement, who was painfully aware that he had not lived up to expectations. The play was said to have been inspired by a classics master at Harrow. Cumberbatch had been a fan of Rattigan's since school days, and now in his mid-thirties, he would be instrumental in helping to revive interest in a playwright who had once been immensely popular, but whose reputation had been neglected.

Just as Cumberbatch had been discouraged from making acting his life, so Rattigan found his father trying to dissuade his son from being creative, and becoming a playwright. 'You can do it in your spare time, old boy,' he was told. Rattigan gained a place at Oxford to study history in 1930, but ended up leaving to pursue opportunities in London theatre. His early attempts got nowhere, and he soon became short of money, but in 1936, his run of rejections ended unexpectedly. A play he had written entitled *French Without Tears* was given a six-week run at short notice as a replacement for a play that had been forced to close. The cast were unknowns, and no one expected it to do well, yet it ran for over 1,000 performances.

Rattigan's second play was a bittersweet comedy about a group who had been the 'Bright Young Things' generation of the 1920s. Too young to have been called up for World War I, they had partied hard during the Twenties and Thirties, always reaching for the drinks tray, and decried any unwelcome conversation topics as a bore. Their interest in politics was almost non-existent, and now, at the end of the 1930s, they had still not faced up to maturity.

He called the play *After the Dance*. Set in the year 1938, it premiered in June 1939, but the ballyhoo surrounding it would be short-lived. After being staged a mere 60 times, the outbreak of World War II in September of that year forced its closure. Rattigan found it hard to write again once war broke out. Either he suffered writers' block, or a breakdown of sorts. He visited a psychiatrist, who suggested he went off to serve in World War II. He got into the Royal Air Force, where he began writing what would become *Flare Path*. After the war ended in 1945, he would enjoy a string of successes on the London stage, among them *The Winslow Boy* in 1946, *The Deep Blue Sea* (1952) and 1954's *Separate Tables*. He also became a noted writer of film screenplays, including adaptations of *The Way to the Stars*, *Brighton Rock* and later, in the 1960s, *Goodbye, Mr Chips*.

But even in peacetime, Rattigan felt deeply uncomfortable with *After the Dance*. He felt that in a time of austerity, Britain would find it hard to accept such detached and hedonistic figures, and so refused to include it in any published anthologies of his works. It was adapted for BBC Television in 1994, but the 2010 stage revival marked the first time it had been performed in London for over 70 years. Even then, during an economic downturn, the escapist and careless bunch of characters it depicted might have been hard to swallow. But Rattigan never sneered at the characters he created, and always respected them, imbuing them with humanity and sensitivity.

Rattigan's hot streak lasted well into the 1950s, but the rise of the Angry Young Men playwrights such as John Osborne later in the decade, with more obviously confrontational works including 1956's *Look Back in Anger*, made him somewhat unfashionable, even though he himself admired many of these new talents.

After Rattigan died of cancer in 1977, aged 66, his work began to be reappraised. 'He was under a dark cloud,' his biographer Michael Darlow remarked in 2011. 'He wanted his reputation to survive, and he was hugely hurt, though he was much too reserved to say it. He said more than once that he would like to write a play that would be done 50 years later.' Rattigan might have been pleasantly surprised to discover that *After the Dance*, a relatively obscure work, would be at the heart of the reappraisal.

Benedict Cumberbatch was cast as David Scott-Fowler, a historian tinkering with a project he was unlikely to finish. Feckless, hard-drinking and self-destructive but loyal, he was wealthy and made £7,000 a year, which in 1939 was around twelve times the earnings of an average British family. He was self-destructive but loyal. 'He's very charming and charismatic – people fall in love with him,' said Cumberbatch, before adding, 'He thinks in very predatory sexual terms. He is a child, like a lot of alpha men.' But he felt a little uneasy about accepting the role of David. Might it be a little too predictable to take, being another upper-middle class part? Did he feel he was 'too right' for it? Finally, he caved in and agreed. Coincidentally, both he and the director of the production, Thea Sharrock, had seen the Karel Reisz stage revival of *The Deep Blue Sea* starring Penelope Wilton in 1993.

Armed with a reading list, Cumberbatch tried to find out as much as he could about Terence Rattigan. Part of his homework included a return visit to Harrow School for the making of *The Rattigan Enigma*, a BBC4 documentary to mark the centenary of the playwright's birth. He had always felt passionately that Rattigan's plays were far from outdated, and still had a profound validity and relevance in the twenty-first century. For the voice of David, he sought inspiration from the clipped tones of Trevor Howard, the stalwart of classic British films of the 1940s, among them *Brief Encounter*.

David Scott-Fowler was typical of Rattigan characters with deep emotional scars, where unspoken behaviour was just as revealing, if not more so, than the words they would utter. A perfect example occurs at the end of the play. David discovers that his wife has taken her own life, and alone on stage, steps out on to the balcony, leans over the edge, looks down, and pauses for a few seconds, seconds in which it is made clear that he knows what has happened is his own fault.

The revival of *After the Dance* opened at the National Theatre on London's South Bank in June 2010. It was an emotional occasion for Cumberbatch's whole family, especially dad Timothy. 'He started to weep when he was telling me how proud he was. I didn't know what to do. I just held on to him. I said, "You're not crying out of relief that I got through it, are you?" And he said, "No, you stupid boy. I'm crying because you were so wonderful."' The acclaim went far beyond his own family, of course. Critics paid tribute to his performance. 'While Cumberbatch's physical pose is remarkable,' wrote the London *Evening Standard*, 'it's his voice that is the real marvel: dense as treacle, but unerringly precise.'

After the Dance would be the biggest winner at the 2011 Olivier Awards the following March. It picked up four gongs, including Best Costume Design, Best Actress (for Nancy Carroll as David's wife, Joan), and Best Actor in a Supporting Role (Adrian Scarborough). If Cumberbatch was not recognised in an individual capacity, the production as a whole won the Best Revival category. It was an appropriate and deserved winner, in the year that marked the centenary of Rattigan's birth.

Several other Rattigan plays enjoyed revivals that year – *Flare Path* (directed by Trevor Nunn), his final completed work, 1977's *Cause Célèbre* – plus exhibitions and a season of his films at the British Film Institute. The director Terence Davies was working on a screen adaptation of *The Deep Blue Sea*. Nine Rattigan plays from the BBC Television archive – featuring Judi Dench, Sean Connery and Michael

Gambon – were dusted off for a special DVD box set. But it was *After the Dance*, sidelined for decades, that got the ball rolling for the Rattigan centenary year.

It was during the rehearsals for *After the Dance* in early 2010 when Cumberbatch's next film opportunity emerged. He was contacted by Tomas Alfredson, the Swedish director of the vampire flick, *Let the Right One In*. Cumberbatch made it clear that he would not have time to read a script but was happy to meet up. When they did so, he had a bit of a shock. 'The first thing that Tomas said to me was, "What did you think of the script?" I told him I hadn't read it and he just looked at me, mouth agape. I felt awful.' Cumberbatch's charm rescued the situation, and he went away to bone up and sent a written apology to the director. He was duly hired and indeed made such an impression that he would work with Alfredson again in 2012 – this time on a TV commercial for Hiscox insurance.

The film role Alfredson offered him in 2010 was Peter Guillam, the MI6 protégé of George Smiley, in a big-screen version of *Tinker Tailor Soldier Spy*. The creation of the novelist John le Carré, previously it had been a BBC television series at the end of the 1970s, with Alec Guinness in the starring role. Born in 1931 as David John Moore Cornwell, le Carré had worked for MI5 and MI6 in his late twenties, during the Cold War, a period in which secret assassinations had been carried out by British intelligence. He quit MI6 in 1964 to become a full-time author of over 20 novels.

Tinker Tailor Soldier Spy tells how MI6's lugubrious

George Smiley is brought out of retirement to identify the mole working at the heart of the Secret Intelligence Service. Smiley enlists the assistance of Guillam (Cumberbatch) to root out the enemy. Le Carré works have an abundance of figures with moral ambiguity, but Guillam was one character with a clear sense of right and wrong. 'He sees what he is fighting for as the right and good cause,' said Cumberbatch, 'and, in a way, he wants to be part of something heroic, like the Hot War, where the lines were very clearly delineated and undivided.'

Ahead of filming, Cumberbatch undertook some typically unusual research in preparing for the part of Guillam. He flew to Morocco, his first holiday break alone. 'I was in Essaouira. Because my character was a spy originally stationed in North Africa, I walked the streets alone at night, imagining what it was like for him – the oppressive doorways, the dark alleys.'

Alfredson had hired quite a cast: Gary Oldman, John Hurt, Mark Strong, Colin Firth, Toby Jones, Ciaran Hinds, Kathy Burke. Cumberbatch was in awe of his co-stars – 'That's a call sheet I'm going to frame and keep for ever.'

Previewed at the Venice Film Festival in early September 2011, *Tinker Tailor Soldier Spy* opened in Britain two weeks later, and would subsequently win Best British Film at the 2012 BAFTA Awards. John le Carré gave the adaptation the warmest of blessings, calling it 'a film that works superbly, and takes me back into byways of the characters that the series of 32 years ago didn't enter.' To those who believed that the remake was an act of heresy, especially in relation to

Gary Oldman succeeding Alec Guinness's masterly portrayal of George Smiley, le Carré insisted: 'If Alec had witnessed Oldman's performance, he would have been the first to give it a standing ovation.'

He also felt that the tougher remake of his original story was a vital decision. 'The television version was made, in a curious way, as a love story to a fading British Establishment. It was done with great nostalgia. The *Tinker Tailor Soldier Spy* that has now been made is without sentiment, sexier, grittier and crueller. It had to be.' Part of the reason for the blunter tone was simply down to time. The BBC series had been a six-part serial. This was a mere two hours, what Gary Oldman described as 'a real tightening of the screw'.

* * *

Tinker Tailor Soldier Spy was not the only film role Cumberbatch accepted while performing in Rattigan's *After the Dance*. As the play neared the end of its run at the National Theatre, he was all set to take some time off. He told close friends that he was about to take a break, 'unless Spielberg calls. A week later, I had to eat my words. Nobody will believe me, but there we are.'

On the day *After the Dance* closed, Cumberbatch met Steven Spielberg. The actor was late for their meeting, as he was unable to find a parking space for his motorbike, but this did not stop him landing a key role in the director's next picture, *War Horse*. He couldn't quite believe it. 'It's the standard actors' joke – "What are you doing after this?"

"Oh, if Spielberg doesn't call then I'm going to go on holiday". But a week after I'd said that, I got the call to say I had the job. It's one of those moments you never forget – I just fell off my chair.'

To be hired by Spielberg was such a thrill – 'It was the most grown-up moment of my life. I was told I couldn't tell anyone. I was walking around with this huge grin on my face and couldn't speak with excitement.' But he did give the esteemed director some advice about his character. 'I told him that the officers mustn't look like doomed upper-class fools, there has to be something heroic about their charge, and he agreed.' For the mixture of 'doomed and heroic' in his own character of Major Jamie Stewart, Cumberbatch sought inspiration from *The Charge of the Light Brigade*'s Trevor Howard, aka Lord Cardigan. The versatile Howard had also been his muse while preparing to play David Scott-Fowler. 'I could not believe it was the same actor,' Cumberbatch told *The Sunday Times*.

It would appear that the Spielberg opportunity put paid to the chances of *After the Dance* transferring to Broadway. Cumberbatch had been asked to be part of the American run but the film opportunities coming his way made it an impossibility and so he declined and the project was dropped. 'It was a shame there was never any talk of finding anyone else,' said the Olivier-winning Nancy Carroll, who had played opposite him as Joan. 'We all missed it.'

Yet for his part, Cumberbatch felt that going to Broadway he might miss out on cinematic opportunities – 'I've never really made a head-over-heart decision like that before, but there's a bit of momentum and I'd like to keep myself available for films. Because I would like to sit at the big table.' And it seemed a place had been set for him – by none other than Steven Spielberg.

Spielberg had been advised to see the National Theatre production of *War Horse* by his producer collaborator Kathleen Kennedy. It had been based on Michael Morpurgo's 1982 book of the same name for children. He had written it after encountering veterans of the First World War in a pub. It tells the story from the viewpoint of Joey the colt, who is sold to the Army and used on the trenches as a packhorse.

On seeing the ambitious stage production, a dazzled Spielberg knew that it must be remade for cinema. The filmmaker had often used World War II as a backdrop to his projects (*Schindler's List* and *Saving Private Ryan*), but had not yet done the same with World War I. *War Horse* would redress the balance, and for the first time since 1998's *Saving Private Ryan*, a Spielberg film would be shot in the UK.

Spielberg did not want an 'all-star cast' for *War Horse*. He sought talented but relative unknowns, of the calibre of David Thewlis, Emily Watson, Peter Mullan and Benedict Cumberbatch. The central role of Albert Narracott, a farmhand in Devon who searches for his colt, Joey, in France's killing fields and who pretends to be older in order to enlist for service, would be filled by a young actor called Jeremy Irvine. Much fêted for his work with the Royal Shakespeare Company and the National Youth Theatre, Irvine was relatively unknown to most of the general public and the international film world. The film would reunite

Cumberbatch with his old school friend Patrick Kennedy (for the first time since *Atonement*), but the real star of the film, in his opinion, was Joey the colt, 'half a tonne of 35mph joy'.

After Spielberg had made visits to the Imperial War Museum in South London to conduct background research, shooting began on *War Horse* in the late summer of 2010. An adaptation was written by Lee Hall and Richard Curtis, the latter hired after Spielberg happened to watch a repeat of the TV series *Blackadder Goes Forth*, also set during the First World War.

As the moustachioed cavalry officer Major Jamie Stewart, Cumberbatch was playing a part which required him to ride a horse, something he had not done since the age of twelve. 'I saw the storyboards, and nearly shat myself. Some extremely good horsemanship is going to be required, and I'm hoping they won't be relying entirely on me.' At least he wouldn't be participating in the more hazardous sequences, though. For those, he would replaced by a stunt double.

His first day on the *War Horse* set took place in August 2010, just days after *Sherlock* debuted on television. The first scene shot was a battle sequence, of a cavalry charge against German troops. 'It was a hell of a way to start. It was a screaming charge and not breathing for what felt like five minutes, though it was probably two and a half, and nearly fainting.' Relations between the man and his horse mostly went well. 'The trust forms through proximity... giving him his hay bag, washing him down, being close and touching. He's so calm, he starts falling asleep on my sleeve.'

Working on *War Horse* made Cumberbatch understand a

little better the experiences of British troops stationed in Afghanistan. 'The First World War is obviously very different,' he conceded, 'but I did get an awareness of the sheer numbers of men on the ground fighting for a common purpose and for freedom, and although the mechanism of the two wars is different, the spirit is the same.'

It was while on the set of *War Horse* that Cumberbatch was to unwittingly stumble into the frame for a future television role. The veteran playwright Sir Tom Stoppard was returning to the medium for the first time in nearly 30 years, writing an adaptation of a long-forgotten series of novels from the 1920s. Stoppard saw him dressed as Major Stewart, and held back from saying a word – for now. 'I was in First World War clobber,' said Cumberbatch, 'although I was thin and moustachioed and ginger for that part.' What Stoppard had in mind for him was a role from the same time period, but a very different sort of character.

CHAPTER 13

TIETJENS

It was clear to Benedict Cumberbatch that a factor in his success was the perception that he was from a relatively privileged background, and had landed many roles of that type. 'I was brought up in a world of privilege,' he told the *Radio Times* in December 2011. 'Being a posh actor in England, you can't escape class-typing. I realised quite early on that, although I wasn't trying to make a career speciality of it, I was playing slightly asexual, sociopathic intellectuals.' Proud as he was of his achievements, he maintained that typecasting was a hazard and a trap for the long-term career. 'The further away you can get from yourself, the more challenging it is. Not to be in your comfort zone is such great fun.'

It was hard for Cumberbatch to shake off the 'posh' tag. His itinerary through the English public school system meant he had the posh accent to go with it, and he had spent some time trying to tone it down. 'My voice is way too posh,' he once protested. 'We're not even a very posh family.'

Many early roles that brought him to prominence did little to challenge the perception of him as posh, something he was happy to concede, at least to begin with. 'I was a priggish shit in *To the Ends of the Earth*, and I was a priggish shit in *Starter for 10*,' he chuckled disarmingly in 2007, 'and who knows, that could be my lot. I can't deny I lack knowledge of that type.' After all, 'I went to Harrow.'

Later, he would grow increasingly frustrated with the stereotype. He didn't want to be complacent, nor to be typecast. 'That's the thing I've been kicking against,' he said, 'to try and shift class and period and perception all the time.'

If he wasn't being cast as someone posh, it was as someone clever or creative: scientists, mathematicians, artists. With each part, he conducted extensive background research. 'I suppose it's flattering that you look like someone who could think this stuff. But it's a confidence trick. You're actually someone who, before shooting begins, has desperately been mugging up on the books he half-finished during gap year.'

What he truly had no time for was a cultural world that was for the financially comfortable – 'I don't want it to be only the sons and daughters of Tory MPs who get to see my plays. I'm interested in art for all.' He was opposed to the coalition government's proposed cuts on arts funding. 'People are going to be shocked at how it will affect the volume of output and choice that they're used to at the moment. The Arts provide a massive return of revenue, employment and hold national prestige.'

Given his public school background, it was only a matter of time before Cumberbatch would be drawn into the evergreen debate about the British class system. As cuts to the Arts sector were proposed, could it be that acting might only be a career option for those with moneyed backgrounds? It was striking that in the twenty-first century, many of the most prominent and in-demand British actors had been educated via the public school system. The Old Etonian Eddie Redmayne had been a contemporary of Prince William. Dominic West, another Eton boy, had been at school with Prime Minister David Cameron. Then there was Tom Hiddleston, Damian Lewis (both Eton), and so the list went on.

Cumberbatch also may have had a slight advantage over others, given that both his parents had been successful actors for many years. But what of opportunities for actors who had neither wealth, nor privileged education, nor family connections behind them? It is hard for many actors to make a living wage. Equity, the performers' union, estimates that at any one time, some two-thirds of actors are unemployed. How can those with little or no money survive in such a precarious profession?

Rob James-Collier, Thomas the footman in *Downton Abbey*, would reignite the ongoing debate about class in the acting profession. The Stockport-born actor told the *Radio Times* in March 2012 that he had no 'posh' leanings and said that getting a professional foothold in acting was hard without money behind you. 'You have to work for a year with no money. How on earth are you going to finance that?'

It was not unlike the internships of other professions that, if unpaid, would be only available to those from wealthy families. Prior to landing a part in *Coronation Street*, James-Collier had supported himself in the hunt for acting jobs by working in factories and as a labourer. 'Because you've done the horrible jobs it gives you an even grittier determination to succeed. If I had a comfort blanket, I wouldn't have been as passionate and driven. When you get there, you really do appreciate it because you know where you've been.'

Louise Brealey, who as pathologist Molly Hooper appeared alongside Cumberbatch in *Sherlock*, still juggled acting with journalism and TV producing. In arts and media, she argued, those from affluent backgrounds were at an advantage. 'It's getting more difficult all the time for kids from poorer backgrounds to break in, because you're expected to work for nothing in endless internships. Without someone bankrolling you, that's impossible. The upshot is that working-class voices will be heard even less frequently than they are already.'

It did seem as if, bar the soaps such as *Emmerdale*, *Coronation Street* and *EastEnders*, popular blue-collar dramas had faded from most peak-time TV. The *Radio Times*' Gareth McLean wondered if there could ever be modern-day reflections of working-class Britain like *Auf Wiedersehen, Pet*, *Clocking Off* or *Boys from the Blackstuff*. 'Where are those shows now?' McLean wrote. 'The only time you see working-class life on TV is when they go back to people's houses on *The X Factor* or *Britain's Got Talent*.'

But Cumberbatch dismissed claims that there was any kind

of 'private school elite' in acting. He described himself as 'definitely middle-class'. 'People have tried to pull together a pattern,' he told the *Mail on Sunday* in May 2013, 'because Tom Hiddleston, Eddie Redmayne, Damian Lewis and I were all privately educated. But James McAvoy, Michael Fassbender and Tom Hardy weren't, and they're equally talented. It's just lazy.'

It's considered bad form to complain if you're both famous and wealthy, and if you weren't poor to start with, that's even worse. Cumberbatch felt he couldn't win, when it came to discussing his origins: 'You either come across as being arrogant and ungrateful if you complain about it, or being snooty and overprivileged if you bathe in it.'

On the face of it, a five-part television drama series called *Parade's End* did little to alter the perception of Cumberbatch as one of the screen's top portrayers of the upper-middle class and above. It was set in Edwardian England around the time of the outbreak of the First World War, and he played a government statistician called Christopher Tietjens, with Rebecca Hall co-starring as his socialite wife Sylvia. As Sylvia begins an extra-marital affair, he falls for a free-spirited suffragette called Valentine Wannop, played by the Australian Adelaide Clemens. Based on material from a set of four novels written by Ford Madox Ford in the 1920s, it was adapted by Sir Tom Stoppard, his first contribution to television drama in nearly 30 years.

Cumberbatch felt a special kind of connection towards Christopher Tietjens, a physically cumbersome and emotionally undemonstrative Yorkshireman whose quiet loyalty, intelligence and patriotism he found truly heroic and inspirational. 'He's not just another toff in a period drama,' he said. 'I have such a huge affection for Christopher – more so than almost any other character I've played. I sympathise with his care, his sense of duty and virtue, his intelligence in the face of hypocritical, self-serving mediocrity and his love for his country. That is what leads me to love this fat, baggy bolster of a blockhead.'

He later said that he had based his visual interpretation of the character (as a 'very intelligent but rather oafish buffoon') on Boris Johnson, the mayor of London, who had a habit of making gaffes during speeches, a trait that endeared him to some, but not to others. To fill out for the part, he needed to put on a fair bit of weight. 'There was a lot of rubbish food and drinking alcohol without worrying about it... lots of beer, wine, chips, the most amazing proper steaks and goulashes.'

But he was advised not to over-egg the Borisisms. 'They stopped me going the whole hog because they wanted a pin-up. He's got to be seen as sexually attractive, or why would someone as beautiful as Valentine fall for him?' The onscreen chemistry between her and Christopher would indeed be intense. 'He is so inspiring and overwhelming in the best possible way,' Adelaide Clemens gushed of her co-star. 'We were feeding each other's curiosity. He is so in control of his craft.'

Though he shared the icy-cold wit of Cumberbatch's Sherlock Holmes, Tietjens was a much more considered and stately thinker, someone who doesn't reach rapid conclusions, but who seems to already possess inbuilt wisdom. Although the man originated in a quartet of novels relatively few had read, the obscurity of the character was advantageous for Cumberbatch. He saw the role as a blank canvas, and an opportunity to make the part his own. He had also vowed to avoid upper-class British characters for a time, feeling that he was in danger of being typecast, and being too associated with such figures. But Tietjens was too much of a temptation to turn down. He accepted the challenge.

Parade's End had been adapted for television once before – as one of the earliest dramas made for the BBC's second TV channel, BBC2. It aired in December 1964, with Ronald Hines as Tietjens, and a young Judi Dench as Valentine. BBC Radio 3 had mounted a production in 2003, with Tom Goodman Hill as Tietjens. The plans for the new version were officially announced in September 2011, around a year before broadcast. Comparisons were immediately drawn between it and the ITV series *Downton Abbey* – which had launched in 2010, and had become one of the network's biggest drama hits in years. On the face of it, the two series did indeed share certain similarities. Both were set around the same time – namely the period before and during the First World War – and both dealt with social tensions surrounding the English aristocracy.

Parade's End's producers insisted any similarities were superficial and coincidental, especially as the concept for the series had been hatched some time before *Downton Abbey* had reached the screen.

'I can honestly say,' said executive producer Damien Timmer, 'that we started off doing this before any of us had ever heard about *Downton Abbey*.' 'Just because things are set in a similar period,' argued Ben Stephenson, drama head at the BBC, where a TV version of Sebastian Faulks' WWI novel *Birdsong* was also in the pipeline, 'doesn't mean that they are the same.'

Sir Tom Stoppard had finished writing his adaptation of *Parade's End* in 2009, a year before *Downton Abbey* launched. Stoppard was in no doubt as to why the Edwardian period was so fascinating for millions of viewers a century later. 'It was the last period of social history among the top half of the English class system. In the case of 1914 [the outbreak of World War I], there is a sense of an important page being turned, never to be turned back again.' *Parade's End* contained many themes like post-war trauma, shell-shock and remembrance of lives lost that would remain relevant in the twenty-first century.

Ford Madox Ford, the author of the original novels, had himself served in World War I. Born in 1873 in Surrey as Ford Hermann Hueffer, he had a German father, but changed his name just after World War I as he felt it sounded too German. The four novels he wrote between 1924 and 1928 and covering the period 1912 to the early 1920s, and later favourites of Anthony Burgess and Graham Greene, did not lend themselves easily to visual adaptation. They were modernist, bordering on experimental, and many of the themes and treatments would be hard to transfer directly. 'You have the problem that there's a lot of interesting stuff going on in the novel,' Tom Stoppard added, 'without necessarily having the dramatic momentum or even the physical concrete dimension to it.' Stoppard confessed to being a little out of date on the matter of writing for television. He hadn't written anything for the medium since the BBC's *Squaring the Circle* in 1984 – 'I write talkies. I wrote *Parade's End* in the same spirit as I write stage plays.'

The main reason for the delay in bringing *Parade's End* to life as a television series was mostly a financial one. With a star-studded cast including Anne-Marie Duff, Miranda Richardson and Rupert Everett, as well as old friends and colleagues of Cumberbatch's such as Roger Allam, Rebecca Hall and Patrick Kennedy, the sheer cost of the lavish project required international backing. There were over 100 speaking parts, and nearly 150 different locations (from Yorkshire to Belgium), a vast number for a five-part television series. Eventually, HBO, the American cable network, and home to *The Sopranos*, *Six Feet Under*, *The Wire* and *Curb Your Enthusiasm*, agreed to co-fund with the BBC. The total bill for the series was around £12 million, the most expensive drama series yet made for BBC2.

Cumberbatch was formally offered the part of Tietjens in early 2011, and filming began in the late summer of that year. One location shoot took place in Belgium, at Ypres, site of some of the most intense battles of the First World War. 'When I got into the trench, with one of those tin hats on,' Cumberbatch recalled, 'I realised you're standing basically in a grave. Everything above you is exploding and anything over the edge is death. With the tin trench helmet on, you hardly see any sky. The practicality of just moving around was hard enough and you're supposed to be a fighting machine. Going up a ladder knowing you are walking into gunfire goes against every instinct of what it is to be a human being.'

'You never quite get used to imagining how it must have been for men my age, 100 years ago,' he added. 'It's a duty as an actor to respect their memory in a way, and you do feel an almost patriotic pressure to get it true and right.'

He narrowly escaped injury during the Belgium shoot. During the making of a dream sequence which involved an explosion, it went off in his face – 'It was terrifying. I was engulfed in flames.' Fortunately, he suffered no damage apart from his hair, eyebrows and eyelashes being singed, and none of this damage would be permanent.

From a twenty-first century perspective, of course, the events of World War I still had resonance for many, many people. 'We're living through a time where we are fighting wars with equally tragic realities for our soldiers and their families,' said Cumberbatch. 'We are living in times of political hypocrisy, and there aren't that many really good people. And Christopher is just that – a good man.'

The relevance of *Parade's End* in 2012 didn't stop at war either. 'People are asking questions about how we behave as a society,' commented director Susanna White, 'the environment, money, politicians and the NHS, and that's all in *Parade's End*. It's asking big questions about society and how we behave. Even the love triangle asks what happens if you marry the wrong person. I think there is a lot which will still chime with people.'

Parade's End would be broadcast on BBC2 in late August and September 2012. In the week before broadcast, Benedict Cumberbatch would become headline news because of a handful of remarks he made in interviews to promote the show. Invited to comment on the notion that his new series could be classed as 'a thinking person's *Downton Abbey*', he dismissed any comparisons as 'crude' and 'a danger', but later (while naming no names) promised that the five-parter would not be 'some crappy, easily digestible milk-chocolate on a Sunday evening... It's going to be hard work, but it will pay dividends if you stick with it.'

So was *that* a veiled criticism of *Downton Abbey*, already a hit on Sunday nights? One couldn't be sure, although Cumberbatch then celebrated his new series as 'funny, pointed, but also three-dimensional. We're not serving purposes to make some clichéd comment about "Oh, isn't it awful the way there's this upstairs-downstairs divide." It's a little bit more sophisticated.'

It was a slow news week. Parliament was in recess for the summer. The London 2012 Olympics had just finished, and the Paralympics were yet to take place. And Cumberbatch was now a star in a way he hadn't been even two years before, so anything he said would be instantly quotable. The press picked up his remarks and ran with them, engaging in much comment and debate. Was this deliberate provocation, to have a dig at the competition, or simply to send up the question put to him?

Yet if he did mean *Downton Abbey* on that occasion, he wasn't alone in making the comparison. 'I think we've got to signal to people that they're not going to turn on and get something cosy like *Downton Abbey*,' said Susanna White. 'It's television that makes demands on you – if you go away to make a cup of tea, you'll be lost.'

It may have required concentration, but plenty of viewers were prepared to sit tight and pay close attention. *Parade's End* premiered on Friday nights, traditionally an evening for entertainment rather than drama, but over 3 million viewers saw the first episode, immediately making it BBC2's highest rated drama series since *Rome* (another HBO co-production) in 2005. Perhaps even more surprisingly, the collection of the original books became a bestseller, zooming into the Amazon top 10 chart. And the presence of Benedict Cumberbatch was undoubtedly a key factor in the success of the series, with his brooding silences wowing the critics. 'There's something of the Alan Rickman about him,' said the *Guardian*. 'One drowsy droop of an eyelid, one slip of the planes of his face, can convey either wry honest amusement or withering contempt.'

It was generally agreed that any comparison between *Parade's End* and *Downton Abbey* held little water, and the fuss died down, only to flare up again – more directly this time – only a few weeks later. In an interview with *Reader's Digest* magazine, Cumberbatch believed that the second series of *Downton Abbey* was inferior to the first, and had 'traded a lot on the sentiment'. He was quoted as branding it as 'fucking atrocious'.

Inevitably, the showbiz desks of newspapers – both tabloid and broadsheet – rang round to find if anyone connected with *Downton Abbey* would give a right of reply. Series creator Julian Fellowes stepped into the fray, fully aware of what the phrase 'good copy' meant: 'I have known Ben since he was a little boy and I couldn't be fonder of him. I am quite sure what he said has been taken out of context and does not at all reflect his real feelings. [It's] all part of a surge of interest in television drama, which can only be good news for all of us.'

Cumberbatch confirmed what he had said had been a private joke. 'Anyone who knows me, including my friends Julian Fellowes and Hugh Bonneville, just laughed when they read it.' He went on to say that in his opinion the second run of *Downton Abbey* lacked the sharpness of the first series, 'but what Julian does is great – it's good Sunday night telly.' In a subsequent interview, he would groan about the perceived slagging. 'I've got family and friends in it. My dad was in the Christmas special, for God's sake.'

Even beyond this, other Cumberbatch soundbites seeped into the mass media. At around the same time, he had told the *Radio Times* that he was tired of being 'castigated as a moaning, rich, public school bastard', followed by: 'It's all so predictable, so domestic, so dumb. It makes me think I want to go to America. I wasn't born into land or titles, or new money, or an oil rig.' The A-word of 'America' sounded an alarm bell of the notion that he'd decamp to the States at any moment as he would get away from posh roles there.

It was an over-reaction, delivered with his tongue lodged firmly in his cheek. Besides, he had been asked about America before, back in 2007. He had been seduced by the glamour of it: 'It was the red carpet treatment all the way – limousines, first-class flight – it was dreamy.' But he didn't want to relocate, and was irritable about the assumption from the press that he would move to Hollywood at the first possible opportunity. 'Which is kind of tiresome, but people still think it sells papers.'

Radio Times had become a publication that would customarily hit the headlines of a Tuesday morning for its star interview. It would crank up the controversy level of the interviewee, saying something as a joke and to garner attention would send it to the press. So it was with the Cumberbatch interview. The epitome of a storm in a teacup, but in a quiet week for news in the middle of summer, it was a jumping-off point for a subject that never seems to be off the agenda in the UK: the class system.

Reaction in the press was swift, although there was less outrage than wry amusement. Writing in the *Independent* about his protestations, Viv Groskop (a Cumberbatch fan) wrote that it was faintly ludicrous simply because 'Benedict Timothy Carlton Cumberbatch has a name of exceptionally ridiculous proportions. One so silly no novelist would dare to propose it. The Americans so don't deserve that name!' Others pointed out that Harrow's annual fees (£30,000 in 2012) were only just below the average annual salary for a British male, and that over half the British medallists at the Olympics had been in private education.

Generally cordial, courteous and entertaining in interviews, Benedict Cumberbatch could feel anger about media privacy. Happy to promote and discuss his work, he found the prying into people's personal lives to be unnecessary and unpleasant. Speaking to National Public Radio in the USA in 2012, he talked of his unease towards the British press: 'We're living in an era where there's an awful lot of soul-searching, with the Leveson Inquiry, and [Rupert] Murdoch being held out to task, and just being exposed for the fraudulent, pathetic, abhorrent behaviour that is rife in all our media.' Cumberbatch's difficult experiences with the press about his own life were relatively minor, but even so, for an A-lister to be this outspoken about the tabloids was unusual. It underlined his ambivalence towards national and international fame.

CHAPTER 14

VICTOR AND
THE CREATURES

In late 2010, Benedict Cumberbatch was limbering up for what would be his most high-profile stage role yet. In November, he joined forces with fellow acting titans like Sir Ben Kingsley, Samuel West, Romola Garai, Tom Hiddleston and Gemma Arterton for a special one-off charity show at South London's Old Vic theatre. *The Children's Monologues* was a dozen monologues, compiled by a team of playwrights from the testimonies of 250 children in South Africa. The original raw material had been gathered by the charity Dramatic Need, who had asked the children to each select a specific day in their life which had brought them either joy or sadness. The replies they received were both tragic and disturbing, including accounts of illness, violence and sexual abuse.

The director Danny Boyle, who organised the Old Vic

performance, described many of the stories as being like a punch in the stomach. 'They have that directness that you find with children anywhere. They can't compartmentalise or filter traumatic stuff so they just say it.' Cumberbatch was proud to be associated with the evening. 'One of the privileges of doing something as high profile as *Sherlock* is the effect that you can have, that you can help raise awareness or even money for a good cause. It's an extraordinary position to be in.'

The special evening took place just as he and Boyle were preparing the ground at the nearby National Theatre for an ambitious stage project in early 2011. Cumberbatch was to co-star in a radical re-interpretation of Mary Shelley's tale, *Frankenstein*. In an unusual twist, he and fellow lead actor Jonny Lee Miller would play two parts – the scientist Victor Frankenstein and the Creature he created – swapping roles for each performance. 'Every other night they reinhabit each other,' said Danny Boyle. 'They are mirrors of each other. And it'll make the play interesting for the actors to do – they won't be able to settle and they'll be constantly sparring.'

Danny Boyle's background, before working in television and cinema, was in theatre. He had been a director at London's Royal Court for five years (1982–87). Later, he was the director of *Shallow Grave*, *Trainspotting*, *28 Days Later*, *Slumdog Millionaire* and *127 Hours*. But he hadn't directed any theatre in 15 years. During this period, he was also preparing for the opening ceremony of the London 2012 Olympics and in fact described *Frankenstein* as a 'little mini-sabbatical', a distraction from the Olympic job – a task that took two full years of preparation.

To have two lead actors in a play swap roles on a nightly basis was relatively unusual, but not completely unprecedented. Way back in 1935, John Gielgud and Laurence Olivier had faced each other in Gielgud's production of *Romeo and Juliet*, switching back and forth between Romeo and his foil, Mercutio. Nearly 40 years later, in 1973, Ian Richardson and Richard Pasco tried the same thing with Richard II and Bolingbroke. As did Mark Rylance and Michael Rudko in a 1994 London production of Sam Shepard's *True West*, a play examining the stormy relationship between two brothers.

Nick Dear was responsible for adapting *Frankenstein* for 2011. When one of his drafts suggested opening the play from the Creature's perspective, Danny Boyle realised it, 'gave the Creature his voice back'. This prompted him into switching the lead roles around. 'Starting from the Creature's point of view was the key to unlocking the adaptation,' he went on. 'Once you don't start with Victor Frankenstein, you need to balance the Creature with his obsession with his creator. So we rebalanced our approach by double casting the actors.'

The double casting would leave no room for ego, and from day one of rehearsals, relations between the two were harmonious. 'The dialogue between us is selfless and co-operative,' said Cumberbatch. 'If there's something really good that he does, I will ask if I can incorporate it.' 'We're not precious,' added Jonny Lee Miller. 'We're more of a team. We find it constructive to talk to each other about what looks good, what doesn't.'

The dynamic between the two actors was highly rewarding. They could share their concerns, and feel like a team. 'No one's precious about it,' said Jonny Lee Miller. 'We're watching each other a lot, and taking things from each other.' There were a few drawbacks, though: a lack of time being one. 'It's double the workload,' explained Cumberbatch, 'but not double the rehearsal time.' Another difficulty concerned learning the lines. This was complicated. One actor could start learning one part, only to find himself thrown by the other performer's cues. 'Having both characters on the same page is a distraction,' admitted Cumberbatch. But Danny Boyle observed that this seemed appropriate: the two lead characters should become 'the same in a way... two strands of the same part... They're the creator and son, and the obligation in that relationship is very close.' If there was a matinee performance as well as an evening one, the leads would remain in the same part for that particular day, but even so it demanded stamina and concentration. Plus, for whoever was playing the Creature, becoming black and blue was part of the job. 'You come off stage with a cut on your lip, your wrists are bruised and you've just shed 5lb,' summed up Cumberbatch. Still, as ordeals go, it was a rewarding one.

Getting the right actors, Boyle acknowledged, had been vital. Having cast Cumberbatch, he had worked with Jonny Lee Miller on *Trainspotting* 15 years earlier, but had had no contact since. For Boyle to involve an actor he knew well

(Miller, by now a regular on American TV's *Dexter*) and another he did not (Cumberbatch) was conscious. The actors needed to be bold and commanding, to fill the spacious stage. But Boyle soon knew he had the right men for the job: 'The job of director is mostly fuelling actors. They are insatiable. And Benedict and Jonny are like a Venn diagram – they cross over constantly.'

Like the revamp of *Sherlock*, Boyle and Dear's twenty-first century take on *Frankenstein* was both thoroughly modern and yet close in spirit to the source material. Mary Shelley's original text was written in 1816, during a period when she had two poets in her life: her husband Shelley, and Byron. 'She sees Byron as the noble savage in the Creature,' explained Cumberbatch, 'whereas she sees Shelley as this obsessive social misfit. So her novel makes sense of the psychodrama she found herself in.'

Yet, the grotesque figure of the Creature (which required 90 minutes in make-up before the curtain could go up) would not be based on its most famous screen incarnation inhabited by Boris Karloff in James Whale's 1931 movie. This time there was to be no bolt in the neck, and the Creature would even gradually acquire language skills, and be able to talk back to his creator. Others to play the Creature had included Robert De Niro and Christopher Lee, but both Dear and Boyle wanted to bypass the story's horror film connections and instead concentrate on the ideas explored in Shelley's original novel, which was in its day extremely futuristic in its vision. 'Shelley is looking forward to the technological revolution,' explained Nick

Dear. '200 years on from when she wrote it, our technology is such that we are achieving now what she had nightmares about.'

For the audience, the play – two hours long with no interval – presented a tricky conundrum, of who to root for, and empathise with: the creator or the Creature. Victor Frankenstein has no real interest in procreating with his fiancée Elizabeth. As for the Creature devised by Victor, he longs to be helpful and decent (a humane attitude largely missing from his inventor's character), but he is shunned by society, and as a result fights back in a destructive and aggressive fashion.

Under-15s were discouraged, if not actually banned, from attending *Frankenstein*, partly because of the nudity (the Creature was naked and caked in blood and gore for most of the first half-hour), but also because of a rape scene. Many youngsters sneaked in regardless, and *Guardian* writer Catherine Bennett took her 13-year-old daughter to see it. She was baffled by the age restrictions. 'It is hard to see why the theatre decided to exclude so many potential converts,' she wrote, 'unless it was a fear of how younger teens might react [when] the piteous monster comes to life and learns to wriggle, then stagger, completely naked until his maker chucks him a large cloak.'

'You can explore all these ideas – prejudice, not fitting in, love, revenge, original sin, nurture and nature – when you have a man creating a life,' commented Jonny Lee Miller. '[The Creature] has a fully grown brain because it comes from an adult male corpse. But he's a baby, yet he learns very quickly. So the story is also about the growing and education of a man, which goes very wrong.'

This was a whistle-stop tour of human evolution, and when the play opened in February 2011, it immediately attracted feverishly enthusiastic notices. 'Manages to be both graphic and subtle,' said the *Independent*. 'The most viscerally exciting and visually stunning show in town,' ventured the *Telegraph*. And the *Guardian* paid tribute to 'an astonishing performance' by Cumberbatch. But for the most part, critics refused to place one actor's performance over the other. Both were praised equally.

Part of the reason why it was so hard to get tickets was that some of the audience booked for multiple shows. Cumberbatch would see the same faces in the front row of the Olivier for several nights in a row. 'Two young women from China saw every performance,' he said. 'I asked them, "How do you afford the time and the money?" And they just said, "Oh, it doesn't matter. We love you." I used to be in the audience, I used to obsess about things, but I don't understand this.'

For those unable to get tickets (so, most people), there would be an alternative. Two special live broadcasts of the play (on 17 March) were relayed via more than 400 cinemas or arenas around the world, including just over 100 in Britain. Obviously the cinema showing of the performance could never hope to match the live experience but with the play selling out so quickly, how else would people be able to see it? In addition, having the performance relayed via cinema, it could still be a shared experience, just like theatre.

Cumberbatch and Miller's sterling work on *Frankenstein* would be recognised when the nominations were announced for the 2011 London *Evening Standard* Theatre Awards. They were in contention for Best Actor, alongside Dominic West, James Corden, Jude Law, Ralph Fiennes and Kevin Spacey. But how would the judging panel be able to favour one over the other if they were choosing a Frankenstein actor? It just didn't seem right to separate them, and the panel knew it. So, on 20 November, they were heralded as joint winners of the category, a first in the 57-year history of the Awards. At the 2012 Olivier Theatre Awards, the two would again share a Best Actor gong.

* * *

In the wake of *Sherlock* becoming an international television hit, further Sherlock Holmes adaptations had been emerging. A second Guy Ritchie film with Robert Downey Jr. and Jude Law was released in 2011, the same year that Arthur Conan Doyle's estate agreed that a new Holmes story could be published. Anthony Horowitz was chosen to write it, and *The House of Silk* duly became the first Sherlock story since Conan Doyle's 13-part *Return of Sherlock Holmes*, finished in 1905. But in 2012, American television would adapt the Holmes/Watson relationship for a new primetime series, *Elementary*, set in contemporary New York City. For Sherlock Holmes himself, they were to select a potentially controversial lead.

It transpired that the CBS network in the US had initially

wanted to remake the BBC's *Sherlock* series. 'We said "No",' said Sue Vertue at Hartswood Films. 'We could have gone for financial gain but we wanted to keep creative control.' Even though the characters of Sherlock Holmes and John Watson had been re-imagined hundreds of times in films, plays, and TV and radio programmes, the stylised look of Hartswood's *Sherlock* was highly distinctive, and the executives there would be watching *Elementary* very closely indeed to make sure it didn't ape their series too faithfully. 'It will be annoying if they use elements that can be traced to our show rather than the original stories,' said Vertue. Her husband, *Sherlock* co-creator Steven Moffat, wasn't best pleased either: 'They've just decided to go off and do one of their own, having been turned down by us to do an adaptation of our version. What if it's awful? If there's this unrelated rogue version of *Sherlock* going around and it's bad, it can be bad for us. It degrades the brand.'

So it was ironic that the lead actor hired for *Elementary* had a connection to the British Sherlock. CBS's choice was Jonny Lee Miller, Benedict Cumberbatch's co-star in *Frankenstein*. Miller's Holmes would be a drug addict who was just out of a rehabilitation centre in Manhattan. The casting choice for Watson, though, was a bigger departure: Lucy Liu, who would play a former surgeon called Dr Joan Watson. Liu welcomed the opportunity not just to make Watson female but an Asian-American. 'Watson's ethnicity is a very big deal,' she said. 'I didn't grow up seeing people like myself in films. Although it's quite different now, it's still a slow process.'

Miller had adored Cumberbatch's portrayal of Holmes. After each showing of *Sherlock* aired, the two had chatted warmly about it. 'I would call him up like a groupie,' recalled Miller, 'and we had a discussion about this project as well. I wanted to reassure him about how different this was: it's another country and a whole lot of vibe.' In light of this, an unwelcome Cumberbatch quote in the British free-sheet *ShortList* was potentially awkward. He was quoted as saying he had told Miller that he would have preferred him to turn down the *Elementary* job, 'but you've got a kid to feed, a nice house in L.A. and a wife to keep in good clothes. When they waft a pay cheque at you, what are you going to do?'

A displeased Cumberbatch soon hit back, insisting he had been misquoted. 'I never said that Jonny took the job for the paycheck, nor did I ask him not to do it. What I said is I would have preferred not to be in the situation where we will again be compared because we are friends. I know for a fact his motivations were to do with the quality of the script and the challenges of this exceptional role.' He looked forward to Miller's Sherlock Holmes and wished him the very best of luck with it.

In any case, insisted Miller, *Elementary* was for a different audience: 'We've made our Sherlock Holmes rougher around the edges. It examines Holmes's flaws and how damaged he is. You see him struggle.' With CBS being a mainstream commercial network in America, it might have a bigger audience too, given that PBS, which broadcast *Sherlock*, was unavailable to some of the US. 'The BBC show is very popular,' added Miller, 'but it hasn't been seen by most of America.'

Elementary premiered on the CBS network in September 2012, and began showings on Sky in the UK the following month. Critics in the States approved, with *The New York Times* saying that Miller's Holmes was a 'likeable hangdog... showing the glint of mania, without the pyrotechnics that Cumberbatch brings to his performance in *Sherlock*'.

Where Cumberbatch's *Sherlock* had been about fast-moving plot, Miller's *Elementary* was more about Holmes's brooding and addictive psyche, a complexity of character in keeping with the groundbreaking US cable TV hits like *The Sopranos*, *Breaking Bad* and *Boardwalk Empire*. 'Our Sherlock has emerged with a tiny kernel of self-doubt where one previously never existed,' said Rob Doherty, series creator of *Elementary*, and formerly a writer/producer on *Medium*. 'It's not something we are going to speak to very often, but I think it's one of the things that drives him.'

Ultimately, Cumberbatch approved of Miller's take on Holmes. 'He sent me some messages,' said Miller, 'when he'd first seen the show. He's been very supportive the whole way.' Although they were friends, after all, with inbuilt loyalty. 'I'm pretty sure he wouldn't have sent me a text message saying, "You suck!"'

The co-existence of *Elementary* and *Sherlock* meant that the possibility of restaging *Frankenstein* on Broadway with its two National Theatre leads would not take place. There was also a problem finding a suitable venue. 'I don't think there's any theatre that's right for it,' bemoaned Cumberbatch. 'The Olivier is an old-fashioned acting theatre with this incredible machinery and a drama in the middle of it. There aren't many places like it.' Another stumbling block to transferring *Frankenstein* to the States seemed to be Cumberbatch's schedule. Jonny Lee Miller's career had blasted into international orbit some time before, and now it was Benedict's turn.

CHAPTER 15

CUMBERBATCH INTERNATIONAL

Benedict Cumberbatch had always been the sort of actor who would take 'big parts in small films, and small parts in big films'. Even now, on the brink of international stardom, that maxim would remain. He had not abandoned independent cinema. *Wreckers*, a British drama with a tiny budget, which opened in the UK just before Christmas 2011, was a case in point. He co-starred with Claire Foy as a recently-married couple, who move back to the small Suffolk village where he had been raised, but whose idyllic life is disturbed by the arrival of his troubled sibling, Nick (Shaun Evans). Nick, like Dr John Watson, had been in service in Afghanistan, and back on Civvy Street was in a tormented state, but once under pressure, David would show Dawn (Foy) a side of him that was testier and tenser.

After *Wreckers*, though, much of Cumberbatch's film

shoots would be conducted abroad. Though several of his film appearances had been seen in the USA, he remained cautious about ever moving there and attempting a full-time Hollywood career. 'You've really got to commit to make it there,' he had said in 2007. 'I'm in a lucky position now that I can get enough good work to have a career here.' Five years on, in 2012, he would spend much of the year filming overseas.

The move into big-time cinematic roles had been a dream of his for some time, although the 'star' system of the movie world was a far cry from the ensemble nature of theatre. Compared to the community spirit of theatre, in which the cast, director and crew worked as a whole, cinema is more of a star-led medium, in which individual actors are encouraged to compete for being the star on which a picture depends. 'It's all about a graph. You are commodified in a way that doesn't really happen in theatre,' he had told Mark Lawson of the *Guardian* in 2008. 'Does this person tick the gay box, the married-couples box, the under-25 box and so on?' It could be another kind of typecasting, but as ever, Cumberbatch would keep moving, refusing to be trapped as one character.

He had been especially eager to participate in an action flick. 'I want to have my Daniel Craig moment! I want to run around a desert, shooting guns at aliens and looking like I barely have to take a breath. I'd love to do all that shit!' *Star Trek Into Darkness* marked his entry into action-packed blockbusters, thanks to an impromptu and unorthodox audition piece he sent to the director J.J. Abrams.

He had been wary and even critical of Hollywood big-budget action films, what he called 'cookie cutters, two-dimensional villains and the English transition of an actor being from a different culture. We'd better give him the bad guy role and a cape, and just make him be really horrible'. But when Benicio Del Toro, rumoured to be playing the villainous Khan, dropped out of the project around Christmas 2011, Cumberbatch was made aware that Abrams was interested in casting him: 'He fleshed out the whole world of the rest of the script, and there's a purpose and intention to his otherwise violent and pretty distressing actions that make it really intriguing.'

With all the casting directors in the UK on holiday over the Christmas period, he decided to send his audition via his smart phone. His best friend Adam Ackland offered his kitchen as an audition location. 'I squatted under the one good overhead light, with Adam's wife Alice balanced on two chairs holding my iPhone, and Adam feeding the lines to me off-camera,' he told journalist Siobhan Synnot. 'We eventually shot three takes of each scene. Then it took me a day to work out how to compress the file and email it to J.J.'s iPad.'

Abrams was also away over the festive season, so once the file was sent, all he could do was to wait. He had found a way of relaxing himself in auditions of all kinds: 'I try to imagine I'm the only person they're seeing that day, because it could be overwhelming to try to fulfil everyone's expectations rather than the people nearest to you in the creative process – be it your director, fellow actors, writers.'

After New Year, Abrams contacted Cumberbatch by email with a cryptic invitation: 'You want to come and play?' The actor was confused. 'I said, "What does this mean? Are you in town, you want to go for a drink? I'm English, you've got to be really straight with me on this. Have I got the part?"'

He had been successful, but euphoria turned to self-doubt. 'It's very flattering to be offered work without an audition, but it also brings pressure because you haven't won it. You haven't proved your ability to do that role.' His sure-footedness briefly deserted him when he began work on this, his first Hollywood blockbuster. It felt quite intimidating for him to reach the studio, and meet a room of five producers and many crew members. 'I was the Brit abroad,' he told the *Daily Mirror*. 'I was terrified. I was jet-lagged and must have looked as white as a sheet, with dark rings around my eyes.' The director, J.J. Abrams, was also a bit startled, though. 'Everyone stood a little bit taller when he was around.'

Cumberbatch had been cast as the intergalactic baddie Commander John Harrison (aka Khan), a ruthless and vengeful rogue officer, who had plotted a bomb attack in London, then a raid on Starfleet's Californian nerve-centre, before beaming up on Kronos, the Klingons' planet. The USS *Enterprise* was called back to Earth from an expedition in deep space to find an 'unstoppable terror' had destroyed the fleet. Harrison was not a cardboard villain, but a complex individual, exactly the sort of bad guy role that Cumberbatch always celebrated. 'The action he takes has intent and reason,' he explained. 'He is not a clearly good or evil character. There's a lot of reasoning and motivation behind what he does. He has a moral core, he just has a method that's pretty brutal in our world.'

Cumberbatch soon found his feet on the *Star Trek* shoot, finding it a supportive company, but because he had been cast relatively late, his appearance needed urgent attention. For one thing, the hair department on *Into Darkness* had some work to do. Khan needed to have dark hair, the opposite of Captain James T. Kirk's blond. 'The day he flew in, he walks in with super-short blond hair,' said the film's hair department head, Mary L. Mastro. 'We had two weeks to darken and lengthen his hair.'

Similarly, Cumberbatch's six-foot frame needed filling out as Harrison was made of bulkier stuff. Every day for two weeks, in preparation, he trained for two hours and ate 4,000 calories: chicken, potatoes, broccoli, protein shakes. He later described the process as force feeding himself 'like a foie gras goose': 'It was the most physical demand that's ever been made of me for the screen. It was horrible. You turn into an absolute creature from hell!' By the time the shoot went ahead, he had gone from a 38 chest to a 42, but was quick to point out that gaining weight wasn't in itself skilful acting. 'I've always been a bit po-faced that all you need to do to be put in the hallowed halls of method acting is put on shitloads of weight. The effort involved deserves some credit, but it doesn't make a performance.'

As part of his preparation, he also underwent some basic martial arts training, learning how to move and throw a punch. Supervising his progress was his stunt double, Martin de Boer. 'I've had actors who want to be an action star, but don't want to put in the work. He was the opposite: "I want to train as much as I can."' But the more dangerous stunts would be out of bounds for Cumberbatch; it was simply too risky. 'If something happens to him we're all screwed,' noted de Boer. 'That's why I'd be on the wire, not him.'

Ironically, Cumberbatch had been no particular *Star Trek* fanatic, prior to seeing Abrams' reboot of the brand in 2009, but once seen, he was hooked. 'Lo and behold, the Trekkie in me was reborn. The Trekkie world is phenomenally rich and entertaining, but at its core, it's about humans and being human and how to aspire to a greater democracy than we have. Emotions are ramped up and men cry in this film.'

For him it was vital that characterisation and story were central to *Star Trek*. He told *The LA Times* in May 2013: 'They're such condensed, incredibly beautifully drawn characters that are very now, even though it's a future-scape with loads of rich, imaginative detail for fans to obsess over. The actual core content of the story is universal in time and place.'

The *Star Trek* shoot would last four months, and for a time, Cumberbatch's parents came to stay with him in the US. One day, they accompanied him to the set. Wanda Ventham, herself a veteran of sci-fi shows like *UFO* and *Doctor Who*, was amused by the endless takes. 'It went on all day, just to get Ben in this bloody spaceship. At one point, I said to them, "You know, when I was doing *UFO*, it only took me three takes to get to the Moon!"'

When *Into Darkness* (Abrams' second *Star Trek* movie, and the twelfth film in all) opened in the UK in May 2013, critics recognised the moral core of Harrison. 'A piece of full-on, chilly, orotund Shakespearean villainry,' wrote *Scotland on Sunday*. 'It's a kick to see Cumberbatch roar, glower and run through glass windows like a weaponised Duracell bunny.'

The rest of the cast included Chris Pine (Captain Kirk), Zachary Quinto (Spock) and Zoe Saldana (Lt Uhuru). There were opportunities for mischief on the shoot, and predictably the British comedy actor Simon Pegg (in the role of Scotty) was one of the main exponents of such tomfoolery. One stunt took place at a nuclear fusion laboratory in California called the National Ignition Faculty. Pegg warned Cumberbatch that special precautions had to be taken while they were shooting there. In particular, he would need to protect himself with some special 'neutron cream'. 'I was convinced that I had to put dots of this cream on my face,' said the fall guy for the prank. 'There was also a disclaimer I had to sign, basically saying, "I'm aware of the physical dangers of working in this environment." God knows what else I've signed in my life that I might have got into trouble for.'

Also featuring in the cast, as Dr Carol Marcus, was Alice Eve, whose connection with Cumberbatch stretched back to 2006's *Starter for 10*. Like him, she was the offspring of two actors, in her case Trevor Eve and Sharon Maughan, and suggested that growing up in a family of thespians could be challenging: 'The energy and the passion was fantastic to be around – but that has its other side, too. There was a lot of socialising. I think it was because of the unsettled nature of an actor's life that I ended up seeking out a very structured education.' For Cumberbatch, it had been Harrow, then Manchester University. For Eve, it was Westminster School and Oxford, 'where the rules were rigid and people had a rigidity in their approach to life that I wasn't familiar with.'

At the end of the *Star Trek* shoot in the summer of 2012, Cumberbatch had sneaked in to record a guest voice for *The Simpsons*, before jetting back to the UK to read some war poetry at the Cheltenham Literary Festival, participate in a *Sherlock* event at the Edinburgh Television Festival, and do a round of interviews for the premiere of *Parade's End* on BBC2. By late August, he was back in the USA filming *12 Years a Slave*, Steve McQueen's adaptation of Solomon Northup's 1850s autobiography, which detailed his experiences of being kidnapped and sold into slavery. McQueen described the memoir as 'the Anne Frank book of America... a meditation on family, freedom and love'. He found it both gripping and harrowing. 'I was trembling. Every page was a revelation. I was upset that I didn't know the book, then I realised no one knew about it.'

Solomon Northup was a talented violinist with a young family, but was struggling to find employment. On the street of New York's Manhattan one day in 1841, he was approached by two strangers offering him work. Although the state of New York had already outlawed slavery, many other US states had not, and the next thing Northup knew, he was in Washington, DC, then in New Orleans. The two strangers had drugged him. Over the next 12 years, he was sold as an enslaved person three times, forced to pick cotton, beaten numerous times, and faced a lynching. He was finally rescued when a Canadian called Bass, who was heavily involved in abolishing slavery in North America, stepped in, and sent a message back to New York. As a free man, Northup could not sue the men who had sold him into slavery (it was illegal for him to give evidence in court against white people), but he could at least publish a memoir.

When *12 Years a Slave* was published in 1853, it sold around 30,000 copies, and Northup strived to help other enslaved people be freed over the next decade. Sadly, his own story has an uncertain and mysterious postscript. In 1863, he travelled to the state of Vermont to help free slaves, where-upon he disappeared. Little was known about what happened next.

For the film adaptation of *12 Years a Slave*, Cumberbatch was cast as Ford, one of Northup's slave owners. The character was meant to have a little more of a conscience than some of his contemporaries, but he was still presiding over a plantation 'in which brutality reigns untrammelled'. Having read the memoir, and other relevant books for research with titles including *Cultivation and Culture* and *We Lived in a Little Cabin in the Yard*, he flew to New Orleans to join a cast which included Chiwetel Ejiofor (as Northup), Michael Fassbender, Brad Pitt and Paul Giamatti, but he was still familiarising himself with America. 'I feel slightly terrified about the heat, and about being a day player because it's far harder to hit the ground running, but it'll be fascinating.'

Several scenes in the film would be unsparing in how they depicted the conditions under which Northup and others suffered. Steve McQueen, born in London to Grenadian parents, was unapologetic about the brutality of his adaptation. 'My responsibility is this: either I'm making a film about slavery or I'm not. It was mental and physical torture, and people have to remember why I as an individual am sitting here today – I'm here because members of my family went through slavery. Fact.'

Another of Cumberbatch's projects to be filmed in the United States was another adaptation. *August: Osage County* had been a Pulitzer Prize and Tony-winning stage drama written by Tracy Letts, and transferred to the screen with a cast that included Julia Roberts and Meryl Streep. Centred round the family of an alcoholic father (Chris Cooper), even while it was being made, it was already being talked about as a possible Oscar winner in 2014.

Cumberbatch, who would co-star as Charles Aiken, had first met Meryl Streep at the Golden Globes. Star-struck, he found it surreal to discover that she was a *Sherlock* fanatic, as was Ted Danson. He was then given some advice on 'how to handle all this'... from George Clooney. It just didn't seem real – hanging around superstars he had been watching on the screen since childhood. He would wobble and freeze during one scene of *August: Osage County*: 'We had one scene around the table with Meryl, and I just couldn't act. I was in awe of her. She is spellbinding to watch.'

Tracy Letts, who had adapted his stage play for the film version, had originally intended that the whole cast should be comprised of American actors. He relented when Cumberbatch and Ewan Macgregor were both spotted. 'I guess I lost the fight,' he told US newspaper, the *Philadelphia Inquirer*. 'They're lovely fellows and they do a great job.' In October 2013, the film would win an Ensemble Acting Prize at the Hollywood Film Awards.

* * *

Benedict Cumberbatch had begun a hectic 2013 with yet another film shoot, one which would open before either *August: Osage County* or *12 Years a Slave*. *The Fifth Estate* was to be the second Cumberbatch film with a connection to Steven Spielberg, whose DreamWorks company were making it. He had landed the part in October 2012. It would focus on the controversial exploits of the Australian Julian Assange, who had founded the whistleblowing website WikiLeaks in 2006, but since June 2012 had been living under sanctuary at the Ecuador Embassy in London in the light of two controversies. At the time of writing, he remains a wanted man in Sweden for sexually assaulting two women, while the US authorities are also still trying to extradite him for leaking hundreds of confidential and classified documents on his website for public consumption, material which had originated from military and international government sources.

The Fifth Estate was based on a book called *Inside WikiLeaks: My Time with Julian Assange at the World's Most Dangerous Website*, written by the hacker Daniel Domscheit-Berg. James McAvoy was originally slated to play him, until filming commitments on the *X Men* film, *Days of Future Past*, made him pull out. He was replaced by Daniel Bruhl, who had risen to prominence in the Quentin Tarantino 2009 movie, *Inglourious Basterds*.

Filming on *The Fifth Estate* began in early 2013 in Iceland, where WikiLeaks had been launched, seven years earlier. The day before the cameras started rolling, Cumberbatch received a lengthy email from the man he was playing: Julian Assange himself. 'It was a very considered, thorough, charming and intelligent account of why he thought it was morally wrong for me to be part of something he thought was going to be damaging in real terms, not just to perceptions but to the reality of the outcome for himself. He characterised himself as a political refugee, and with [Bradley] Manning awaiting trial, and other supporters of WikiLeaks who have been detained or might be awaiting detention, and the organisation itself – all of that being under threat if I took part in this film.'

In his letter to Cumberbatch, Assange had described the book that the filmmakers had chosen to adapt as 'deceitful' and 'toxic': 'I believe it will distort events and subtract from public understanding. It does not seek to simplify, clarify or distil the truth, but rather it seeks to bury it.' He went on to say that although he believed the actor was 'a decent person, who would not naturally wish to harm good people in dire situations', nonetheless Cumberbatch would be 'used, as a hired gun, to assume the appearance of the truth in order to assassinate it. In the end, you are a jobbing actor who gets paid to follow the script, no matter how debauched.'

Cumberbatch stood firm and shot back an email of his own, stressing the film was furthering a debate and not casting judgement. 'This is not documentary, this is not a legally admissible piece of evidence... It's a starting point, that should both provoke and entertain...' The claim that he was a 'hired gun' especially stung him, though: 'He accuses me of being a "hired gun" as if I am an easily bought cipher for right-wing propaganda. Not only do I NOT operate in a moral vacuum but this was not a pay day for me at all. I've worked far less hard for more financial reward.' Cumberbatch had been driven by integrity, not by celebrity or money, to work on *The Fifth Estate*, but he still acknowledged that the correspondence with Assange had made him truly analyse his motives for accepting the lead role in the first place. 'It gave me real cause for concern... it galvanised me into addressing why I was doing this movie.'

But he believed his motives were good ones: he believed in civil liberties, democracy, and the rights of the general public to question those in charge. He had also felt compelled to explore the controversial character of Assange: 'I wanted to create a three-dimensional portrait of a man far more maligned in the tabloid press than he is in our film, to remind people that he is not just the weird, white-haired Australian dude wanted in Sweden, hiding in an embassy behind Harrods.'

The film's director Bill Condon, previously at the helm of two *Twilight* movies, agreed it was a discursive piece of work about the impact of WikiLeaks, and how information was spread in the digital age: 'This film won't claim any long view authority on its subject, or attempt any final judgment. We want to explore the complexities and challenges of transparency in the information age and, we hope, enliven and enrich the conversations WikiLeaks has already provoked.'

As ever, Cumberbatch was striving to understand Assange's qualities and failings in a rounded character study, rather than branding him good or evil. He elaborated: 'I said, listen, this film is going to explore what you achieved, what brought you to the world's attention, in a way that I think is nothing but positive. I'm not acting in a moral vacuum. Whatever happens, I want to give as much complexity and understanding of you as I can.'

To help him get this right, he had conducted plenty of background research. He felt the key to Assange partly lay in his difficult childhood: 'To have been a child in a single-mother relationship, being pursued around the country by an abusive stepfather who was part of a cult – to be taken out of any context where he could discover who he was in relation to other people – well, to then become a teenage hacktivist, and evolve into a cyber-journalist, to me makes perfect sense. And he's still a runaway today – he can't form those human relationships that other organisations have.'

Assange continued to be unhappy with the concept of the film. Via videolink from his refuge at the Ecuadorian Embassy, he detailed why to a gathering of students at the Oxford University Union.

'It is a lie upon lie. The movie is a massive propaganda attack on WikiLeaks and the character of my staff.'

Cumberbatch persisted with the idea of a meeting in

person. Assange refused, but the email correspondence continued. 'I wanted to give a fair account of him,' the actor told *Time Out*. 'The moral responsibility was very much part of the job. He was having none of it as far as a meeting goes. He felt that a meeting would condone a film he felt was too poisonous an account. He got hold of an old script and all sorts of issues blew up when we were filming. We had a discussion, though, which was good. If Julian is feeling that way, politically he's right not to let [a meeting] happen, because it would be like a blessing.' All the same, when Assange eventually saw footage of Cumberbatch's performance in the film, he was unimpressed with his attempt at an Australian drawl. 'We're all used to foreign actors trying to do Australian accents, and when you hear a Brit trying to do your own accent, I can't tell you how grating it is.'

The filmmaker Oliver Stone, who did manage to secure a meeting with Assange at the Embassy, took a dim view of both the prospect of *The Fifth Estate* and a documentary called *We Steal Secrets*, made by Alex Gibney. He said that the film was likely to be 'unfriendly' and went on: 'I don't think most people realize how important WikiLeaks is and why Julian's case needs support. Julian Assange did much for free speech and is now being victimised by the abusers of that concept.'

Later, Cumberbatch would tell *New York Magazine* a little more about his encounter with Assange. 'He asked me not to do it, and I said to him, "Well, somebody is going to do it, wouldn't you rather it's someone who has your ear, who could steer the film to a place that's more accurate or balanced?" The tabloid image of him, what he fears is going to be promoted – that weird, white-haired guy wanted for rape – is so far from what he did.' To his mind, however you viewed the man, he had provided 'a massive service, to wake us up to the zombie-like way we absorb our news'.

The issue of the sexual assaults allegation would be glossed over in the final cut of *The Fifth Estate*. The completed film was intended to be more of a general overview on the divide between the public and the confidential in the modern world, rather than a specific biography of Julian Assange.

Empathy was Cumberbatch's watchword. He was striving to create as three-dimensional a portrait as possible. 'I think to try to go into this realm of "thumbs up or thumbs down" is so limiting,' he said. 'You want to find what's human about him.' Director Bill Condon concurred with this way of thinking: 'Watching the movie is the experience of being impressed and turned off by Assange every five minutes.'

In August 2013, Cumberbatch made his own oblique protest. Filming was nearing completion on the third series of *Sherlock* in London, and he had a message for some loitering paparazzi. He donned a hoodie and held up a message for the cameras. 'Go photograph Egypt and show the world something important,' it read. Two days later, he held up a series of messages referring to the detention of David Miranda, partner of the *Guardian*'s Glenn Greenwald. It was an oblique reference to Schedule 7 of the UK's Terrorism Act, which gives police the power over passengers to stop and search them at airports.

Cumberbatch had written the following in relation to David Miranda, highlighting his own concerns about the British government's stance on civil liberties: 'Hard drive smashed, journalists detained at airports... Democracy? Schedule 7 prior restraint. Is this erosion of civil liberties winning the war on terror? What do they not want you to know? And how did they get to know it? Does the exposure of their techniques cause a threat to our security or does it just cause them embarrassment?'

The Fifth Estate opened in British cinemas early in October 2013. One fan of his portrayal of Julian Assange was Prime Minister David Cameron, who viewed some of the film for an ITV discussion programme called *The Agenda*. Cameron described Cumberbatch's take on Assange as a 'brilliant fantastic piece of acting... The twitchiness and everything of Julian Assange is brilliantly portrayed.' He was less convinced by how the film tackled the subject of confidentiality, though. 'There is an interesting bit when he says some of these documents are confidential,' he told *The Agenda*'s host, Tom Bradby. 'People's lives are at risk, and of course he is thinking of the people who have leaked them. Actually you also need to think about the people whose lives are at risk because they have been leaked.'

Cameron's doubts about the film were not the only ones to be voiced. Some critics considered it inappropriate that the matter of the sexual assault allegations towards Assange was confined to a brief onscreen caption at the tail end of the picture. Others concluded the subject under discussion was too large and sprawling to be contained in a single two-hour story, especially for a saga that was ongoing and incomplete.

But the most common complaint about *The Fifth Estate* from critical circles came with how it dealt with the character of Assange. 'The filmmakers haven't made up their minds yet,' wrote the *Independent*, 'whether Assange is a visionary champion of free speech or an autocratic and "manipulative asshole" with a personality skirting on the autistic end of the spectrum.' The tendency for the film to lean towards the latter may have contributed to Assange being dismissive of the released version.

The general feeling was that, while Cumberbatch gave a good performance in the central role, the film surrounding him was less formidable, and lacked substance. 'Cumberbatch is brilliant,' wrote Mark Kermode in the *Observer*, 'getting the peculiar vocal and physical mannerisms of Assange just so, playing him as saint and sinner, perfectly capturing his shabby charisma. Yet the film never allows him to show his teeth, withholding not only judgment but also clear direction. *The Fifth Estate* feels strangely unfocused, uncertain of how to deal with its slippery enigma.'

Coolly received by critics, *The Fifth Estate* would fare even worse with the public, even with Benedict Cumberbatch in his first lead role. In its opening weekend in US cinemas, it took around £1 million at the box office, barely one-tenth of the £16 million budget. Lagging well behind the fortunes of blockbusters like *Captain Phillips* (starring Tom Hanks) and the Sandra Bullock/George Clooney sci-fi thriller *Gravity*, it was a commercial flop, and did little better even in the UK. Then again, it was not a subject that lent itself naturally to a populist movie, and not all movies need to be populist ones. Even as an A-lister, Cumberbatch would continue to sign up for all kinds of film projects, not just guaranteed hits.

* * *

In between zooming back and forth from the USA on projects like *12 Years a Slave*, *Star Trek Into Darkness* and *August: Osage County*, Cumberbatch had been spending a fair bit of time out in New Zealand, where he had become an addition to the cast of Peter Jackson's epic remake of J.R.R. Tolkien's *The Hobbit*.

Cumberbatch's co-star in *Sherlock*, Martin Freeman, had been cast in the role of Bilbo Baggins early in 2011, but feared that five months of work out in Wellington would clash with the second series of *Sherlock*, back in the UK. However, after the first seven weeks of *Hobbit* filming, Jackson allowed Freeman to fly back for Watson duties, concentrating for the time being on scenes which would not feature him. Even so, it was indicative of what a worldwide splash *Sherlock* had made, that a television series with a fraction of the budget of *The Hobbit* could borrow back its lead actor. For Jackson, they had no choice but to revise the schedule, simply because they had the Bilbo Baggins they wanted. 'We stopped shooting for six weeks,' he explained. 'We didn't have anyone else we wanted for Bilbo. If you don't get that casting right, the film is simply not going to work, no matter how much you spend.'

It was at the BAFTA Television Awards of May 2011 when

Freeman let slip that Benedict would be joining him in Middle Earth. Cumberbatch was initially slow to confirm the nature of his involvement, but eventually revealed that he would be the voice of Smaug the dragon. His addition to the vast cast list came at around the same time that the Australian comedian Barry Humphries, aka Dame Edna Everage, was also signed up to play the Goblin King. Cumberbatch and Freeman had become firm friends on *Sherlock*. Now they would also be working together on the other side of the world, and it was in January 2012 that Cumberbatch made his first visit to the *Hobbit* set.

Working on *The Hobbit* was a great honour for Cumberbatch. The Tolkien book had been a childhood favourite, 'the first imaginary landscape I had in my head'. His father Timothy had read the story to him when he was seven. 'I'd say, "Just do Gollum, what would Gollum say now, Dad?" And he'd do the voice. He was brilliant at it.'

In *The Hobbit*, he would play two roles. One was a necromancer. The other was Smaug, a huge, sinister fire-breathing dragon, hundreds of years old. As Smaug, though, he would hardly encounter his fellow cast members, as this was one of the many sections of the film which would use Peter Jackson's ingenious motion capture techniques. He would stand before a green screen, while wearing a suit covered in raised dots. 'It's a sort of grey all-in-one jumpsuit,' he summarised, 'with a skullcap, a Madonna headset and Aboriginal-like face paint. You feel like a tit in all that gear, but Peter is so lovely, you soon forget.'

It has often been assumed that, as with Andy Serkis (aka Gollum) in the *Lord of the Rings* trilogy and *The Hobbit*, Cumberbatch's involvement in *The Hobbit* was simply to provide the voice for Smaug and the Necromancer. Not so. While his physical likeness would not be present onscreen, the physicality and body movements of his characters would be. 'My voice, my motions,' he told *New York Magazine*. 'I worked my ass off to create that dragon.'

Ahead of the motion-capture work on *The Hobbit*, he prepared for life as a dragon by researching animation, and by visiting the Komodo dragons housed at London Zoo to analyse their posture and movement. 'They have some amazing ones. Snakes too. So I've been going there to see how the skeleton moves differently, what the head movements are like.' Playing the Creature on stage in *Frankenstein* ('very full-on and corporeal') had helped him to inhabit an entity between man and beast but in the end, he found he just had to seek inspiration from inside his own mind, and discard any inhibitions. 'It's very freeing,' he told *Total Film* magazine in 2012, 'once you put the suit on, and the sensors. I've never felt less encumbered, actually. And you have to be. You have to be free. You just have to lose your shit on a carpeted floor, in a place that looks a little bit like a mundane government building. It was just me as well, with four static cameras, and all the sensors.'

After all that, the Weta workshop crew would 'work their magic' with special effects to develop his physical movements. But the spirit of the actor would remain. 'As an actor, you can do weight loss, weight gain, put on silly noses, crazy accents, move like a dragon, inviting people to look at the fireworks and admire how different you're being,' said Cumberbatch in late 2011. 'But with acting like that [i.e. Smaug], it's all about look-at-me, when what you should be doing is helping the audience care about the person they're watching.'

As *The Hobbit* film grew from one to two movies, and finally to a trilogy, opening at consecutive Christmases from 2012–14, Benedict Cumberbatch would be needed more and more in New Zealand, and would fly back and forth for further motion capture sessions, and if time allowed, a spot of his latest passion of skydiving. Not that there was much spare time these days for one of the most in-demand actors in the business.

'I'm playing a really big game now,' said Cumberbatch of his move into blockbuster movies. 'I'm going into studios to meet executives and heads of production, and asking: "What have you got on your slate?". And they say, "This and this and this." And you know there are five actors ahead of you who have first refusal, so there will be fallow periods now. But I can't afford another five months in the theatre, or another big TV gig. I think it's time. I don't have any dependants. I'm interested in just playing the game a little bit, because it gives you a lot more choice. It gives you power. If you become indispensable to that machine it gives you a greater variety, which is what I always wanted.'

But then he always intended his career to last, rather than make a splash too early and then find the parts drying up – 'I've never wanted to be an adolescent flash in the pan.' He cited Brad Pitt, his co-star in *12 Years a Slave*, or George

Clooney, as the kind of actors whose privileged position in film he aspired to: 'They're great people to emulate as a business model.' Those who get film screen net – in other words, a share of the box-office receipts. 'There are about five people in the world who can do that.'

CHAPTER 16

THE A-LISTER

As Benedict Cumberbatch headed out to Ibiza in July 2013 to officiate at the wedding of his friends Seth Cummings and Rob Rinder, he prepared himself for an autumn in which several of his projects were ready and waiting to hit our screens. At the Toronto International Film Festival in early September, he would feature in no fewer than three pictures. *The Fifth Estate* would open in Britain a month later, with *12 Years a Slave* and *August: Osage Country* set to follow. November brought a short film called *Little Favour* (available through iTunes, and co-starring Colin Salmon and Nick Moran), while Christmas time would bring *The Desolation of Smaug*, the second part of Peter Jackson's *Hobbit* trilogy. 'I had a really busy year last year, and the beginning of this year,' Cumberbatch said in autumn 2013, 'and all of them are coming home to roost in the same year, which is quite extraordinary.'And as if that wasn't enough Benedict Cumberbatch, there was still some unfinished business at St Bart's Hospital ...

After the double whammy of *Sherlock*'s second series and *Parade's End*, Benedict Cumberbatch had been showered with accolades at awards ceremonies: the Critics' Choice Television Award for Best Actor in Los Angeles, Virgin Media Award for Best TV Actor, a Specsavers Crime Thriller Award for *Sherlock*, and the Broadcasting Press Guild Award for Best Actor (for *Parade's End*, one of four gongs the series picked up at that ceremony). He seemed somewhat more bemused when *The Sun*'s readers voted him Sexiest Man, beating David Beckham and One Direction to the title two years running. 'I am very flattered. I don't know about being the sexiest man in the world. I am barely the sexiest man in my flat, and I'm the only guy living there.'

Even when he lost out on a prize, there was sometimes a feeling that he had been robbed. When Dominic West won a deserved BAFTA Award for the powerful television film *Appropriate Adult* (about the lives of murderers Fred and Rose West), he professed to feeling surprised. 'Even my sister was rooting for Benedict,' he announced from the stage. Other nominations of note for Cumberbatch's acting included the National Television Awards, the Golden Globes, plus the 2012 Primetime Emmy Awards, for which his work on 'A Scandal in Belgravia' earned him an Outstanding Lead Actor in a Miniseries or Movie nomination. The other esteemed nominees were Woody Harrelson (*Game Change*), Clive Owen (*Hemingway & Gelhorn*), Idris Elba (*Luther*) and two of the leads of *Hatfields & McCoys*: Bill Paxton and Kevin Costner. Owen, Elba and Cumberbatch were far from being the only British nominees at the 2012 Emmys. Armando Iannucci and Simon Blackwell's political sitcom *Veep* was much touted in the comedy category, *Homeland*'s Damian Lewis (Outstanding Lead Actor), and the inevitable nominations for Julian Fellowes' *Downton Abbey* and its lead actor, Hugh Bonneville.

It may have seemed that Cumberbatch should have won more of his categories, but because *Sherlock* and *Parade's End* were not star vehicles but ambitious ensemble pieces where he was cast in a central role, it felt that the successes of the series were also significant. Both series received numerous prizes, both at home and internationally. In 2012, *Parade's End* triumphed in four categories: Best Drama Series, Best Actor (Cumberbatch), Best Actress (Rebecca Hall), plus a Writer's Award for Sir Tom Stoppard.

When *Sherlock* co-creator Steven Moffat won a Special Achievement Award at BAFTA in 2012 for his work both on that series and *Doctor Who*, Cumberbatch helped pay tribute to the man who allowed him to bring Sherlock to life. Moffat in his view was 'a word machine. His name is a byword for quality family entertainment.'

Elsewhere, Cumberbatch had been involved in two consecutive victories of Best TV Drama at the South Bank Sky Arts Awards – *Sherlock* in 2012, *Parade's End* the year after. Plus, at the end of 2012, *Sherlock* was voted the Television Show of the Year in a *Radio Times* poll, beating the likes of *Homeland*, *Twenty Twelve* and *The Thick of It*.

Such was his standing in the film and theatre fraternity that in early 2013, he was appointed as part of a jury alongside the likes of Kevin Macdonald and Sam Mendes in a vote for the BAFTA Rising Star Award. The shortlist comprised Juno Temple, Andrea Riseborough, Elizabeth Olsen, Alicia Vikander and (the only male nominee) Suraj Sharma.

When it came to his own attitude to awards, though, Cumberbatch insisted that while it was nice to be recognised, and undoubtedly nice to win, prizes could never be the main reason for entering his profession. Indeed, he denied that he was a competitive person. 'You have to be a little bit, for acting roles, but you try to kid yourself they are not competition, otherwise it drives you mad.'

* * *

There was never really much mystery about whether there would be a third series of *Sherlock*. Within minutes of series two finishing in January 2012, Steven Moffat tweeted the following: 'Of course there's going to be a third series – it was commissioned at the same time as the second. Gotcha!' Even so, the second had tackled head-on some of the biggest stories in Conan Doyle's canon for a reason – out of caution that the show might not be automatically recommissioned, especially since the BBC had chosen to end some of its drama productions after two runs. 'We're working on the principle there's no point in deferred pleasure,' Moffat said. 'When we went to the second series, we thought we'd do the three big ones, which are Irene Adler, the Hound and the Final

Problem. We thought we might as well get to them now. What if we never got to them?'

But audiences faced an agonising two-year wait before a third series, partly down to the hectic work schedules of the stars and writers. The huge popularity of *Sherlock* in the first place had made Cumberbatch and Freeman such bankable and sought-after performers in international cinema. As a result, it was a challenge for Steven Moffat and Mark Gatiss (themselves busy men) to clear space in everyone's diary in order to make series three. 'It's a problem by accident and design,' Moffat told the *Radio Times*. 'We have two of the biggest film stars in the world playing the leads in our show. But they seem to like doing it and we hope we can hang on to them for a bit.'

Almost inevitably, some of the cast and crew would not be able to return. For a time, it looked as if Paul McGuigan, the director of most of the first six episodes, would be back. 'It feels like we all belong to it,' he said. 'As a small group we always challenge each other.' But in March 2013, just before shooting was due to begin, it was announced that he had projects over in North America. One was an adaptation of *Frankenstein*, the other a new biopic about Brian Epstein, the original manager in the 1960s of The Beatles and Cilla Black, but who died in 1967 at the age of just thirty-two. The film would be called *The Man Who*, and would be co-produced by Tom Hanks.

Nor would James Moriarty, aka Andrew Scott, be returning to *Sherlock*. He had bowed out in the final scenes of series two during the St Bart's rooftop confrontation with

Holmes. 'I don't think there could have been any better exit for a character like that,' he said. He was well aware that the potency and terror with Moriarty lay in making his appearances sparing. To have him coming back again and again risked making the character stale or even a pantomime villain of a figure. There were only so many occasions a truly evil persona could re-appear and not become over-familiar. And so Scott moved on, soon gravitating to a Channel 4 drama called *Dates*.

So just how had Sherlock Holmes survived the fall from the roof of St Bart's? All sorts of weird and wonderful theories had been circulating. Maybe something or someone else had fallen off the roof – a dummy, by any chance? Perhaps when Holmes fell, he had somehow landed safely. Possibly there was a doppelganger of *Sherlock*, or was Moriarty (already shot) disguised as him? Or was John Watson hallucinating, due to taking the Baskerville drug (a hangover from the previous story)?

It was, insisted a mischievous Steven Moffat, none of these possibilities. He said there was something else that no one seemed to have noticed. 'It's something Sherlock did that was out of character, but which nobody has picked up on.' This was no trick, no cheat; it was a genuine solution to the mystery, but Moffat wondered if the millions of potential Sherlocks watching the show around the world might solve it ahead of the third series airing. 'My problem is that the audience is more fiction-literate than ever. In Shakespeare's day, you probably expected to see a play once or twice in your life; today, you experience four or five different kinds of fiction every day. So staying ahead of the audience is impossible.' And by now, it was quite an audience. The BBC had sold the first two series to a staggering 234 territories around the world, from Australia and the US to Iran and Kazakhstan.

Certainly, no one on the production was giving very much away. Everyone was keeping mum about what would happen next. Not that they were much more clued-up anyway. 'Even we are kept in the dark about the scripts now,' said Martin Freeman. 'At the end of the last series, neither Benedict nor I knew what was going to happen afterwards.' About all he would say was that *Sherlock* had obviously faked his own death, and given the title of their continuing series, that was a given. The mystery was how he had faked his own death. The fanbase was feverishly waiting for the answer. But that's how it should be, argued Cumberbatch. The public didn't really want to know the answer before the next episode. 'It's not paranoia, it's not absurd control. It's about giving the audience what they secretly want. Like a kid with a box of chocolates, once you've eaten them all you feel sick.'

What was promised for series three was a deepening of Sherlock's character. If not quite maturing, he might be becoming more humane. 'It's about him coming to terms with the fact that he can do a better job if he has a little bit of morality, feeling and emotion,' said Cumberbatch, 'and to be able to play with those things without necessarily being taken over by them.' But ultimately, Sherlock would still be driven by the attitude that his life was about a game. 'It's very apparent in the books that his glee and his joy comes at the beginning of the case and when he's solved it. The game is on. He's an animal on the scent.'

Once again, the third series would consist of three feature-length episodes. It would open with 'The Empty Hearse', an appropriate choice as it referenced Conan Doyle's *The Adventure of the Empty House*, the story which brought back Sherlock back from the dead in 1903. But the Sherlock team would be mixing the traditional with the contemporary, as ever. The other two stories were announced as 'The Sign of Three', in which Watson would meet the love of his life, and 'His Last Vow', in which Sherlock would turn spy for his country – with his villainous foil being Charles Augustus Magnussen, played by Lars Mikkelsen, the lead in the Danish cult crime drama serial *The Killing*. The series continued to revel in meta-references. 'The Sign of Three' would find Watson getting married to Mary Morstan, played by Martin Freeman's real-life partner, Amanda Abbington. 'The Empty Hearse', meanwhile, would introduce to viewers Sherlock's parents, revealed as Cumberbatch's own mother and father, Wanda Ventham and Tim Carlton.

Filming began in earnest for the third series in March 2013, with locations including Bristol, Cardiff and Cheltenham. Occasionally, slivers of information would enter the public domain, as in April when the production was back on the roof at St Bart's Hospital to film the rest of the scene after Cumberbatch was seen to jump. Though the actor stood on a platform, a stunt double actually performed the jump.

The shoots in Bristol and Cheltenham had led some fans to turn up in the hope of getting to meet the stars, as well as surreptitiously taking photographs and uploading them to the Internet. Eventually, Sue Vertue had to beg them to stop. She wrote on the official *Sherlock* Tumblr.com blog: 'Our London shooting schedule is punishing, and will really give us very little time to interact with you... Also... the majority of fans and indeed ourselves would REALLY appreciate it if you didn't post pictures or spoilers or ideally our daily locations.'

Mostly fans complied with Vertue's public request, although some would still benignly gather at certain shoots, no matter how remote the location might be. 'We were shooting in the middle of Wales,' she recalled. 'Suddenly there's a bunch of them at the end of this deserted lane. They are all really sweet, and they've known some spoilers for months, but nobody has posted anything. It's like a bunch of best mates. Admittedly, it's a bunch that's thousands and thousands of people.' These, then, were benevolent onlookers, content and able to keep secrets.

Even so, a veil had to be drawn over some of the proceedings. For months, theories had been circulating as to how Sherlock had survived the fall from St Bart's, and the production team had painstakingly ensured that the filming of the crucial survival scene could not lead to spoilers being leaked. In order to put onlookers off the scent, extra material was shot, but the solution to the mystery was only clarified and revealed after filming was completed. In other words, the solution was only unveiled when the footage was edited together, one of the reasons that the lead actors could be truthful when they said they had no idea how Sherlock Holmes had survived the fall. 'We knew right from the start how we were going to do it,' revealed Mark Gatiss. 'By the time we came to actually do it we really had to address the fact it had become so huge, and there are really only so many ways you can jump off a building onto the pavement.' In truth, though, the survival of Holmes was not based on fantastical elements, but logic. 'There's nothing magical,' Moffat would point out. 'It's not *Doctor Who*.' For Gatiss, the key to the longevity between Holmes and Watson lay not only in their friendship. 'It's because Sherlock as a character brings order to chaos. That's the consolation he provides.'

By the end of the summer of 2013, series three's final scenes had been shot. On 15 December that year, after a week in which a trail had attracted over three million hits on YouTube, 'The Empty Hearse' was shown before a specially invited 500-strong audience at the BFI in London. Afterwards, Cumberbatch, Martin Freeman, Steven Moffat and Mark Gatiss participated in a question and answer session. A mini-episode, 'Many Happy Returns', was released on the BBC's iPlayer service on Christmas Day, with 1.5 million viewing it in the first week.

On New Year's Day 2014, 'The Empty Hearse' was given its television premiere on BBC1, followed by the rest of the new series. The third series was watched overall by nearly 12 million people in Britain alone, the highest audience for a drama series in the UK in over a decade (apart from *Doctor Who*). In August 2014, Cumberbatch, Freeman and Moffat would all win Emmy Awards in the US for their work on series three.

The appeal of *Sherlock* now stretched right around the

globe. Even in China, the series had a fanatical cult audience, thanks to the existence of online streaming services and pirate digital technology. There, Cumberbatch had been awarded a special nickname – 'Curly Fu', as a reference to his curly hair. When British Prime Minister David Cameron visited China in December 2013, he was asked if his government could pressurise the Chinese authorities into organising the screening of new episodes of *Sherlock* more quickly. The BBC specially made series three available on a video hosting website called Youku.com.

Elsewhere, the fan fiction about his and Watson's characters continued to proliferate. Cumberbatch was flattered, but only up to a point. 'It's part of the love people have for the show, even if a few of them are quite fanatical about it,' he said, 'but it's not really what we're doing.'

* * *

As with any career, there are lots of what-ifs and curiosities in Cumberbatch's past. He was apparently considered a strong contender by some for *Doctor Who* after David Tennant's departure from the role, but he was happy enough for Matt Smith to take on the part of the Timelord. 'David and I talked about it, but I thought it would have to be radically different. And anyway I didn't really like the whole package – being on school lunchboxes.' He soon dashed those rumours completely, in any case. He had never been offered the role, and in any case, would have turned it down. 'Jumping on to school stages and giving out prizes, and saying, "I am the Doctor",' he sighed to the *Sunday Times*. 'It's not where I want to go.' It was tricky enough having the feverish fanbase of *Sherlock*, although Steven Moffat liked the notion that Cumberbatch might yet play the Doctor's arch-enemy, The Master. 'Fans will love the idea of the man who plays Sherlock taking on the Doctor. Benedict is the perfect choice if schedules can work.'

In a curious way, as Sherlock, Cumberbatch had inherited exactly the kind of mystique that had always been the hallmark of classic *Doctor Who*. Waris Hussein, director of the very first *Doctor Who* story for the BBC way back in 1963, told BBC Radio 4's *The Reunion* in 2013 that he was disappointed with the growing references to sexuality in *Doctor Who*. 'Recently the Doctor was actually snogged by his new companion. Once you have that on screen, people anticipate them getting together. The person who is mysterious and unavailable now is the new Sherlock. There's been a strange transference, because Sherlock was the type of mysterious character I always wanted the Doctor to stay.'

Cumberbatch was even suggested as a possible replacement for Matt Smith in *Doctor Who* before Peter Capaldi was selected as his successor. But it always seemed an improbable and impractical suggestion, especially with *Sherlock* still being so popular. How could someone play both parts?

Any A-list actor finds their name associated with numerous projects, whether or not they sign up in the end. A big screen version of *Frankenstein*, with Guillermo Del Toro directing, and to potentially feature Cumberbatch, has been mooted, as has the part of Brian Epstein in *Sherlock* director Paul McGuigan's biopic *The Man Who*. At the time of writing, both of these projects remain possibilities rather than certainties, as did the whisper that he might soon become a nemesis of Daniel Craig's James Bond. 'It would be a childhood ambition fulfilled,' promised a statement from Bond HQ. 'Playing a Bond villain is one of the plum roles in film history and he'd jump at the chance.' Especially since his previous Bond audition had gone nowhere. It was for a computer game. 'This seemed like the best chance to play Bond I'd get. I went along to this shabby, sweatbox in Soho. After a two hour wait, they made me leap over sofas. The worst of it was, I did it.' He wasn't called back.

A mysterious omission from the Cumberbatch CV which hardly anyone has seen is *The Dark Side of the Earth*, a sci-fi story made in 2008 about a hypochondriac who inhabits a sealed body suit. Despite being an expensive project, it never reached the public domain. Cumberbatch misfires are few and far between, and it remains to be seen if *The Dark Side of the Earth* emerges in some form or other in the future.

He had turned some things down flat. Hollywood asked him to be in a screen version of *Dracula*. He said no. 'I've been fighting it rather than being in it,' he told the *Radio Times*. 'I don't like to repeat myself too much. There are too many vampire franchises.' He pulled out of the horror flick *Crimson Peak*, to be replaced by Tom Hiddleston. He was supposedly being considered for a new *Star Wars* film as 'a Darth Vader-style villain', but denied any association with it. He was even offered the part of King Edward VIII for

Madonna's directorial feature film debut, *W.E.* He was invited to her home expecting a brief chat and a readthrough at most, but she suggested a dress rehearsal. 'I ended up in a suit and tie with Madonna operating the camera herself. We walked around the room trying to do the scene, with her going, "This shot's not working, I don't know why."' The part went to James D'Arcy, although given the ferocious critical reception the released film got, Cumberbatch may have had a lucky escape.

* * *

Besides, he had quite enough on his plate in 2013. After filming *The Fifth Estate* early in the year, he took the place of Leonardo DiCaprio in *The Imitation Game*, the real-life story of the mathematician Alan Turing, with Keira Knightley co-starring. At Bletchley Park in Buckinghamshire, Turing had been instrumental in inventing the modern computer. He had also been the man who had helped to crack the German Enigma code during World War II, helping to save thousands of lives in the process, but who was persecuted in post-war Britain for his homosexuality and arrested in 1952. Given the choice between being sent to prison or put on probation, so long as he would take hormonal treatment to reduce his sex drive, Turing opted for the latter. But two years later, just before his 42nd birthday, he took his own life. Only in 2009, following an Internet campaign, was an official public apology made – by then-Prime Minister Gordon Brown – for the 'appalling way'

Turing had been treated. Finally, in 2013, nearly sixty years after his death, Turing was granted a posthumous pardon.

When he was offered the part of Turing, Cumberbatch was in the middle of filming *Star Trek: Into Darkness* for J.J. Abrams. He dimly remembered the play *Breaking the Code*, written by Hugh Whitemore in 1986 and televised by the BBC in early 1997 with Derek Jacobi delivering a bravura performance as Turing. But beyond that, he knew little of the scientist and so the script of *The Imitation Game* gave an introduction to an uncompromising, fiercely intelligent figure. 'You get embroiled in this mystery both of the code and who this man is, and breaking the code, and that eureka moment and the joy of that, and then the devolution into the tragedy. And the emotional impact of what injustice he was served and the excruciating reality of that is only magnified when you realize I didn't know this. Why don't I know this?'

Cumberbatch, in his research for the role of Alan Turing, had come to regard him as 'someone who was caring and loving, as well as someone who was very determined and often in isolation. If any young person's ever felt... like an outsider, then this is definitely a film for them. It's about a hero for them.' He remained concerned about bigotry and intolerance around the world. He told *Out* magazine: 'People are being beheaded in countries right now because of their beliefs or sexual orientations. It's terrifying. If you're going to sell yourself as a leading man in Hollywood, to say "I'm gay", sadly, is still a huge obstacle. We all know actors who don't want to talk about it, or bring it up, or who deny it.'

While Cumberbatch's performance as Turing was generally

praised, there was criticism from some quarters about the film overall. *The Imitation Game* contrives a situation where Turing is collaborating closely with John Cairncross, who happened to be a spy for the Soviet Union at the time. Though both men worked at Bletchley Park, it was not in the same department, a fact confirmed by both Turing's biographer Andrew Hodges and Cairncross's own autobiography. This might be brushed aside as a tiny historical inaccuracy, but it leads to a more troubling rewriting of the past. When Turing discovers that Cairncross is a spy, Cairncross threatens to 'out' him, and so effectively – for a time – he covers up the spy's activities. Writing in *The Guardian*, the historian and critic Alex von Tunzelmann described this as 'wholly imaginary and deeply offensive – for concealing a spy would have been an extremely serious matter. Were the makers of *The Imitation Game* intending to accuse Alan Turing, one of Britain's greatest war heroes, of cowardice and treason?' Any biopic treads a fine line: how do you make an interesting life into a compelling feature film? While *The Imitation Game* received plenty of plaudits, some of those who knew their history questioned whether it had gone too far in its pursuit of dramatic tension.

* * *

In October 2014, *The Imitation Game* was previewed at the London Film Festival, and was on general release a month later, which more or less coincided with a rare public announcement about Benedict Cumberbatch's personal life.

On Wednesday 5 November, in its Forthcoming Marriages column, the *Times* newspaper in London published a six-line notice. It read: 'The engagement is announced between Benedict, son of Wanda and Timothy Cumberbatch of London, and Sophie, daughter of Katharine Hunter of Edinburgh and Charles Hunter of London.'

Relatively few of the Cumberbatch faithful might have been regular readers of the *Times* Notices section, but it did not take long for the shock news to reverberate through the media. Suddenly, Benedict Cumberbatch's days as a single man were now numbered.

Benedict and fellow actor Sophie had known each other for some time. In fact, they had first met over five years earlier, on the set of the film *Burlesque Fairytales*. Two years Benedict's junior, she had previously attended St Paul's School in London and then Oxford University before TV and film appearances beckoned (*Midsomer Murders*, *Vanity Fair*, *Torchwood*, Stephen Poliakoff's *Friends and Crocodiles*).

It was impressive that the couple had succeeded in keeping their relationship low-key for so long. In June 2014, a couple of articles whispered that Benedict was no longer single, but no name appeared. Even after he was first publicly photographed with Sophie, at the French Open tennis tournament in September 2014, press speculation was relatively muted. On the other hand, by continuing to mostly let his work rather than his personal life do the talking, Benedict Cumberbatch had been able to distract the world of showbiz gossip.

Benedict and Sophie's first high-profile appearance

together was at the New York premiere of *The Imitation Game*, just days after the *Times* notice. Benedict expressed gratitude for a torrent of good wishes that followed the engagement announcement. 'One of the most incredible things about getting engaged,' he said, 'which we had no idea would be coming back our way, is the amount of love that just comes flooding back.'

In his words, 'as a nomad with no dependants', Cumberbatch was content to still use his home city of London as a base, and 'pack a suitcase and travel' whenever appropriate. There were rumours in December 2014 that he might relocate to Los Angeles with his fiancée, but bigger news was to come. On 7 January 2015, it was officially announced to the media that Benedict and Sophie were to become parents. The following month, on Valentine's Day itself, the couple married at St Peter and St Paul Church in Mottistone on the Isle of Wight.

* * *

There comes a point in an A-list star's career when they are so famous that they are somehow everywhere and nowhere at the same time: everywhere because of their prolific output and because they are forever being talked about, yet nowhere because actual sightings off screen became comparatively rare, save for the very occasional chat show appearance or press interview.

This neatly encapsulated the year 2014 for Benedict Cumberbatch. Almost everything he did or said became headline news. He seemed especially ever-present in January: as well as the premiere of *Sherlock*'s third series on television, *12 Years a Slave* and *August: Osage County* both opened in British cinemas. Yet, behind the scenes, he was involved in a fresh raft of projects and cameos, which would encompass work for radio, television, cinema and, perhaps most excitingly of all, stage.

In February, two more *Rumpole* dramas were taped for Radio 4. Then, towards the end of that month, he took part in the final recording of *Cabin Pressure*. The broadcast of the two-part episode ('Zurich'), in which his character Martin Crieff was poised to leave the tiny MJN Airline for a larger Swiss one, was delayed until Christmas 2014, but deservedly met with plaudits – a fitting send-off for the most inventive and consistently funny radio sitcom in many years.

These were not his only contributions to the Radio 4 airwaves in 2014. A decade earlier, when still a relative unknown, he had been an integral part of the station's 60th anniversary of D-Day. Now, to mark the occasion's 70th anniversary, he was to be a newsreader. Over the weekend of 6–8 June 2014, he joined Toby Jones and Sir Patrick Stewart to voice new recordings of the BBC's original news bulletins from 1944.

As far as the world of celluloid is concerned – and the IMDB website reflects it – Cumberbatch is a particularly busy man. Future projects in various stages of completion include the war drama *The Yellow Birds*, the gangster flick *Black Mass* (for which he replaced Guy Pearce as Bill Bulger), and the big screen adaptation of R.C. Sheriff's *Journey's End*. All are some way off release, as is *Jungle Book: Origins*, Andy Serkis' ambitious motion capture reinvention of the Walt Disney classic of 1967, itself based on Rudyard Kipling's stories, for which Cumberbatch would play the tiger Shere Khan. In late 2014, it was announced that he would be playing Doctor Strange in a remake of the Marvel comic book, and there was also the long-awaited *The Lost City of Z*, an adaptation of *City of Angels*, and a favourite of Cumberbatch's from his youth, in which he would portray the Amazonian explorer, Percy Fawcett. 'In order to get the whole film noir detective thing,' he explained, 'I smoked a lot and drank a lot of whisky. I used to smoke quite a bit and it deepened my voice.' Filming was due to begin on this last project in Belfast, Northern Ireland, in early 2015.

In fact, Cumberbatch was almost in danger of being typecast as Being In Almost Anything. If the press was to be believed, he was tipped to star in just about every lead role. Some were nothing more than mere rumour – the voice of Dangermouse, or Lucian Freud, for instance – and a cameo in a future instalment of the *Star Wars* movie franchise was ruled out by its director, J.J. Abrams.

In 2014 itself, though, actual new film releases starring Benedict Cumberbatch were confined to the winter months. There was a nine-month gap between *12 Years a Slave* and *August: Osage County* (both in January) and no fewer than three films at the close of the year: *The Imitation Game* (still only his second feature film in a starring role), the animated feature *Penguins of Madagascar*, and the finale of Peter Jackson's *The Hobbit* trilogy, subtitled *The Battle of the Five*

Armies. At Christmas 2014, the first and third of these were both in the top five at the UK box office.

Even as he entered the realms of superstardom, Cumberbatch could still be versatile with the roles he accepted. 'You get to flex different muscles,' he told US TV talk show host Charlie Rose. 'For me, it's variety. There's not one that stands out or defines me, even though *Sherlock*'s success is extraordinary. People draw comparisons to the intelligence of some of them, or the oddness of some of them, [or] the outsider hero qualities of some of them. But I equally do the guy next door as I did in *August: Osage County*, or the comedian as I do in *Penguins of Madagascar*, playing a talking wolf.'

Occasionally, as in the Rose interview, Cumberbatch would emerge into the media glare as himself. While the world waited for further films to appear in 2014, he appeared on a panel at the Hay-on-Wye literary festival in May. Even a good-natured stunt during an interview for MTV in November, when he was challenged to impersonate eleven fellow actors in one minute (among them, Michael Caine, Alan Rickman, Sean Connery and Jack Nicholson), would pinball around the media.

For television, *Sherlock* was on hiatus, with filming of a special and fourth series not scheduled to begin until January 2015. In the interim, Cumberbatch participated in a segment on arithmetic for the US children's programme *Sesame Street* with Muppets Count von Count and Murray Monster. In addition, he began work on a lavish series for the BBC of the historical drama *The Hollow Crown*. He was to play King

Richard III, with one of his co-stars being Judi Dench (as Cecily, Duchess of York). The two had known each other since he was a boy; she had opened Brambletye's prep school theatre way back in the late 1980s.

The one area he had neglected in recent times had been stage work, but as with television, his triumphant return would be marked in Shakespearean fashion. His last stint in British theatre had been *Frankenstein* in 2011, and now he would return to the London stage in the summer of 2015 as Hamlet. Curiously, as recently as 2013, he had batted away suggestions that he might like to play such a role. 'It's been inflicted on audiences too much. I mean, fucking Jasper Carrott will be doing it next! It's like there's a queue. I think we're just seeing people do their Hamlet, that's where it goes wrong.'

Regardless of Cumberbatch's reservations, then, only a year later he was officially announced in the part. It was his first Shakespearean stage role in over a decade – since his four open-air Shakespeare plays in 2001–02, in fact. 'I don't know if there is such a thing as a right age to play the part, but 36 or 37 seems appropriate to me, so I need to do it before long.' The production, to last 12 weeks, would open at the Barbican in August 2015, just a few weeks after its lead had turned 39 years old. The director would be Lyndsey Turner, associate director of the Crucible Theatre in Sheffield, and who had just directed *Machinal* on Broadway. There was a mad rush for tickets, but fans were assured that cinemas were likely to show the production as part of National Theatre Live.

And what of other future ambitions besides acting?

Directing is a possibility, partly so that he can experience the making of a film from conception to completion. 'As an actor you are never there for every heartbeat of it.'

* * *

In his late thirties, Cumberbatch has unwittingly become a role model, partly through his work but also through the fame which has accidentally engulfed him. He is an ambassador for the Prince's Trust, and frequently takes part in events for the charity. In October 2012, he cycled the Palace to Palace bike ride, westwards from Buckingham Palace to Windsor Castle in Berkshire. The distance was 45 miles, or 72 kilometres. 'I don't get the opportunity to cycle much so it was fantastic to take part on such a beautiful route through London. It's worth it for such an important cause. The Prince's Trust is a charity which I am passionate about helping. With so many young people struggling to find work in the UK, I feel it's vital we do everything we can to make sure all young people have the opportunities to succeed.'

Sherlock has made him a star, but for how much longer could that show continue, in the light of all his other work? Its executive producers Steven Moffat and Mark Gatiss certainly hope it could carry on. 'We love the idea of the audience growing up with the show and the characters growing too,' Gatiss said just as series three was nearing completion. 'There is something lovely in the idea of Benedict and Martin aged 55 sitting at a fireplace, being the age we associate with Holmes and Watson.'

Television drama in Britain had become event TV once again. Just as soaps, reality TV and sport had become water-cooler topics, so primetime drama with large casts was becoming equally popular: *Downton Abbey*, *Call the Midwife*, *Broadchurch*, international crime dramas like *The Killing*, *Top of the Lake* and *Wallander*. DVD box sets had become the currency of TV drama, with a story arc over many episodes, as in a novel.

The trend for star vehicles, where an actor had an exclusive contract with a network and had shows created for them, had waned. 'We are mostly dealing with ensemble casts,' said one ITV executive. '*Broadchurch* was actually an ensemble drama with a cast of actors who all had a brilliant role to play.' Even *Sherlock* was not really a star vehicle for Benedict Cumberbatch, but more about his association with Dr John Watson. Just as Cumberbatch's parents, Wanda Ventham and Timothy Carlton, had not had series built around them, but had appeared in numerous series as resident cast members, Cumberbatch had rarely been The Star of something.

In the case of *Sherlock*, it may be that keeping the series occasional and lean, at just three episodes per series every couple of years, could ensure that it lasts for some time yet. It enables the main cast and indeed its writers to also work on other things. 'There is a traditional model of making television,' explained Steven Moffat, 'where you make an awful lot of episodes over five, six or seven years, until you get utterly sick of it and never make the show again.' Why not, then, take breaks to keep the creative process fresh?

Despite hectic diaries for both the lead actors and writers, more Sherlock will follow, with a special lined up for Christmastime in 2015, and with series four currently scheduled for early 2016. 'In Martin and Benedict,' explained Mark Gatiss, 'we accidentally cast two of the hottest film actors on the planet. But that brings its own attendant problems – everyone's schedules are incredibly tight.'

Elsewhere, the Sherlock Holmes industry shows little sign of abating, at the time of writing. *Elementary,* with Jonny Lee Miller as Holmes, continues on American television. Sir Ian McKellen has been cast as an elderly Sherlock for a Bill Condon movie, scheduled for 2015, called *Mr Holmes*. And Benedict Cumberbatch remains happy to play Sherlock for the foreseeable future, provided he is not tied to the role year in, year out.

The extraordinary fame that this series has brought him risked locking him into being perceived for just one role, always a peril for an actor. But there's another side to that fame. When you're that well-known, and that respected, you can use that power and clout for other projects. For someone as ambitious and curious as Cumberbatch, he looked forward to a time when he would not be solely defined by the popular media as Sherlock Holmes. '[*Sherlock*] gives you the power to do the kind of work you want to do. So obviously, some of it's constructive. That's the bit I'm interested in.' As he told the *Daily Telegraph* late in 2014, 'I'm interested in working in 40 years' time. I'm in it for the long game.'

SOURCES

BBC, *Belfast Telegraph*, *Coventry Telegraph*, *Daily Express*, *Daily Mail*, *Daily Mirror*, *Daily Record*, *Daily Star*, *Daily Telegraph*, *Design Week*, *Express on Sunday*, *Financial Times*, *Glasgow Herald*, *Guardian*, *The Harrovian*, *Hollywood Reporter*, *Independent*, *Independent on Sunday*, *Irish Independent*, *Irish Times*, ITV, *LA Times*, *Mail on Sunday*, *Marketing Week*, National Public Radio, *New York Times*, *Northern Echo*, *Observer*, *Out*, PBS, *The People*, *Philadelphia Inquirer*, *Radio Times*, *Reader's Digest*, *Scotland on Sunday*, *Scotsman*, *SFX*, *ShortList*, *The Stage and Television Today*, *Sun*, *Sunday Mail*, *Sunday Telegraph*, *The Sunday Times*, *Sydney Daily Telegraph*, *Time Out*, *The Times*, *Total Film*, *USA Today*, *Variety*, *Western Morning News*, *World Entertainment News Network*, TheWrap.com,

SELECTED
CREDITS

STAGE

2001: *11 June–8 September*
A MIDSUMMER NIGHT'S DREAM (Role: Demetrius)
Open Air Theatre, Regent's Park, London
Presented by: New Shakespeare Company
Revival of the play written by: William Shakespeare
Directed by: Alan Strachan
Cast included: Martin Turner (Theseus/Oberon), Rebecca
Johnson (Hippolyta/Titania), Paul Kemp (Philostrate/Puck),
Philip York (Egeus/Attendant to Oberon), Gideon Turner
(Lysander), Candida Benson (Helena), Rebecca Callard

(Hermia).

2001: *15 June–22 August*

LOVE'S LABOUR'S LOST (Role: Ferdinand, King of Navarre)

Open Air Theatre, Regent's Park, London

Presented by: New Shakespeare Company

Revival of the play written by: William Shakespeare

Directed by: Rachel Kavanaugh

Cast included: Adrian Schiller (Berowne), Gideon Turner (Longueville), Daniel Crowder (Dumaine), Candida Benson (Princess of France), Rebecca Johnson (Rosaline), Rebecca Callard (Maria), Lottie Mayor (Katherine), Martin Turner (Boyet).

2002: *5 June–5 September*

ROMEO AND JULIET (Role: Benvolio)

Open Air Theatre, Regent's Park, London

Presented by: New Shakespeare Company

Revival of the play written by: William Shakespeare

Directed by: Dominic Hill

Cast included: Alan Westaway (Romeo), Laura Main (Juliet), Adam Levy (Tybalt), John Hodgkinson (Mercutio).

2002: *10 June–7 September*

AS YOU LIKE IT (Role: Orlando)

Open Air Theatre, Regent's Park, London

Presented by: New Shakespeare Company

Revival of the play written by: William Shakespeare

Directed by: Rachel Kavanaugh

Cast included: Jon Cartwright (Duke Frederick), Caitlin Mottram (Celia), Rebecca Johnson (Rosalind), John Hodgkinson (Touchstone), Abigail Langham (Audrey).

2002: *25 July–3 September*
OH! WHAT A LOVELY WAR (Roles: Various)
Open Air Theatre, Regent's Park, London
Presented by: New Shakespeare Company
Revival of the musical entertainment by: Joan Littlewood, Charles Chilton, Gerry Raffles, and members of the original Theatre Workshop Cast
Directed by: Ian Talbot

2003: *15 May–28 June*
THE LADY FROM THE SEA (Role: Lyngstrand)
Almeida Theatre, London
Revival of the play by: Henrik Ibsen
Directed by: Trevor Nunn
Cast included: Natasha Richardson (Ellida), Claudie Blakley (Bolette), Geoffrey Hutchings (Ballested), Louisa Clein (Hilde), John Bowe (Dr Wangel), Tim McInnerny (Arnholm).

2005: *16 March–30 April*; 23 May–6 August***
HEDDA GABLER (Role: George Tesman)
*Almeida Theatre, London; **Duke of York's Theatre, London
Revival of the play by: Henrik Ibsen
Adapted and directed by: Richard Eyre
Cast included: Eve Best (Hedda Tesman), Gillian Raine

(Juliana Tesman), Sarah Flind (Berthe), Lisa Dillon (Thea Elvsted), Iain Glen (Judge Brack), Jamie Sives (Eilert Loevborg).

2006: *16 March–29 April*
PERIOD OF ADJUSTMENT (Role: George Haverstick)
Almeida Theatre, London
Revival of the play by: Tennessee Williams
Directed by: Howard Davies
Cast included: Lisa Dillon (Isabel Haverstick), Jared Harris (Ralph Bates), Sandy McDade (Dorothea Bates).

2007: *21 September–15 December*
RHINOCEROS (Role: Bérenger)
Royal Court Theatre, London
Revival of the play by: Eugène Ionesco
Directed by: Dominic Cooke
Cast included: Jasper Britton (Jean), Zawe Ashton (Daisy), Paul Chahidi (Dudard), Lloyd Hutchingson (Botard), Graham Turner (Monsieur Papillon).

2007: *1 November–15 December*
THE ARSONISTS (Role: Eisenring)
Royal Court Theatre, London
Revival of the play by: Max Frisch
Directed by: Ramin Gray
Cast included: Zawe Ashton (Anna), Will Keen (Biedermann), Paul Chahidi (Schmitz), Jacqueline Defferary (Babette).

2008: *24 April–7 June*
THE CITY (Role: Chris)
Royal Court Theatre, London
Directed by: Katie Mitchell
Written by: Martin Crimp
Cast includes: Hattie Morahan (Clair), Amanda Hale (Jenny), Child (Matilda Castrey or Ruby Douglas; alternate performances).

2008: *16–26 September*
CARYL CHURCHILL 70TH BIRTHDAY EVENT (Guest Reader)
Royal Court Theatre, London
'Far Away' reading
Directed by: Martin Crimp
Readers included: Deborah Findlay, Hattie Morahan.

2010: *1 June–11 August*
AFTER THE DANCE (Role: David Scott-Fowler)
Lyttelton Theatre, National Theatre, London
Presented by: National Theatre Company
Written by: Terence Rattigan
Directed by: Thea Sharrock
Cast included: Nancy Carroll (Joan Scott-Fowler), Adrian Scarborough (John Reid), Faye Castelow (Helen Banner), Giles Cooper (Dr George Banner), Pandora Colin (Julia Browne), John Heffernan (Peter Scott-Fowler), Jenny Galloway (Miss Potter), Juliet Howland (Moya Lexington),

Nicholas Lumley (Williams), Lachlan Nieboer (Cyril Carter), Giles Taylor (Lawrence Walters), Richard Teverson (Arthur Power).

2010: *14 November*
THE CHILDREN'S MONOLOGUES (Participant/Reader)
Old Vic, London
Produced and organised by: Danny Boyle
Monologues adapted and compiled by: Lynn Nottage, Bola Agbaje, Polly Stenham, Kwame Kwei-Armah, and others
Cast included: Nikki Amuka-Bird, Romola Garai, Tom Hiddleston, Sir Ben Kingsley, Eddie Redmayne, Samuel West.

2011: *22 February–2 May*
FRANKENSTEIN (Alternating roles: Victor Frankenstein/ The Creature)
National Theatre, London
Directed by: Danny Boyle
Adapted by: Nick Dear, based on the novel by Mary Shelley
Cast includes: Jonny Lee Miller (alternating roles: The Creature/Victor Frankenstein), Karl Johnson, Naomie Harris (Elizabeth Lavenza), Ella Smith, George Harris.

FORTHCOMING STAGE WORK

2015: *5 August – 31 October*
HAMLET (Hamlet)
Barbican, London

Directed by: Lyndsey Turner
Revival of the play written by: William Shakespeare
[Rest of cast unknown at time of writing.]

TELEVISION

2000: *30 January*
HEARTBEAT (Role: Charles)
ITV (Sunday, 2000–2100)
(Featured in one episode: 'The Good Doctor')
Directed by: Paul Walker.

2002: *8–9 June*
FIELDS OF GOLD (Role: Jeremy)
BBC1 (two parts: Saturday, 2105–2235; Sunday, 2105–2200)
Directed by: Bill Anderson
Produced by: Liza Marshall
Written by: Ronan Bennett, Alan Rusbridger
Cast included: Anna Friel (Lucia Merritt), Phil Davis (Roy Lodge), Max Beesley (Mark Hurst), James Fleet (Alan Buckley), Mark Strong (Dr Tolkin), Phyllis Logan (Rachel Greenlaw), Alphonsia Emmanuel (Karen Delage).

2002: *9 October*
TIPPING THE VELVET (Role: Freddy)
BBC2 (Wednesday, 2100–2200) (Cumberbatch features in Part 1 only of this three-part drama)

Directed by: Geoffrey Sax
Adapted by: Andrew Davies, from the novel by Sarah Waters
Cast included: Rachael Stirling (Nan Astley), Keeley Hawes
(Kitty Butler), Johnny Vegas (Gully Sutherland), Alexei Sayle
(Charles Frobisher).

2002: *19–20 October*
SILENT WITNESS (Role: Warren Reid)
BBC1 (Saturday, 2105–2205; Sunday, 2100–2200)
(Cumberbatch features in the two-part story, 'Tell No Tales')
Directed by: John Duthie

2003: *9 May*
CAMBRIDGE SPIES (Role: Edward Hand)
*BBC4 (Friday, 2200–2300)(Cumberbatch features in Part 2
only of this four-part drama)*
Directed by: Tim Fywell
Cast included: Toby Stephens (Kim Philby), Tom Hollander
(Guy Burgess), Rupert Penry-Jones (Donald Maclean),
Samuel West (Anthony Blunt).
*[This episode was first broadcast on terrestrial television on
BBC2 the following Friday, 16 May 2003, at 2100]*

2003: *2 June*
SPOOKS (Role: Jim North)
BBC1 (Monday, 2100–2200)
Features in the episode 'Legitimate Targets'
Directed by: Bharat Nalluri

2003: *29 June–6 July; 19 July–9 August*
FORTYSOMETHING (Role: Rory Slippery)
ITV1 (Sundays, 2100–2200 (eps 1 and 2); Saturdays, around 2300–0000 (eps 3–6))
(Cumberbatch appears in **all six episodes** of the series)
Directed by: Hugh Laurie (eps 1 and 2), Nic Phillips (eps 3–6)
Series cast included: Hugh Laurie (Dr Paul Slippery), Anna Chancellor (Estelle Slippery), Neil Henry (Daniel Slippery), Joe Van Moyland (Edwin Slippery), Lolita Chakrabati (Surinder), Peter Capaldi (Ronnie Pilfrey), Sheila Hancock (Gwendolen)
(After two episodes, due to unexpectedly low ratings, the series was shifted to a late-night slot on Saturdays, and replaced in its Sunday peak time slot by repeats of *Midsomer Murders*.)

2004: *18–20 February*
DUNKIRK (Role: Lt Jimmy Langley (all episodes))
BBC2 (Wednesday–Friday, 2100–2200)
1: Retreat
2: Evacuation
3: Survival
Directed by: Alex Holmes
Cast included: Timothy Dalton (Narrator), Simon Russell Beale (Winston Churchill).

2004: *11 April*
HEARTBEAT (Role: Toby Fisher)
ITV1 (Sunday, 2000–2100)
Features in the episode **'No Hard Feelings'**

Directed by: Judith Dine
2004: *13 April*
HAWKING (Role: Stephen Hawking)
BBC2 (Tuesday, 2100–2230)
Directed by: Philip Martin
Cast included: Michael Brandon (Arno Penzias), Tom
Hodgkins (Bob Wilson), Peter Firth (Fred Hoyle), Lisa Dillon
(Jane Wilde), John Sessions (Dennis Sciama), Tom Ward
(Roger Penrose), Phoebe Nicholls (Isobel Hawking), Adam
Godley (Frank Hawking), Bertie Carvel (George Ellis), Alice
Eve (Martha Guthrie), Carolina Giammetta (Lidia Sciama).

2005: *25 February; 3 March*
NATHAN BARLEY (Role: Robin)
Channel 4 (Fridays, 2200–2230)
(Cumberbatch appears in **episodes 3 and 4 only** of this six-
part series)
Directed by: Chris Morris
Written by: Chris Morris and Charlie Brooker
Main Cast: Nicholas Burns (Nathan Barley), Julian Barratt
(Dan Ashcroft), Claire Keelan (Claire Ashcroft), Richard
Ayaode (Ned Smanks), Spencer Brown (Rufus Onslatt),
Charlie Condou (Jonatton Yeah?), Noel Fielding (Jones),
Stephen Mangan (Rod Senseless), Rhys Thomas (Toby), Ben
Whishaw (Pingu)

2005: *6–20 July*
**TO THE ENDS OF THE EARTH (Role: Edmund Talbot
(all episodes))**

BBC2 *(Wednesdays, 2100–2230)*
Directed by: David Attwood
Cast included: Jared Harris (Captain Anderson), Jamie Sives (1st Lieutenant Summers), Sam Neill (Mr Prettiman), Denise Black (Mrs Brocklebank), Richard McCabe (Mr Brocklebank), Victoria Hamilton (Miss Granham), Paula Jennings (Zenobia), Robert Hobbs (Lieutenant Cumbersham), Daniel Evans (Parson Colley), Charles Dance (Sir Henry Somerset), Cheryl Campbell (Lady Somerset).

2005: *5 September*
THE MAN WHO PREDICTED 9/11 (Narrator)
Channel 4 (Monday, 2100–2200)
Produced by: Steve Humphries

2005: *31 October–5 December*
BROKEN NEWS (Role: Will Parker (all episodes))
BBC2 (Mondays, 2130–2200)
1: Tomato Flu
2: Missing Island
3: Half Way There Day
4: Crime
5: Bolivian Crisis
6: Hijack
Directed by: John Morton
Produced by: Paul Schlesinger
Written by: John Morton and Tony Roche
Series cast included: Claudia Christian (Julia Regan), Duncan Duff (Richard Pritchard), Sharon Horgan (Katie

Tate), Kim Wall (Phil Curdridge), Tom Goodman-Hill (Joe Reed), Sarah Hadland (Claire), Phil Nichol (Josh Cashman), Darren Boyd (Nick Burnham).

2007: *23 September*
STUART: A LIFE BACKWARDS (Role: Alexander Masters)
BBC2 (Sunday, 2100–2230)
Directed by: David Attwood
Cast included: Tom Hardy (Stuart Shorter), Nicola Duffett (Judith Shorter), Claire-Louise Cordwell (Karen Shorter), Edna Doré (Gran), Frank Mills (Granpa), Candis Nergaard (Sophie).

2008: *6–20 January*
PICTURE THIS (Narrator)
Channel 4 (Sundays, 1900–2000)
Produced and directed by: Tom Coveney
Panel: Martin Parr, Brett Rogers, Alex Proud

2008: *17 February–16 March*
THE LAST ENEMY (Role: Stephen Ezard (all episodes))
BBC1 (Sundays, 2100–2225 (ep 1), 2100–2200 (eps 2–6))
Directed by: Iain B. MacDonald
Series cast included: Max Beesley (Michael Ezard), Anamaria Marinca (Yasim Anwar), Robert Carlyle (David Russell), David Harewood (Patrick Nye), Eva Birthistle (Eleanor Brooke), Geraldine James (Barbara Turney), Christopher Fulford (George Gibbon), Iona Serban (Nadir).

2009: *10 May–14 June*
SOUTH PACIFIC (Narrator (all episodes))
BBC2 (Sundays, 2030–2130)
1: Ocean of Islands
2: Castaways
3: Endless Blue
4: Ocean of Volcanos
5: Strange Islands
6: Fragile Paradise
Series Producer: Huw Cordey
Executive Producer: Fiona Pitcher
[The series was broadcast in the USA under the title **Wild Pacific**.*]*

2009: *12 August*
THEATRE LIVE!: THE TURNING POINT (Role: Guy Burgess)
Sky Arts 1 (Wednesday, 2100–2200)
Directed by: Fiona Laird
Written by: Michael Dobbs
Series presented by: Sandi Toksvig
Cast included: Matthew Marsh (Winston Churchill).

2009: *13 September*
AGATHA CHRISTIE'S MARPLE: MURDER IS EASY (Role: Luke Fitzwilliam)
ITV1 (Sunday, 2000–2200)
Directed by: Hettie Macdonald

Cast included: Julia McKenzie (Miss Marple), Steve Pemberton (Henry Wake), Shirley Henderson (Honoria Waynflete), Sylvia Syms (Lavinia Pinkerton), James Lance (Dr Geoffrey Thomas), Hugo Speer (James Abbot), Anna Chancellor (Lydia Horton), Jemma Redgrave (Jessie Humbleby), David Haig (Major Hugh Horton), Tim Brooke-Taylor (Dr Edward Humbleby).

2009: *6–13 December*
SMALL ISLAND (Role: Bernard)
BBC1 (Sundays, 2100–2230)
Directed by: John Alexander
Cast included: Naomie Harris (Hortense), David Oyelowo (Gilbert), Ruth Wilson (Queenie), Ashley Walters (Michael).

2010: *5 April*
VAN GOGH: PAINTED WITH WORDS (Role: Vincent Van Gogh)
BBC1 (Monday, 1710–1830)
Directed by: Andrew Hutton
Presented and produced by: Alan Yentob
Cast included: Jamie Parker (Theo Van Gogh), Aidan McArdle (Paul Gauguin), Rowena Cooper (Anna Van Gogh), Christopher Good (Theodorus Van Gogh).

2010: *9–23 May*
STEPHEN HAWKING'S UNIVERSE (Narrator)
Discovery Channel (UK) (Sundays, 2100–2200)
Writer and co-narrator: Stephen Hawking

Directors: Martin Williams, Nathan Williams, Ian Riddick *(The three-part series had premiered on the Discovery Channel in the USA on 25 April 2010. Its UK terrestrial premiere came via Channel 4 from 18 September–2 October 2010.)*

2010–present:
SHERLOCK (Role: Sherlock Holmes)
BBC1
Unaired Pilot (made 2009; included on Series 1 DVD, released 30 August 2010)
Directed by: Coky Giedroyc
Written by: Steven Moffat
Cast included: Martin Freeman (Dr John Watson), Una Stubbs (Mrs Hudson), Rupert Graves (Inspector Lestrade), Zawe Ashton (Sgt Sally Donovan), Phil Davis (Jeff), Louise Brealey (Molly Hooper).
Series 1 (July–August 2010):
1.1: A Study in Pink *(25 July 2010; Sunday, 2100–2230)*
Directed by: Paul McGuigan
Written by: Steven Moffat
Cast included: Martin Freeman (Dr John Watson), Una Stubbs (Mrs Hudson), Rupert Graves (Inspector Lestrade), Vinette Robinson (Sgt Sally Donovan), Phil Davis (Jeff), Louise Brealey (Molly Hooper).
1.2: The Blind Banker *(1 August 2010; Sunday, 2030–2200)*
Directed by: Euros Lyn
Written by: Steve Thompson
Cast included: Martin Freeman (Dr John Watson), Una

Stubbs (Mrs Hudson), Louise Brealey (Molly Hooper), Zöe Telford (Sarah), Paul Chequer (DI Dimmock), Gemma Chan (Soo Lin Yao).

1.3: The Great Game *(8 August 2010; Sunday, 2100–2230)*
Directed by: Paul McGuigan
Written by: Mark Gatiss
Cast included: Martin Freeman (Dr John Watson), Una Stubbs (Mrs Hudson), Rupert Graves (Inspector Lestrade), Vinette Robinson (Sgt Sally Donovan), Mark Gatiss (Mycroft), Louise Brealey (Molly Hooper), Andrew Scott (Moriarty), Zöe Telford (Sarah), John Sessions (Kenny Prince), Haydn Gwynne (Miss Wenceslas).

Series 2: January 2012
2.1: A Scandal in Belgravia *(1 January 2012; Sunday, 2010–2140)*
Directed by: Paul McGuigan
Written by: Steven Moffat
Cast included: Martin Freeman (Dr John Watson), Una Stubbs (Mrs Hudson), Rupert Graves (Inspector Lestrade), Mark Gatiss (Mycroft Holmes), Andrew Scott (Jim Moriarty), Louise Brealey (Molly Hooper), Lara Pulver (Irene Adler), Oona Chaplin (Jeanette), Danny Webb (DI Carter)
2.2: The Hounds of Baskerville *(8 January 2012; Sunday, 2030–2200)*
Directed by: Paul McGuigan
Written by: Steven Moffat
Cast included: Martin Freeman (Dr John Watson), Una Stubbs (Mrs Hudson), Rupert Graves (Inspector Lestrade), Mark Gatiss (Mycroft Holmes), Andrew Scott (Jim Moriarty), Louise

Brealey (Molly Hooper), Russell Tovey (Henry Knight), Amelia Bullmore (Dr Stapleton), Clive Mantle (Dr Frankland).

2.3: The Reichenbach Fall *(15 January 2012; Sunday, 2030–2200)*

Directed by: Toby Haynes

Written by: Steve Thompson

Cast included: Martin Freeman (Dr John Watson), Una Stubbs (Mrs Hudson), Rupert Graves (Inspector Lestrade), Mark Gatiss (Mycroft Holmes), Andrew Scott (Jim Moriarty), Louise Brealey (Molly Hooper), Katherine Parkinson (Kitty Riley), Vinette Robinson (Sgt Sally Donovan), Tanya Moodie (Ella), Jonathan Aris (Anderson).

Mini-Special: December 2013

Many Happy Returns (25 December 2013; originally available on BBC iPlayer)

Written by: Mark Gatiss and Steven Moffat

Cast included: Martin Freeman (Dr John Watson), Rupert Graves (DI Lestrade), Jonathan Aris (Anderson)

Series 3: January 2014

3.1: The Empty Hearse *(1 January 2014; Wednesday, 2030–2200)*

Directed by: Jeremy Lovering

Written by: Mark Gatiss

Cast included: Martin Freeman (Dr John Watson), Una Stubbs (Mrs Hudson), Rupert Graves (DI Lestrade), Mark Gatiss (Mycroft Holmes), Amanda Abbington (Mary Morstan), Louise Brealey (Molly Hooper), David Fynn (Howard Shilcott)

3.2: The Sign of Three *(5 January 2014; Sunday, 2100-2225)*

Directed by: Colm McCarthy
Written by: Steve Thompson
Cast included: Martin Freeman (Dr John Watson), Una Stubbs (Mrs Hudson), Rupert Graves (DI Lestrade), Mark Gatiss (Mycroft Holmes), Amanda Abbington (Mary Morstan), Vinette Robinson (Sgt Sally Donovan), Lara Pulver (Irene Adler), Louise Brealey (Molly Hooper), Alastair Petrie (James Sholto)
3.3: His Last Vow *(12 January 2014; Sunday, 2100-2230)*
Directed by: Nick Hurran
Written by: Steven Moffat
Cast includes: Martin Freeman (Dr John Watson), Una Stubbs (Mrs Hudson), Rupert Graves (DI Lestrade), Mark Gatiss (Mycroft Holmes), Amanda Abbington (Mary Morstan), Louise Brealey (Molly Hooper), Lars Mikkelsen (Charles Augustus Magnussen), Lindsay Duncan (Lady Smallwood)

2010: *14 October*
HAVE I GOT NEWS FOR YOU (Guest Host)
BBC1 (Thursday, 2100–2130)
Director: Paul Wheeler
Team captains: Ian Hislop, Paul Merton
Guests: Victoria Coren, Jon Richardson

2011: *28 July*
THE RATTIGAN ENIGMA: BENEDICT CUMBER-BATCH ON TERENCE RATTIGAN (Presenter/Narrator)
BBC4 (Thursday, 2100–2200)

Produced and directed by: Sally Thomson
Executive producer: Michael Poole
Contributors: Adrian Brown, Michael Darlow, Terence Davies, Jean Dorney, David Hare, Benedict Nightingale, Thea Sharrock.

2011: *7 August (USA)*
CURIOSITY: DID GOD CREATE THE UNIVERSE?
(Narrator)
Discovery Channel (USA) (Sunday, 2000–2100 EST)
Executive producers: Simon Andreae, Alan Eyres, John Smithson, Susan Winslow, Ben Bowie
Presented by: Stephen Hawking.

2012: *17 March*
ARENA: THE DREAMS OF WILLIAM GOLDING
(Reader)
BBC2 (Saturday, 2130–2300)
Directed by: Adam Low
Contributors included: John Carey, Stephen King, Nigel Williams.

2012: *13–27 September*
STEPHEN HAWKING'S GRAND DESIGN (Narrator)
Discovery UK (Thursdays, 2000–2100)
1: The Meaning of Life
2: The Key to the Cosmos
3: Did God Create the Universe?
Directed by: Dan Clifton, Matthew Huntley
With: Stephen Hawking

2012: *24 August–21 September*
PARADE'S END (Role: Christopher Tietjens)
BBC2 (Fridays, 2100–2230)
Directed by: Susanna White
Written by: Tom Stoppard, based on the novels of Ford Madox Ford
Series cast included: Rebecca Hall (Sylvia Tietjens), Roger Allam (General Campion), Adelaide Clemens (Valentine Wannop), Rupert Everett (Mark Tietjens), Miranda Richardson (Mrs Wannop), Sasha Waddell (Glorvina), Janet McTeer (Mrs Satterthwaite), Anne-Marie Duff (Edith Duchemin), Patrick Kennedy (McKechnie), Rufus Sewell (Reverend Duchemin), Stephen Graham (Vincent MacMaster).

2012: *31 October*
FRANKENSTEIN: A MODERN MYTH (Narrator/ Contributor)
Channel 4 (Monday, 2305–0010)
Directed by: Adam Low
Readers: David Bradley, Daniel Ings, Sarah Mowat
Contributors: Dr Gwen Adshead, Philip Ball, Danny Boyle, Nick Dear, Daisy Hay, Stephen Hebron, Philip Hoare, Jonny Lee Miller, Miranda Seymour, Helen Wallace, John Waters.

2012: *8–15 November*
WWI'S TUNNELS OF DEATH (Narrator)
Channel 5 (Thursdays, 2000–2100)
1: The Killing Fields (8 November 2012)
2: Earthquaking the Ridge (15 November 2012)

Directed by: John Hayes-Fisher
Experts: Alexandra Churchill, Peter Doyle, Paul Reed.

2013: *10 February (USA)*
THE SIMPSONS (Role: Voice of Alan Rickman/Prime Minister)
Fox (USA) (Sunday, 2000–2030)
(Season 24, Episode 12: **'Love is a Many Splintered Thing'**)
Directed by: Michael Polcino
Voice cast included: Dan Castellaneta, Julie Kavner, Nancy Cartwright, Yeardley Smith, Harry Shearer.
Guest voices included: Zooey Deschanel (Mary Spuckeler), Max Weinberg, Robert A. Caro.

2013: *2 November*
LIVE FROM THE NATIONAL THEATRE: 50 YEARS ON STAGE (Role: Rosencrantz)
BBC2 (Saturday, 2100–2315)
Directed by: Nicholas Hytner
Participants included: James Corden, Judi Dench, Ralph Fiennes, Derek Jacobi, Helen Mirren, Maggie Smith, Roger Allam, Simon Russell Beale, Frances de la Tour, Christopher Eccleston, Alex Jennings, Rory Kinnear, Adrian Lester, Anna Maxwell Martin, Andrew Scott, Penelope Wilton

FILM

2002
HILLS LIKE WHITE ELEPHANTS (Role: The Man)
Written and directed by: Paige Cameron
Cast included: Greg Wise (The American), Emma Griffiths Main (The Girl), Todd Boyce (The Husband), Paige Cameron (The Woman).

2003
TO KILL A KING (Role: Royalist)
Directed by: Mike Barker
Cast included: Tim Roth (Oliver Cromwell), Dougray Scott (Sir Thomas Fairfax), Olivia Williams (Lady Anne Fairfax), James Bolam (Denzil Holles), Corin Redgrave (Lord de Vere), Finbar Lynch (Cousin Henry), Julian Rhind-Tutt (James), Adrian Scarborough (Sergeant Joyce), Jeremy Swift (Earl of Whitby), Rupert Everett (King Charles I).

2006
AMAZING GRACE (Role: William Pitt the Younger)
Directed by: Michael Apted
Cast included: Ioan Gruffudd (William Wilberforce), Albert Finney (John Newton), Michael Gambon (Charles Fox), Youssou N'Dour (Oloudah Equiano), Bill Paterson (Lord Dundas), Toby Jones (Duke of Clarence), Ciaran Hinds (Lord Tarleton), Romola Garai (Barbara Spooner), Rufus Sewell (Thomas Clarkson).

2006
STARTER FOR 10 (Role: Patrick Watts)
Directed by: Tom Vaughan
Cast included: James McAvoy (Brian Jackson), Alice Eve (Alice Harbinson), Rebecca Hall (Rebecca Epstein), Mark Gatiss (Bamber Gascoigne), Charles Dance (Michael Harbinson), Lindsay Duncan (Rose Harbinson), Dominic Cooper (Spencer), James Gaddas (Martin Jackson), Catherine Tate (Julie Jackson), James Corden (Tone).

2007
INSEPARABLE (Roles: Joe/Charlie)
Directed by: Nick White
Cast included: Natalie Press (Jean), Dylan Byrne (Son), Bijan Daneshmand (Doctor), J.D. Kelleher, Richard Shanks (Heavies).

2007
ATONEMENT (Role: Paul Marshall)
Directed by: Joe Wright
Cast included: James McAvoy (Robbie Turner), Keira Knightley (Cecilia Tallis), Harriet Walter (Cecilia Tallis), Brenda Blethyn (Grace Turner).

2008
THE OTHER BOLEYN GIRL (Role: William Carey)
Directed by: Justin Chadwick
Cast included: Mark Rylance (Sir Thomas Boleyn), Kristin

Scott Thomas (Lady Elizabeth Howard), Jim Sturgess (George Boleyn), Natalie Portman (Anne Boleyn), Scarlett Johansson (Mary Boleyn), Eric Bana (Henry Tudor).

2009
BURLESQUE FAIRYTALES (Role: Henry Clark)
Written and directed by: Susan Luciani
Cast included: Anna Andresen (The Mermaid), Stephen Campbell Moore (Peter Blythe-Smith), Jim Carter (The Compère), Lindsay Duncan (Ice Queen), Barbara Flynn (Mrs Argyle), Sophie Hunter (Annabel Blythe-Smith), Anna Lanyon (Queen of Hearts), Kevin Howarth (Jimmy Harrison).

2009
CREATION (Role: Joseph Hooker)
Directed by: Jon Amiel
Cast included: Paul Bettany (Charles Darwin), Martha West (Annie Darwin), Jennifer Connelly (Emma Darwin), Jeremy Northam (Reverend Innes), Toby Jones (Thomas Huxley).

2010
THE WHISTLEBLOWER (Role: Nick Kaufman)
Directed by: Larysa Kondracki
Cast included: Rachel Weisz (Kathryn Bolkovac), Vanessa Redgrave (Madeleine Rees), Monica Bellucci (Laura Leviani).

2010

FOUR LIONS (Role: Negotiator)
Directed by: Chris Morris
Cast included: Kayvan Novak (Waj), Nigel Lindsay (Barry), Riz Ahmed (Omar), Adeel Akhtar (Faisal), Preeya Kalidas (Sofia), William El-Gardi (Khalid), Mohammad Aqil (Mahmood), Craig Parkinson (Matt), Arsher Ali (Hassan), Alex Macqueen (Malcolm Storge MP), Julia Davis (Alice), Wasim Zakir (Ahmed).

2010
THIRD STAR (Role: James)
Directed by: Hattie Dalton
Cast included: Tom Burke (Davy), J.J. Feild (Miles), Adam Robertson (Bill).

2011
TINKER TAILOR SOLDIER SPY (Role: Peter Guillam)
Directed by: Tomas Alfredson
Cast included: Mark Strong (Jim Prideaux), John Hurt (Control), Colin Firth (Bill Haydon), Gary Oldman (George Smiley), Mark Strong (Jim Prideaux), Tom Hardy (Ricki Tarr), Kathy Burke (Connie Sachs), Toby Jones (Percy Alleline), Ciaran Hinds (Roy Bland), David Dencik (Toby Esterhase), Svetlana Khodchenkova (Irina), Stephen Graham (Jerry Westerby), Simon McBurney (Oliver Lacon).

2011
WAR HORSE (Role: Maj Jamie Stewart)
Directed by: Steven Spielberg

Cast included: Jeremy Irvine (Albert Narracott), Emily Watson (Rose Narracott), Peter Mullan (Ted Narracott), David Thewlis (Lyons), Matt Milne (Andrew), Patrick Kennedy (Lt Charlie Waverly), Robert Emms (David Lyons), Tom Hiddleston (Capt Nicholls), David Kross (Gunther), Celine Buckens (Emilie), Eddie Marsan (Sgt Fry).

2011
WRECKERS (Role: David)
Written and Directed by: D.R. Hood
Cast included: Claire Foy (Dawn), Shaun Evans (Nick), Peter McDonald (Gary), Sinead Matthews (Sharon), June Watson (Miss Hedges), Georgie Smith (Gemma).

2012
GIRLFRIEND IN A COMA (documentary) (Role: Voice of Dante)
Produced and Directed by: Annalisa Piras
Featuring: Bill Emmott.

2012
THE HOBBIT: AN UNEXPECTED JOURNEY (Role: Necromancer)
Directed by: Peter Jackson
Cast included: Martin Freeman (Bilbo Baggins), Ian McKellen (Gandalf), Orlando Bloom (Legolas), Cate Blanchett (Galadriel), Andy Serkis (Gollum), Sylvester McCoy (Radogast the Brown), Stephen Fry (Master of Laketown), Barry Humphries (Great Goblin), Richard Armitage (Thorin), Elijah

Wood (Frodo), Christopher Lee (Saruman), Ken Stott (Balin).

2012

ELECTRIC CINEMA: HOW TO BEHAVE (SHORT FILM) (Role: Humphrey Bogart)

Directed by: Marcel Grant

Cast included: Alexander Armstrong, Gemma Arterton, James Corden, Natalie Dormer, Harry Enfield, Rebecca Ferdinando, Emilia Fox, Tom Hollander, Toby Longworth, Nigella Lawson, Michael McIntyre, Rafe Spall, Olivia Williams.

2013

STAR TREK INTO DARKNESS (Role: Khan)

Directed by: J.J. Abrams

Cast included: Simon Pegg (Scotty), Zoe Saldana (Lt Uhuru), Chris Pine (Captain Kirk), Zachary Quinto (Spock), Alice Eve (Dr Carol Marcus), Noel Clarke (Thomas Harewood), Karl Urban (Dr. 'Bones' McCoy), Anton Yelchin (Chekov), John Cho (Sulu), Bruce Greenwood (Pike), Peter Weller (Marcus).

2013

12 YEARS A SLAVE (Role: William Ford)

Directed by: Steve McQueen

Cast included: Chiwetel Ejiofor (Solomon Northup), Dwight Henry (Uncle Abram), Bryan Batt (Judge Turner), Michael Fassbender (Edwin Epps), Brad Pitt (Bass), Paul Giamatti (Freeman).

2013

THE FIFTH ESTATE (Role: Julian Assange)

Directed by: Bill Condon
Cast included: Daniel Bruhl (Daniel Domscheit-Berg), Peter Capaldi (Alan Rusbridger), Dan Stevens (Ian Katz), David Thewlis (Nick Davies), Alexander Beyer (Marcel Rosenbach), Alicia Vikander (Anke Domscheit).

2013
AUGUST: OSAGE COUNTY (Role: 'Little' Charles Aiken)
Directed by: John Wells
Cast included: Meryl Streep (Violet Weston), Julia Roberts (Barbara Weston), Ewan McGregor (Bill Fordham), Chris Cooper (Charles Aiken), Abigail Breslin (Jean Fordham), Juliette Lewis (Karen Weston), Margo Martindale (Mattie Fae Aiken), Dermot Mulroney (Steve).

2013
LITTLE FAVOUR (short film) (Role: Wallace)
Written and directed by: Patrick Viktor Monroe
Cast included: Colin Salmon (James), Nick Moran (Logan), Julian Shaw (Jimmy), Robert Shannon (Morgan).

2013
THE HOBBIT: THE DESOLATION OF SMAUG (Roles: Smaug/Necromancer)
Directed by: Peter Jackson
Cast includes: Martin Freeman (Bilbo Baggins), Ian McKellen (Gandalf), Richard Armitage (Thorin Oakenshield), Luke Evans (Bard the Bowman), Lee Pace (Thrandruil), Cate

Blanchett (Galadriel), Andy Serkis (Gollum), Christopher Lee (Saruman), Hugo Weaving (Elrond), Billy Connolly (Dain Ironfoot), Orlando Bloom (Legolas), Manu Bennett (Azog), Evangeline Lilly (Tauriel), Stephen Fry (Master of Laketown), James Nesbitt (Bofur), Ian Holm (Old Bilbo).

2014

THE IMITATION GAME (Role: Alan Turing)

Directed by: Morten Tyldum

Cast includes: Keira Knightley (Joan Clarke), Matthew Goode (Hugh Alexander), Mark Strong (Maj. Gen. Stewart Menzies), Charles Dance (Cdr. Alastair Denniston), Matthew Beard (Peter Hilton), Rory Kinnear (Detective Nook), Allen Leech (John Cairncross), James Northcote (Jack Good).

2014

PENGUINS OF MADAGASCAR (Role: Classified (Voice))

Directed by: Simon J. Smith, Eric Darnell

Voice cast includes: Tom McGrath (Skipper), Chris Miller (Kowalski), Conrad Vernon (Rico), Christopher Knights (Private), John Malkovich (Dave), Ken Jeong (Short Fuse), Annet Mahendru (Eve).

2014

THE HOBBIT: THE BATTLE OF THE FIVE ARMIES (Role: Smaug/Necromancer)

Directed by: Peter Jackson

Cast includes: Martin Freeman (Bilbo Baggins), Ian McKellen (Gandalf), Evangeline Lilly (Tauriel), Cate Blanchett

(Galadriel), Richard Armitage (Thorin Oakenshield), Billy Connolly (Dain), Hugo Weaving (Elrond), Christopher Lee (Saruman the White).

FORTHCOMING FILMS

2015 (tbc)
BLACK MASS (Role: Bill Bulger)
Written and directed by: Scott Cooper
Cast scheduled to include: Sienna Miller, Johnny Depp, Joel Edgerton, Kevin Bacon, Peter Sarsgaard, Juno Temple, Dakota Johnson.

2015 (tbc)
THE LOST CITY OF Z (Role: Col. Percival Fawcett)
Directed by: James Gray
Cast scheduled to include: Sienna Miller, Robert Pattinson.

2016 (tbc)
MAGIK (Role: Lewis Clark (voice))
Directed by: Stephen Wallis
Cast scheduled to include: Matthew Goode, Jim Broadbent, Tom Riley, Samantha Morton.

2016 (tbc)
DOCTOR STRANGE (Role: Dr. Stephen Strange)
Directed by: Scott Derrickson

2016 (tbc)
FLYING HORSE (Role: Harry Larkyns)
Written and directed by: Gary Oldman
Cast scheduled to include: Ralph Fiennes, Gary Oldman, Amanda Seyfried.

2017 (tbc)
JUNGLE BOOK: ORIGINS (Role: Shere Khan)
Directed by: Andy Serkis
Cast scheduled to include: Christian Bale, Cate Blanchett, Naomie Harris, Tom Hollander, Peter Mullan, Andy Serkis.

Date Unknown (tbc)
THE YELLOW BIRDS (Role: Sergeant Sterling)
Written and directed by: David Lowery
Cast scheduled to include: Tye Sheridan, Will Poulter.

RADIO

2003: *15–19, 22–26 September*
WOMAN'S HOUR DRAMA: MANSFIELD PARK (Role: Edmund (all episodes))
BBC Radio 4 (Mondays–Fridays, 1045–1100, repeated 1945–2000)
Directed by: Sally Avens
Cast included: Amanda Root (Jane Austen), Felicity Jones (Fanny), Tim Pigott-Smith (Sir Thomas), Liza Sadovy (Lady

Bertram), Julia McKenzie (Mrs Norris), David Tennant (Tom), Toby Jones (Rushworth), Susan Lynch (Mary), James Callis (Henry), Kate Fleetwood (Maria), Gareth Corke (Yates).

2003: *13 December*
PLAY OF THE WEEK: THE COCKTAIL PARTY (Role: Peter Quilpe)
BBC World Service (Sunday, 1830–2000 GMT)
By: T.S. Eliot
Directed by: Marion Nancarrow
Cast included: Ian McDiarmid.

2004: *5 June*
THE SATURDAY PLAY: THE BIGGEST SECRET (Role: Captain Rob Collins)
BBC Radio 4 (Saturday, 1515–1700)
Produced by: Jeremy Howe
Cast included: Juliet Stevenson (Narrator), Claudia Harrison (Cpl Cunningham), Danny Webb (Jack), Kaye Wragg (Gloria), Joseph Tremain (Ray), Ben Tibber (Tim), Colin Stinton (Gen. Eisenhower), Bertie Carvel (Flt. Lt. Parker), Alice Hart (Rosie), Emily Chennery (Lilly), Ricci Harnett (Eddie), Philip Fox (Monty).
[The play was broadcast as part of a day of programmes commemorating the 60th anniversary of D Day.]

2004: *5–9, 12–16 July*
A BOOK AT BEDTIME: THE SURGEON'S MATE
(Reader (all parts))
BBC Radio 4 (Mondays–Fridays, 2245–2300)
By: Patrick O'Brian
Abridged and produced by: Lisa Osborne

2004: *11 August*
AFTERNOON PLAY: KEPLER (Role: Johannes Kepler)
BBC Radio 4 (Wednesday, 1415–1500)
By: John Banville
Directed by: Gemma McMullan
Cast included: Alun Armstrong (Tycho Brahe), Arabella Weir (Barbara Kepler), Gillian Kearney (Sophie), Scott Handy (Longberg), Geoffrey Beevers (Rudolph II), Kenny Baker (Jeppe), Marcella Riordan (Christine), Hannah R. Gordon (Regina), Simon Imrie (Messenger), Kevin Jackson (Court Official).

2004: *23–27 August*
A BOOK AT BEDTIME: MR NORRIS CHANGES
TRAINS (Reader (all parts))
BBC Radio 4 (Monday–Friday, 2245–2300)
By: Christopher Isherwood

2004: *28–29 August*
THE ODYSSEY (Role: Telemachus)
BBC Radio 4

Part 1: 28 August 2004 *(Saturday, 1430–1600)*
Part 2: 28 August 2004 *(Saturday, 2100–2230)*
Part 3: 29 August 2004 *(Saturday, 1500–1600)*
By: Homer, dramatised by: Simon Armitage
Directed by: Janet Whitaker
Cast included: Amanda Redman (Penelope), Tim McInnerny (Odysseus), Janet McTeer (Athena), Frances Barber (Circe), John Wood (Zeus), Mary Wimbush (Eurycleia), Danny Webb (Antinous), Geoffrey Whitehead (King Alcinous), Cheryl Campbell (Queen Arete), Jonathan Keeble (Eurymathus), Barrie Rutter (Cyclops), Adjoa Andon (Calypso).

2004: *13 September*
HEARTS OF OAK: THE FAR SIDE OF THE WORLD
(Role: Narrator)
BBC Radio 4 (Monday, 1530–1545)
By: Patrick O'Brian.

2005: *7 March*
BEYOND THE SURGERY: BAPTISM BY ROTATION
(Reader)
BBC Radio 4 (Monday, 1530–1545)
By: Mikhail Bulgakov, translated by Michael Glenny
[This was the first in a series of four readings (broadcast daily) about authors who had practised as doctors before concentrating on writing. The working title of the series was 'Medical Humanities'.]

2005: *1–8 May, 29 May–5 June*
THE CLASSIC SERIAL: THE RAJ QUARTET (Role: Nigel Rowan)
BBC Radio 4 (Sundays, 1500–1600, repeated following Saturdays, 2100–2200)
Cumberbatch appeared in **episodes 4, 5, 8 and 9** of this nine-part dramatisation.

The Day of the Scorpion (episodes 4–6; Cumberbatch appeared in episodes 4 and 5 only)
By: Paul Scott, dramatised by: Shelley Silas
Produced and directed by: Jeremy Mortimer
Cast included: Lia Williams (Sarah), Geraldine James (Mildred), Alex Tregear (Susan), Nicholas Boulton (Teddie), Mark Bazeley (Ronald), Irene Sutcliffe (Lady Manners), Gary Waldhorn (Count Bronowski), Selina Griffiths (Fenny), Nadim Sawalha (Pandit), Prasanna Puwanarajah (Hari), Bhaskar Patel (Gopal), Marcia Warren (Barbie), Margaret Tyzack (Mabel), Nina Wadia (Aunt Shalina).

A Division of the Spoils (episodes 8–9; Cumberbatch appeared in episodes 8 and 9 only)
By: Paul Scott, dramatised by: Shelley Silas
Produced and directed by: Sally Avens
Cast included: Lia Williams (Sarah), Jeremy Northam (Guy), Gary Waldhorn (Count Bronowski), Shiv Grewal (Ahmed), Mark Bazeley (Ronald), Hugh Dickson (Col. Layton), Matthew Thomas-Davies (Edward), Alex Tregear (Susan), Sam D'Astor (Mak), Stuart McLoughlin (Sergeant).
[The four Scott novels spread across the nine parts of the

serial were as follows:

10–24 April 2005 (parts 1–3): The Jewel in the Crown

1–15 May 2005 (parts 4–6): The Day of the Scorpion
[Cumberbatch appeared in parts 4 and 5 only]

22 May 2005 (part 7): The Towers of Silence

29 May–5 June 2005 (parts 8–9): A Division of the Spoils
[Cumberbatch appeared in parts 8 and 9 only].

2005: *2 July*
FIELDSTUDY: THE FIELD (Reader)
BBC Radio 4 (Saturday, 0030–0045)
By: Rachel Seiffert, abridged by Richard Hamilton
Produced by: Elizabeth Allard.

2005: *12–16, 19–23 September*
A BOOK AT BEDTIME: LE PÈRE GORIOT (Reader)
BBC Radio 4 (Mondays–Fridays, 2245–2300)
By: Honoré de Balzac, abridged by Sally Marmion
Producer: Di Spiers
(Written in 1835, as part of Balzac's series of novels, *La Comedie Humaine*.)

2005: *21 September*
AFTERNOON PLAY: SEVEN WOMEN (Role: Tovey)
BBC Radio 4 (Wednesday, 1415–1500*)
By: J.M. Barrie
Adapted and directed by: Julia McKenzie
Produced by: Bruce Hyman
Cast included: Bill Paterson (J.M. Barrie), Diana Quick (Mrs

Tovey), Alexander Armstrong (Rattray), Harriet Walter (Leonora)
[*Seven Women shared the 45-minute 'Afternoon Play' slot
with another Barrie play, The 12-Pound Look.]

2005: 20 November–11 December
THE CLASSIC SERIAL: THE GLITTERING PRIZES
(Role: Dan (all episodes))
BBC Radio 4 (Sundays, 1500–1600, repeated following
Saturdays, 2100–2200)
Adapted by: Frederic Raphael, from his own novel
Produced and directed by: Pete Atkin
Series cast included: Jamie Glover (Adam), Jemma Redgrave
(Barbara), Damian Lewis (Donald), Robert Bathurst (Alan),
Dominic Hawksley (Mike), Anton Lesser (Bill), Lynsey
Baxter (Lady Frances), Henry Goodman (Lionel), Frederic
Raphael (Narrator).

2006: 7 May
DRAMA ON 3: THE POSSESSED (Role: Nikolai Stavrogin)
BBC Radio 3 (Sunday, 1950–2130)
By: Lou Stein, based on the novel by Dostoyevsky
Cast included: John Sessions (Govorov), Susannah York
(Varvara Petrovna), Paul McGann (Peter Verhovensky),
Anne-Marie Duff (Liza/Marya), Dexter Fletcher
(Virginsky/Kirillov), Roger Lloyd Pack (Liputin/Stepan),
Brian Bovell (Shatov).

2008: *16 February*
THE SATURDAY PLAY: SPELLBOUND (Role: Dr John Murchison)
BBC Radio 4 (Saturday, 1430–1530)
Dramatised by Amanda Dalton from the original book by: Francis Beeching
Directed by: Susan Roberts
Cast included: Hattie Morahan (Constance), Alexandra Mathie (Nurse Deeling), David Fleeshman (Dr Edwardes), Gerard Fletcher (Geoffrey), Christine Cox (Ciceley).

2008: *14 April*
THE AFTERNOON PLAY: GOOD EVENING (Role: Dudley Moore)
BBC Radio 4 (Monday, 1415–1500)
Written by: Roy Smiles
Produced by: Liz Anstee
Cast included: Matt Addis (Alan Bennett), Jonathan Aris (Jonathan Miller), Rory Kinnear (Peter Cook).

2008: *1 May*
THE AFTERNOON PLAY: CHATTERTON: THE ALLINGTON SOLUTION (Role: Thomas Chatterton)
BBC Radio 4 (Thursday, 1415–1500)
Written by: Peter Ackroyd
Directed by: Roy McMillan
Cast included: Adrian Scarborough (Allington), Rachel

Bavidge (Ruth), David Timson (Partridge), Glen McCready (Sam), Liza Sadovy (Mrs Angel), Hugh Ross (Jackman), Jonathan Keeble (Mr Crane), Hugh Dickson (Coroner), Mark Lawson (Himself).

2008: 9, 12–14 May
METAMORPHOSIS (Reader (all parts))
BBC Radio 7 (Friday, then following Monday–Wednesday, 1830–1900)
By: Franz Kafka

2008: 23–27 June
BOOK OF THE WEEK: CASANOVA (Reader)
BBC Radio 4 (Monday–Friday, 0945–1000, repeated same night 0030–0045)
By: Ian Kelly

2008: 6 July
WORDS AND MUSIC: ITALIAN FANTASY (Reader)
BBC Radio 3 (Sunday, 2330–0100)
Also reading: Emily Bruni
[A sequence of poetry and prose (Byron, Browning, ee cummings, Henry James, Elizabeth David, Eleanor Clark), interspersed with music (Berlioz, Respighi and Bob Dylan, among others).]

2008–2014 (four series and two specials):
CABIN PRESSURE (Role: Captain Martin Crieff (all episodes but one*)

BBC Radio 4
Written by: John Finnemore
Produced by: David Tyler
Main cast: Stephanie Cole (Carolyn Knapp-Shappey), Roger Allam (First Officer Douglas Richardson), John Finnemore (Arthur Knapp-Shappey).
Series 1: *2 July–6 August 2008: Wednesdays, 1130–1200*
Series 2: *17 July–21 August 2009: Fridays, 1130–1200*
Special: *25 December 2010: Saturday, 0830–0900*
Series 3: *1 July–5 August 2011: Fridays, 1130–1200*
Series 4: *9 January–13 February 2013: Wednesdays, 1830–1900*
Two-part Finale: *23–24 December 2014: Tuesday/ Wednesday, both 1830–1900*
(*Due to illness, Cumberbatch missed the recording of series 3 episode 3 in 2011. In his absence, Tom Goodman-Hill played the part of Captain Martin Crieff.)

2008: *4–8 August*
AT WAR WITH WELLINGTON (Role: Duke of Wellington)
BBC Radio 4 (Monday–Friday, 1545–1600)
Presented by: Peter and Dan Snow
Producer: Alyn Shipton
Also featuring the voices of: David Westhead, Neil Dudgeon, David Holt, Frank Stirling
[Series in which Peter and Dan Snow introduced extracts from diary entries and letters from soldiers who fought in the Peninsular Campaign.]

2008: *9 August*
BBC WORLD DRAMA: THE TIGER'S TAIL (Reader)
BBC World Service (Saturday, 1900–2000)
[A selection of short stories by Burmese writers.]

2008: *11–15 August*
**WOMAN'S HOUR DRAMA: THE PILLOW BOOK
(Role: Tadanobu)**
BBC Radio 4 (Monday–Friday, 1045–1100)
By: Robert Forrest, inspired by the diary of Sei Shonagon
Cast included: Ruth Gemmell (Shonagon), John Rowe
(Narimasa), Laura Rees (Empress), Caroline Martin (Saisho),
Richard Madden (Emperor), Mark Bazeley (Yukinari),
Colette O'Neil (Tozammi).

2008: *18 August*
SUNSHINE AND SHOWERS: RAINY SEASON (Reader)
BBC Radio 4 (Monday, 1530–1545)
By: DJ Taylor
Producer: Sasha Yevtushenko

2008: *24 September*
**THE AFTERNOON PLAY: THE LAST DAYS OF GRACE
(Role: GF)**
BBC Radio 4 (Wednesday, 1415–1500)
By: Nick Warburton
Produced by: Steven Canny
Cast included: Kenneth Cranham (W.G. Grace), Christopher

Martin-Jenkins (Voice of Cricket).

2008: *27 December*
THE SATURDAY PLAY: TOM AND VIV (Role: Tom)
BBC Radio 4 (Saturday, 1430–1600)
By: Michael Hastings
Produced by: Peter Kavanagh
Cast included: Lia Williams (Vivienne Haigh-Wood), David Haig (Maurice), Judy Parfitt (Rose), John Rowe (Charles), Emily Randall (Louise).

2009–present:
AFTERNOON DRAMA: RUMPOLE (Role: Young Rumpole (all episodes))
BBC Radio 4
Written by: John Mortimer, adapted by Richard Stoneman
Directed by: Marilyn Imrie
1: RUMPOLE AND THE PENGE BUNGALOW MURDERS *(19–26 May 2009; Tuesdays, 1415–1500)*
Cast included: Timothy West (Elder Rumpole), Geoffrey Whitehead (C.H. Wystan), Andy de la Tour (Albert/Peter), Ewan Bailey (Simon), Emma Fielding (Daisy), Jasmine Hyde (Hilda), Stephen Critchlow (Reggie), Matthew Morgan (Bonny), Karl Johnson (Judge/Dr Phillimore), David Shaw-Parker (Lord Jessop).
2: RUMPOLE AND THE FAMILY PRIDE *(9 August 2010; Monday, 1415–1500)*
Cast included: Timothy West (Elder Rumpole), Cathy Sara (Hilda), Elaine Claxton (Liz/Helen), Julian Wadham (Lord Sackbut), Sophie Thompson (Rosemary/Pippa), Joshua

McGuire (Jonathan).

3: RUMPOLE AND THE ETERNAL TRIANGLE *(10 August 2010; Tuesday, 1415–1500)*

Cast included: Timothy West (Elder Rumpole), Cathy Sara (Dorothy), Faye Castelow (Elizabeth).

4: RUMPOLE AND THE MAN OF GOD *(1 March 2012; Thursday, 1415–1500)*

Cast included: Timothy West (Elder Rumpole), Jasmine Hyde (Hilda), Stephen Critchlow (George Frobisher/Mr Pratt), Adrian Scarborough (Rev. Mordred Skinner).

5: RUMPOLE AND THE EXPLOSIVE EVIDENCE *(2 March 2012; Friday, 1415–1500)*

Cast included: Timothy West (Elder Rumpole), Jasmine Hyde (Hilda), Alison Pettitt (Joyce Pringle), Michael Cochrane (Sam Ballard), John Ramm (DI Dickerson), Geoffrey Whitehead (Sir Oliver Oliphant/Philbeam).

6: RUMPOLE AND THE GENTLE ART OF BLACKMAIL *(18 December 2012; Tuesday, 1415–1500)*

Cast included: Timothy West (Elder Rumpole), Jasmine Hyde (Hilda), Louis Tafler-Hyde (Nicholas Rumpole), Stephen Critchlow (Humphrey Grice/Judge Everglades), Faye Castelow (Sue Galton).

7: RUMPOLE AND THE EXPERT WITNESS *(25 December 2012; Tuesday, 1415–1500)*

Cast included: Timothy West (Elder Rumpole), Louis Tafler-Hyde (Nicholas Rumpole), Daniel Weyman (Dr Ned Dacre), Nigel Anthony (Erskine-Brown).

8: RUMPOLE AND THE OLD BOY NET *(20 March 2014; Thursday, 1415–1500)*

Cast included: Jasmine Hyde (Hilda), Nigel Anthony (Erskine-Brown), Ewan Bailey (Sir Cuthbert/Mr Lee), Cathy Sara (Phillida Trant), Stephen Critchlow (Judge Bullingham/Stephen Lucas)

9: RUMPOLE AND THE SLEEPING PARTNERS *(21 March 2014; Friday, 1415–1500)*

Cast included: Jasmine Hyde (Hilda), Nigel Anthony (Erskine-Brown/Judge Gwent-Evans), Cathy Sara (Phillida Trant), Stephen Critchlow (Hugo Lutterworth/Captain Gleason)

2010: *2–3 June*

BLAKE'S 7: THE EARLY YEARS (Role: Townsend)

BBC Radio 7 (Wednesday–Thursday, 1830–1900)

(Cumberbatch appeared in parts 2 and 3 of this five-part revival series)

3: The Dust Run

4: The Trial

Created by: Terry Nation

Written by: Ben Aaronovitch, Simon Guerrier

Cast included: Stephen Lord, Carrie Dobro.

2010: *5 November*

BIG TOE BOOKS (Guest Reader)

BBC Radio 7 (Friday, 1600–1700)

[Cumberbatch was featured in this children's magazine show reading *Silverwing* by Kenneth Oppel.]

2013: *13 January*

DRAMA ON 3: COPENHAGEN (Role: Werner Heisenberg)
BBC Radio 3 (Sunday, 2030–2230)
By: Michael Frayn
Cast included: Simon Russell Beale (Niels Bohr), Greta
Scacchi (Margrethe Bohr).

2013: *16, 18–22 March*
NEVERWHERE (Role: Angel Islington)
BBC Radio 4*/BBC Radio 4 Extra**
**Part 1: BBC Radio 4: 16 March 2013 (Saturday,
1430–1530)*
***Parts 2–6: BBC Radio 4 Extra: 18–22 March 2013
(Monday–Friday, 1800–1830)*
By: Neil Gaiman
Cast included: James McAvoy (Richard Mayhew), Natalie
Dormer (Door), Christopher Lee (Earl of Earls Court),
Andrew Sachs (Tooley), David Harewood (Marquis de
Carabas), Sophie Okonedo (Hunter), Anthony Head
(Croup), David Schofield (Vandemar), Bernard Cribbins
(Old Bailey), Romola Garai (Jessica), Paul Chequer (Gary),
Johnny Vegas (Lord Ratspeaker), Neil Gaiman (Mr Figgis).

AUDIOBOOKS/RECORDINGS

2006: *January*
**CASANOVA: THE VENETIAN YEARS – THE MEMOIRS
OF GIACOMO CASANOVA (Reader)**
CSA Word

Memoirs by: Giacomo Casanova
2008: *August*
DEATH IN A WHITE TIE (Reader)
Hachette Digital
By: Ngaio Marsh

2008: *November*
DOCTOR WHO: FORTY FIVE: FALSE GODS (Role: Howard Carter)
Big Finish Productions
Directed by: Ken Bentley
Written by: Mark Morris
Cast included: Sylvester McCoy (The Doctor), Sophie Aldred (Ace), Philip Olivier (Hex), Lucy Adams (Jane Templeton), Paul Lincoln (Robert Charles/Robot), Jon Glover (Creodont).

2008: *December*
ARTISTS IN CRIME (Reader)
Hachette Digital
By: Ngaio Marsh

2010: *November*
WORDS FOR YOU – THE NEXT CHAPTER (Reader)
Universal Records
25-track charity album of poetry recitations accompanying classical music pieces.
Also featuring: Peter Capaldi, Meryl Streep, Helena Bonham Carter, Terence Stamp, Maureen Lipman, Dervla Kirwan, Peter Capaldi, Rupert Penry-Jones, James Earl Jones.

[Cumberbatch appears on three tracks:
6: Kubla Khan by Samuel Taylor Coleridge (accompanying Modest Mussorgsky/Khovanshtchina, Intermezzo Act 4)
19: Ode to a Nightingale by John Keats (accompanying Gustav Mahler/Symphony No. 5 in C Sharp, 4th Movement – Death in Venice)
24: Jabberwocky by Lewis Carroll (accompanying Richard Wagner/Magic Fire Music (Feuerzauber))

2010: *December*
SHERLOCK HOLMES: THE REDISCOVERED RAILWAY MYSTERIES AND OTHER STORIES (Reader)
BBC Audiobooks/AudioGo
Written by: John Taylor

2012: *September*
MOBY DICK – THE BIG READ (Reader)
Part of Plymouth International Book Festival
Devised by: Philip Hoare, Angela Cockayne
Online at www.mobydickbigread.com

2012: *November*
LATE NIGHT TALES: FRIENDLY FIRES (Narrator/ Contributor)
Late Night Tales Records
[Contributes to one track: 'Flat of Angels' by Simon Cleary.]

2012: *December*
THE SNOWMAN AND THE SNOWDOG (Reader)

Puffin Books e-audiobook
By: Hilary Audus, based on the book, *The Snowman*, by
Raymond Briggs

2013: *February*
THE TEMPEST (Role: Ferdinand)
Naxos Audio Books
By: William Shakespeare
Produced by: John Tydeman
Cast included: Ian McKellen (Prospero), Emilia Fox
(Miranda).

2013: *June*
RÖYKSOPP: LATE NIGHT TALES (Narrator/Contributor)
Late Night Tales Records
[Contributes to one track: 'Flat of Angels Part 2' by Simon
Cleary.]

PUBLICATIONS

2009: *July*
INSPIRED* (Contributor)
Shoehorn Publications
Published in aid of the Prince's Trust
[Includes Cumberbatch's account of being car-jacked in
South Africa.]

GAMES

2011: *April*
THE NIGHT JAR (Voice)
iPhone App Game
AMV/Somethin' Else Productions